Lead Follow Love

Lead Follow Love

Authority Transfer Relationships

Reflections by:

Dan Williams   Kevin Casey
Dawn Williams   Katie Casey

Alfred Press
Hubbardston, Massachusetts

Alfred Press
12 Simond Hill Road
Hubbardston, MA 01452

Lead Follow Love:
Authority Transfer Relationships
© 2024 Dan Williams, Dawn Williams, Kevin Casey,
Katie Casey
ISBN 979-8-9887309-2-7

Printed in cooperation with
Lulu Enterprises, Inc.
860 Aviation Parkway, Suite 300
Morrisville, NC 27560

Contents

Dedications

Dan:

In 2006, dawn and I presented classes and workshops in a swing club in Ohio, a fetish fair in Atlanta, a private event in Texas, then two events in Indiana. Next was a kink event in Wisconsin, a Leather club in Ohio, and finally a group in Massachusetts. Every year since then is the same—traveling all over North America to share about healthy power exchange relationships (as well as sacred sexuality and simply fun kink). We really enjoy teaching and are very grateful for the opportunity. We don't charge for our classes or time; if we work something out that is mostly cost-neutral, we are pretty happy. We may even sell enough books that gas on the trip home is paid for. And we get to meet lots of folks and attend a variety of events! Win-win is our view.

When we teach a class or share a workshop, be it Living Power Exchange or Sensual Spanking, things normally have a pattern. In a room of say thirty people, one or two leave pretty early, as they perhaps expected something different (not a big deal at all, sometimes I'm that guy when I attend a class). Then you do your thing and ninety minutes later, everybody applauds, and of the remaining twenty-eight people, twenty leave and head for the next class. Of the remaining eight, six or seven stay to further express their appreciation and tell us what part they liked or a story they are reminded of. These are always enjoyable interactions. Then they leave. Then sometimes there are one or two people who have been waiting for the others to leave. They want your full attention because they want you to know—or sometimes need you to know—that you said "the thing". You've given them the golden thread that solved a long-standing problem they had or just helped them to feel a sense of homecoming—that feeling that you seem so different from everyone else but now they have found their tribe.

I dedicate this book to you—that person who stuck around, that found the bit that filled a void and needed us to know that. And the person who wrote to us out of the blue just to let us know we said something that they found valuable. The couple who stopped us in the hall to tell us what their life looked like after attending an intensive we hosted years back.

Because sometimes, after teaching at hundreds of events and thousands of classes, I think that maybe it is time to do something else. Something that is new and different. Then you, via a random mention on a social media site or contacting us directly or finding us at an event and telling us about a book chapter you used to solve an issue ... this always leaves me with a renewed sense of purpose and a desire to do more. There is a lot of stuff in the world I can't do anything about. But I can help a few people feel like they belong, that their non-standard relationship is healthy, that although they have been told they have to do it one way, the other ways work too and are pretty great.

And in doing this, you remind me it is true for me as well. Here is to your first twenty years, and to my next twenty.

dawn:

To all of our power exchange / authority transfer / hierarchical and Leather friends that have supported us over the years ... I'd love to name you all ... each of you helped us in some way over the last two decades. Whether in listening to us during our struggles, offering advice, or just being yourself and being our friends ... we appreciate you being there for us. I dedicate this book to you.

To our Power eXchange Summit (PXS) staff, volunteers and attendees, the Subs in Service Intensive presenters and attendees, the Columbus Space volunteers and attendees, the Erotic Awakening podcast patrons and listeners, our workshop attendees both in person and online, our supporters during our title year, all of you; you shared your time and energy supporting us and made all these projects not only possible, but successful. I dedicate this book to you.

To our poly partners who have not only put up with all the time and energy we've invested in these projects, but have supported or been part of them. I dedicate this book to you.

To the special individuals that reach out to us and let us know that we did something, said something, shared something personal that spoke to you. You keep us going when we experience "vulnerability hangovers". I'll admit that there are days when we wonder if we have anything left to share. When you've reached out to us, we've taken it as a sign that we need to keep doing what we do. I dedicate this book to you.

To our friends Kevin and Katie. We couldn't have done this book without you. I dedicate this book to you.

To Elsie Dog and Ginger the Poly Pup, both of which you can hear their collars jingle on the podcast; Elsie during the first couple years and Ginger on the last couple of years … I dedicate this book to you.

And of course, to Dan, who has put so much energy into our projects, our relationship, himself and me, as a Leader and a friend, I dedicate this book to you, Belum.

Yes, this is a lot of people. But, it's been a lot of people that have supported us over the years and made all this possible. Thank you.

Kevin:

I bumped into an old friend at a farmer's market ten years after the last time I saw him. We hung out together a few times to see if we were still buddies after a decade. At one point, as he went to leave my home, I asked him if he knew the hiker's knot for shoe tying. He said "Kevin, it is a climber's knot, and I taught you that."

Most of my wisdom is absorbed from someone else. A vital phrase by a teacher at a Kink conference. A book about the qualities of a Leader. Deep conversations with peers that love to mindfully explore. The example Katie provides of loving adoration. A respected elder poking holes in the myths of the BDSM subculture and instead embracing authenticity. The folks who do some strange relationship thing that helps me say "Nope, that's not my path." The academic striving for an unbiased understanding of Authority Transfer. I absorb and integrate.

This book is dedicated to the dozens of folks who have made me wiser, whose thoughts I have integrated into my own, whose example guided my own exploration. Sometimes I can exactly identify who turned on a lightbulb that provided key illumination when I needed it. Sometimes, like with the climber knot, I retain the information but not the source. And sometimes it is simply a whisper or a breeze that I don't even know has changed me, but still influenced where I've landed.

This book is dedicated to all the people who have given me the greatest gift I can imagine: the tools to be the man who deserves to own Katie.

This book is further dedicated to all the people from whom I've absorbed wisdom—I am hopeful that our classes and this book are ways that we pay it forward, and that this honors each of you that gave to me, whether intentionally or not.

Finally, this book is dedicated to all the people who mindfully and intentionally explore Authority Transfer relationships. I am hopeful this book will both inform and challenge. Take this stuff and craft something marvelous.

Katie:

Did you attend one of the many discussion groups Kevin and I moderated across the years? Then this book is partly your creation. The questions folks would pose and consider are here. Yes, we saved all those hundreds of 3x5 cards with your questions scrawled on them. We sorted them down to the toughest ones. We clumped up the similar ones. You might find and remember your question inside this cover. Thank you.

I dedicate my efforts in this book to all the relationship hackers out there. No matter what the style or hierarchy, if you think about, talk about, and work on this stuff, you're my daisies.

So many people just grow up, date, get married or become partners without the deep discussions of what they want and need in a relationship—or in *life*! We have huge thinks and conversations before choosing a career, but rarely do we do the interviews and discussions with potential partners.

My first marriage was a "You like me? I like you too! I now love you! Let's make babies and get married. What?! You don't care about budgeting and living within your means? You don't care about being healthy? You have no interest in becoming a better human and gaining knowledge? You like to count all the Legos and make sure the kids didn't misplace any? You hate spontaneous fun and adventure? Ooops, I made a mistake."

I went forward from that relationship with lessons learned. I learned them the hard way, with tears, sad children, and financial suffering—so I learned them good. I began my journey into being a relationship hacker; into pursuing an Intentional Relationship with conscious effort, controlled emotions, healthy thoughts and adoration. I *never* lose sight of what I have invested in or how valuable this man and this life is.

This book is dedicated to the people who want the same. Who have taken that brutal lesson learned from past failure and are intentionally trying to create something wonderful.

A bad relationship is hard. A good relationship is hard. Choose your hard.

Introduction

This Introduction is probably the hardest part of this book to write. In the other sections each writer keeps their own voice and style. In this intro, we must somehow get four people to agree on how we want to make a first impression, plus convey a lot of really important information. Dan's advice was to start with a bunch of dialogue that ran through his head like a mediocre sitcom. (*Kevin looks around the room.* "Hey guys, weren't we going to work on the intro? Where'd everybody go? Guys??") Katie leaned toward a witty intro. (An Artist, Buddhist, Pagan and Psychologist walk into a writing session. *Insert punchline here.*). Dawn wants to start with an amusing anecdote. (When Kevin and Katie contacted Dan and dawn months after first meeting each other, Dan remembered them all right... "Oh yeah! You're Hot Chick and Suit Guy from Canada..."). Unfortunately for them, I (Kevin) volunteered to do the first draft of this intro and my kinks are complicated sentences, bullet point lists, and worrying about definitions. While you shouldn't judge a book by its cover, it is even more important not to judge this book by its Introduction. Just get through the next few pages and the witty and charming folks will be back in the driver's seat. In the meantime, buckle up, because I'm taking the wheel.

―――――――――◗◗◯◖―――――――――

We had forty-six possible titles for this book. (You can find them all in Appendix One.) The reason we had so many ideas for the title is because this is such an unusual and hard-to-describe creation.

We are two couples (Dan & dawn and Kevin & Katie) who have been engaged in a specialized form of relationship for almost exactly twenty years for each couple. That specialized relationship style will be referred to as Authority Transfer within this book, although you might know it by a variety of other terms, like Power Exchange, Master/slave relationship, Dom/sub relationship, etc.

(As an aside, when the four authors are together, we agree to be clear and honest with each other regarding whether we are "attached" or "not attached" to something. In this case, Kevin was very attached to the use of Authority Transfer as the prevailing term in this book. Katie agreed but is less uptight about it than Kevin. Dan and dawn were largely unattached to the term used, so Kevin's strong attachment was honored.)

Authority Transfer is essentially an umbrella term that is intended to contain and encompass all the various expressions of consensual inegalitarian relationships. Said differently, Authority Transfer is a hierarchical relationship style where one partner turns over authority to the other partner. (There is a more complex and comprehensive definition available, but that is beyond the intent of this work[1]). At the core: One person in the relationship agrees to be the Leader, and has the right and responsibility of decision making and thus "being in charge", while the Follower agrees to support and, well, follow.

Backing up, then: The two couples have each been in a hierarchical relationship with their partner (an Authority Transfer relationship) for twenty years. These are loving couples who deeply adore and cherish their partner. These are couples who rarely disagree with each other and who mindfully use communication and relationship tools on a daily basis. These couples recognize and enjoy the hot and sexy aspects of Authority Transfer, but they have also discovered and honed the pragmatic value.

Our relationships have evolved over those twenty years, becoming more functional, more pleasurable and more customized to the unique individuals involved. That means we know a lot about our personal experience of our own customized relationship—but maybe have insights that would be valuable to others as they evolve their own Authority Transfer relationship. We don't present this book to you and believe that it contains any truths about the way you should design your relationship. We present it to you,

---

[1] Kevin and Dr. Brad Sagarin have a paper in revision for publication. That paper attempts to define and clarify Authority Transfer relationships in the hope to improve the language researchers use and correct some myths and misunderstandings about Authority Transfer relationships that seem to be relatively prevalent.

rather, in the hope that it will help you discover your own truths and spark great conversations with your partner and peers. Your relationship must be yours, as these words illuminate a look at ours.

This book is intended to be a unique way to provide those insights for your reading and consideration. The design of this project is sufficiently exciting that we want to give you a behind-the-scenes glimpse into how this work was created. The process is, in some ways, just as important as the content. Knowing how this book was created will, hopefully, give you a different perspective on the magic contained within.

Step One

Katie and Kevin have run discussion groups about Authority Transfer for many years. For most of that time, they had participants write questions or topics on a 3x5" card so that Kevin could sort and combine them as he saw fit as moderator. They kept those cards for over a decade. To begin this book, Katie went through every card and pulled out the questions that went beyond the 101 level, because the four of us didn't want to write about rudimentary topics. We wanted challenging and interesting writing prompts.

Katie organized and condensed those topics until we had a list of sixty possible writing prompts. We created a spreadsheet, and then the four of us each blind voted (unaware of the votes of the others) which topics we thought should end up in the book. Any topic that got three or four votes is contained in this book. As a bonus, each of us got a "golden buzzer" to include any one question or topic they wanted, even if the others voted it out.

Step Two

All the authors got together for a writing retreat lasting 21 days. Sure, we went for hikes and did yoga and played a lot of board games ... but the majority of this book was carved out during this time together. Here are the rules we followed for each writing:

❖ All questions were assigned a number. We took turns pulling a number out of a tiny box to select the topic, randomly, at the very last minute, before writing.

❖ No talking before, or during, the writing - no planning what to write or discussing or even asking any questions about the topic, unless it was really unclear or unmanageable in the current state. If it required discussion, then the topic was set aside for improvement and was written about on another day when it came out of the box randomly again.

❖ Set a timer for 30 minutes and write, write, write.

❖ When the timer goes off: Hands off keyboards! Yer fuckin' done, mate.

Step Three

After the thirty minutes concluded, we each took turns reading our writing to the others. Each one of us would share our thoughts and hear the perspectives of the others. This often led to additional discussion or revelations as we considered what we heard, or what we realized we entirely neglected to cover in our own writing. Step Three doesn't show up in this book, or anywhere—it was our personal processing to foster our own growth. It was our chance to grow as people, as couples, and as friends.

(We love the idea of this book being used for a book reading or discussion group. Read the question, do your own journal entry, share it with trusted peers! Or just fight about which of the authors would survive longest if dropped into the Star Wars universe.)

Step Four

With absolutely minimal editing, we put that spontaneously birthed essay straight into the book. Edits were only allowed for sentences that got impossibly mangled in the heat of rapid writing. No additions or deletions. No fixing things or making them more clear. No softening any of our blunt proclamations. The essays you have in your hands have been read for blatant disasters and then ripped from their author's clawing hands and dropped into a chapter. Our goal was to make just barely enough edits so that the essays had the delicious smell of fresh-baked spontaneity without the stink of 100% unrefined word vomit.

[Note: Any time we added content after the writing period ended, we placed it inside brackets like this so that you can tell it was added as an afterthought.]

[Also Note: Raven Kaldera at Alfred Press agreed to be our editor and publisher … and also agreed, with some trepidation, (we suspect) to leave the book as raw as possible. Kevin imagined Raven editing while wearing mittens in order to force himself to edit as lightly as possible. The authors want to specifically note here that Raven corrected only what was absolutely needful, and the rest (in his own words) "I pretty much left alone. Goofy jokes, stupid limericks, and all." Thank you, Raven, for your Herculean restraint!]

The Final Product In Your Hands!

We want to reassure you, and make you the promise, that all the super-weird commonalities between some essays are the legitimate result of this writing process. When two authors happened to use the same phrase, reference the same event, have an identical opinion, or had some other outlandish overlap it always made us shake our heads in wonderment. Why did two people happen to mention monkeys, or oatmeal, or puke—in the same writing prompt? One writing had Katie and Dan both referencing cowboys, of all things! Sometimes it was the other member of a couple, so might be attributed to shared experiences or shared language. Oftentimes it was not, though, and how it occurred is beyond us. It happened often enough we wanted to explicitly state again that there was no conversation before or during the writing, and that those nutty similarities are pure happenstance. Also, please keep in mind the chapters were written in a random order, not in the order they appear in the book. This means you might find an occasional time when an author says, "I already talked about this" (or somesuch) and they, in fact, have not talked about it in anything you have read up to that point.

This book is a tapestry of experiences that harmonize yet have counterpoint. The perspectives of the Leaders are sometimes different from the Followers. The perspectives of one couple are sometimes aligned with each other but vastly different from the other couple. As a reader you may find that you resonate with one author in particular. You may find that the opinions of the Followers are more interesting to you than the Leader's opinions. We urge you to consider that the fullness of each topic is captured through examining all the voices, and considering the points of similarity and the equally valuable points of difference. Our truths may not be yours, but the combination of our perspectives is likely to have better answers for you than any one of us alone.

That said, feel free to play the "Make the Grade" game at home using our handy scorecard in Appendix Two. For each topic, you can place a checkmark next to the author who gave you most value, or with whom you resonated. If something we said made a difference in your life, or resonated with you, please let us know! There isn't much financial profit in pouring out your guts like this—knowing we helped you would make this effort worthwhile, because ultimately that's our motivation.

Anyhow, the described writing process means that as a reader you get four unfiltered perspectives on each topic, reflecting a combined eighty years of experience. These are not carefully considered and prepared lectures designed to convey information clearly. These are fucking raw journal entries, shared with vulnerability between friends, and then slipped between two covers and into your hands. You get the journal entries that brought tears to our eyes, read out in the heat of the moment after our writing frenzy. You get the bullet point lists where we only managed to address two of the four points before time ran out. You get to hear our internal dialogue as (relatively often) we start our journal entry with "Wow, this one is going to suck" or something similar. We believe this is the deepest and most impactful look at Authority Transfer relationships available—it is ripped from our hearts as fast as we could type it, with no time to make it pretty. These are the hardest topics we could find, the safest environment to explore them, the harshest time-limit to prevent taking the easy route—and we hope you will agree the result is beautiful. These are our love letters to Authority Transfer, shared with you in trust and vulnerability.

Caveats and General Disclaimer

When we say we are sharing with you in trust, part of what we mean is that we trust you to try to hear our words with kindness and compassion. If you have come into this experience looking for failures, omissions or offense—you're in luck, as there are sure to be many. We were writing with no time to carefully watch our phrasing. Given even a few moments of consideration, we would likely choose to say some things more gently, or with more care. We offer a blanket apology, in advance, for our many failings. We hope that with this early admission of our imperfections, you will be able to remain mindful that our intent is to be caring, loving and appropriate.

Additionally, you might find some topics or statements offensive. The writings include the relatively frequent use of strong language—if the muse meant one of us sprinkled "fuck" throughout the writing, that's what you get. Relatedly, there is a fair amount of honest (but raw) conversation about sex. If cum swallowing and cunt fingering are going to be offensive to you, surprise!! - not only are they here in the intro, but also other places in the book.

We also vowed not to soften or disclaimer every damn sentence in the book, the way we might be cautious in a presentation at a conference. The writing is fast and furious, and we shoot from the hip. We made an agreement with each other not to waste time and energy saying "In my opinion…" or "For me, in my relationship…" or "Some people might maybe find that possibly…" Fuck that. This couple of paragraphs right here are all the disclaimering you get.

Disclaimer: We did our best to be honest, vulnerable and unedited. We are caring, loving people that truly mean no offense. If despite our best efforts to provide a great experience for you, we manage to offend you - we are sorry we've impacted you negatively, as that is contrary to our purpose and intent. That said, this is your fair warning that everything following the word "weirdness" is blunt and pulls no punches. Reading onward contractually obligates you to read with generosity and constitutes consent to be exposed to our words, our wisdom and our weirdness.

Foreword

We're breaking rules all over the place. Normally the "Foreword" for a book goes pretty far … forward. However, we had a special assignment for our Foreword writers, and we wanted you to understand the challenge they faced. Placing the Foreword too far forward would have spoiled the fun!

In keeping with our strange choices, we picked four people to write the Foreword for this book, since four people wrote the book. We tried to pick four people that won't shit the bed in some spectacular maelstrom of drama sometime in the future and make us regret having them appear in our book. We feel really confident about these four folks. We also limited our choices to folks with excellent literary skills because we asked them to commit to following the same rules we followed for our writings: 30-minute time limit, minimal pre-consideration, and no editing their Foreword once the timer goes off.

We picked folks we are pretty sure like us, because the assignment is pretty terrible: read this book and then sum up your experience in 30 minutes. We hope it is as challenging for them as writing each section was for us. Good luck, friends. We are grateful for your willingness to do the job and to do it by our crazy guidelines.

Brad Sagarin

I speak from the heart, but I write from the head. I pore over my words, making sure they say precisely what I need them to say. It's one of the reasons I don't tweet. A 280-character tweet would likely take me hours to write and refine, and by the time I was ready to post it, whatever I was commenting on would be receding into the past.

So this assignment has taken me way out of my comfort zone. Thanks a lot, Kevin.

I really liked this book. It's fun, engaging, and informative, and it gave me a lot of food for thought about my own relationship—this despite the fact that my 27-year relationship has been egalitarian from the start. That's because, although some of the essays in this book are specifically about Authority Transfer relationships, many are just about relationships. Dan, dawn, Kevin, and katie each take a remarkably mindful and intentional approach to their relationships, and the success of their relationships and the insights found throughout this book are a testament to the benefits of such a mindful and intentional approach.

I've already used 8 minutes? AAAAAAAAH!!!!!!

Couple of examples:

I teach an undergraduate human sexuality class, and Kevin and katie have generously visited the class to present on their relationship. My motivation for inviting them was originally to introduce my students to Authority Transfer relationships, and I know that Kevin and katie are fantastic speakers who address some of the thorny questions such as whether feminism is incompatible with Authority Transfer (spoiler alert: it's not). In watching my students respond to Kevin and katie, though, the main thing they absorb is the love, affection, and mutual caring that permeates Kevin and katie's relationship. It is beautiful, and I know of at least one student (who had experienced some very negative relationships in the past) who was profoundly affected by their example. Kevin and katie showed what is possible when people commit to making themselves and their relationship as awesome as possible. It is inspiring.

I know Dan and dawn less well, but one of my first interactions with them stands out in my mind. My research team was at the Power Exchange Summit for the first time, and during the opening ceremonies, I remember Dan telling the attendees that at PXS, everyone has something to learn and everyone has something to teach. This statement, and the sincerity behind it, set a perfect tone for the weekend. It reduced the hierarchy that often permeates such events, inviting everyone to listen to each other with an open heart and to share what they have to offer. It was beautiful.

In the end, I would recommend this book to anyone. Individuals pursuing or interested in an Authority Transfer relationship will gain valuable guidance from some really smart people who are doing AT really well. And individuals pursuing or interested in any type of relationship will learn a lot about what happens when people commit to openness, transparency, communication, and love. It is a lot easier for those of us in egalitarian relationships to meander along on autopilot. Society gives us a script to work from. It's not a great script, but it serves. Kevin, katie, Dan, and dawn show what's possible when you write your own script. They make me want to do the same.

Five minutes left. Good, because there's one more thing I want to get off my chest: I CANNOT BELIEVE THEY WROTE THIS WHOLE FUCKING BOOK IN THREE WEEKS. THREE WEEKS!!! I've been working on a book for over three years, and suffice it to say, I'm not ready to send the draft to anyone to write the forward yet. Congratulations, Dan, dawn, Kevin, and katie, on a job well (and efficiently) done. Maybe I'll have to give those 30-minute writing sessions a try...

Dr. Brad Sagarin
Northern Illinois University
Science of BDSM Research Team

nadine Cutler (slave nadine)

Reading this book was taken in small doses. Read. Laugh. Read. Cry. Read. Digest. And then start another round of reading time.

When I am reading four different voices writing about the same question as they also include specific incidents—funny and hurtful and growth-producing and heartfelt—from their lives, I need to take a break to digest, and I did so with this book. I am happy to have spent time in conversation, live or Zoom room, with the authors, so that I could picture them in my mind as I was reading their words and thus feel connected to them in this additional way. Even without having met them, I imagine I could appreciate the differences between them from their words herein.

What I heard throughout from each was their excitement for co-constructed authority transfer relationships, and their motivation to nurture the container in which they support each other to be, and know themselves and the leader and follower activities that work for them.

One loss for me in this foreword project is not being able to discuss with anyone else (especially my partner) the parts that I laughed with (in recognition) and cried with (in recognition) and laughed at (a funny turn of phrase!). I can hardly wait to finish this foreword to read this book with my partner, my Master.

For people new to hierarchal relationships—the chosen and intentional kind—and for people who have lived such a relationship for many years, I see value in this book.

To the authors: Thank you for talking about being a follower with an expectation that D/s looks a certain way and there is a predetermined image that I had to inhabit. I remember, in the beginning, keeping my hurt inside, and I had tears of recognition and a healing of the loss of being my Self in the beginning of my relationship—of not recognizing that the image did not work for me, and of not immediately sharing this part of me with my partner. When this slave was a new person to authority transfer relationships, I needed to hear about this.

Thank you for writing about hanging in there to hear the other person's experience of (five-minute alarm here) life in the middle of a grumpy or painful episode. After years of working and sharing in an authority transfer relationship, I am happy to hear about this form of devotion to each other's well-being in a relationship and in life.

Enjoy this book! That is not an order. I am excited to think of you enjoying this book, and my gain is feeling accompanied in the world by people who can appreciate this form of relationship.

slave nadine

Joshua Tenpenny

"Hey Josh! Raven told us you'd write a foreword for our book. You have 30 minutes! Your time starts ... NOW."

I am delighted to have been volunteered (volun-told?) for this task. We didn't have much opportunity to hear candid talk from many experienced people when we were first trying to figure out how to make this relationship work, where one person is in charge, and the other has to do what they say. There were some online forums, some mailing lists, but it was mostly skewed towards fantasy, and it was hard to trust that the folks who claimed years of experience were even in a relationship at all. We were both heavily involved in our local kink communities, but neither community was especially supportive of taking things outside of the bedroom. So we'd been working it out on our own for some years when we first went to a meeting of "Masters And slaves Together" (MAsT), and for the first time, met face-to-face with people who were mindfully incorporating some kind of real-world power imbalance into their day-to-day relationships. A few years later, we went to the Master/slave Conference in DC, and had the opportunity to talk with an even wider range of folks, with an eye-opening variety of relationship styles. There was an amazing feeling of kinship, and also, a broadening of perspective as we met folks whose relationships worked very, very, differently from ours.

This book provides a special opportunity for the reader to sit in on a virtual panel discussion lasting sixty hours, where four experienced people give their spontaneous and uncensored answers to some of the most thought-provoking questions they've encountered about these unique relationships. There are countless ways to answer any of the questions posed here, and this book gives just a sample of the internal workings of two relationships.

Reading through this book, you are likely to see things that resonate for you, and feel that wonderful sense of kinship. You are also likely to see things that make you wonder, "Really? That actually works for you?" or think "Yeah, but that would *never* work for us, because...." Fantastic! This book is the start of a conversation, of many conversations, but not the end of it. Bring these conversations to your partners, to your Leather families, to your kink communities.

Bring your conversations on these topics beyond the 101 level where everyone is saying pretty much the same things about trust, communication, integrity, etc. Bring your conversations into the deeply personal, the idiosyncratic, the raw and unfiltered reality of who we are together, and how we make these relationships work.

Joshua Tenpenny, Raven's Boy

Mama Vi

Blast you, Kevin!

You've given me an almost impossible assignment. Worse, I think you knew that when you gave it to me. Thirty minutes. Write my thoughts on this tome in thirty minutes. Grrr. (Do I hear you laughing?)

When I was first asked to read *Lead, Follow, Love* and contribute to the preface of the book, I was honored and also curious. The book is about couples living an *authority transfer* lifestyle and I (though now retired) spent over forty years in M/s. What were the similarities, the differences? What would a book be like that was written by two couples all giving their own perspectives on frequently asked questions? A project like this could challenge even the best of friends

The download arrived. It was printed, punched and placed into a notebook for easy reading. I attacked this new project the way I used to read textbooks. Marker and pen in hand, I underlined and noted passages that struck a chord with my heart or mind or pieces I wanted to go back and reread. By the time I finished a few days later and gazed through the dog-eared and underlined pages I had to laugh at myself. There was not going to be a test on this work. Somehow, I had missed the beauty of the forest, because I was too busy studying the trees. So, it was time to start the book over with a new perspective.

"Don't reread the book with your eyes, read it with your heart and ears."

I found myself looking at the different writing styles and how the personalities of each member of the couples shown through in their answers. Each person described their counterparts through the eyes of friendship and mutual admiration, then each other through the eyes of love and the parameters of their relationship.

I began to *hear* their separate voices as I turned the pages. Dan's straightforward "It begins with me" style is so much present when he talks about inspiring Dawn to be her best and achieve … for him. Kevin's therapist background makes its presence known as he writes about feedback for Katie, checking and analyzing his own behavior before he shares it.

The writing on disappointment resonated so much with me. Dawn wrote about always wanting Dan to be proud of her and how it was the motivation for all of her actions. When she wrote of disappointing him as the *ultimate* punishment for her and how she internalized it, I thought she was reciting my own words back to me. Learning to separate an action or situation that disappoints from being a personal disappointment is not always an easy lesson to learn.

Katie's writing on transparency and vulnerability showed me one of the major differences between our chosen lifestyles, so much so that I discussed her portion with my partner Jill. Was there a little bit of envy in Katie's ability to be vulnerable with Kevin? Maybe. Those of us who chose the collar way back in the 70's were to serve. That occasionally meant getting *it* done no matter what the cost. Not showing the emotional bumps and bruises. It didn't mean we didn't have them; just that we were not supposed to express them to our owners. If Owner didn't ask, property didn't share. How things have changed. Or have they just evolved as they should?

By the last entries I realized that I was not just a reader of pages, but someone privileged to be party to honest and informative discussions between good friends. I was the silent listener in an ongoing conversation; a conversation filled with honesty, wisdom, emotion and love.

Now I'm on my third read-through of this wonderful piece of writing. *Lead, Follow, Love* is a relationship manual, not just for the authority transfer lifestyle, but also for any people in love.

To those who pick up these pages, allow your eyes to *lead*, your brain to *follow* and your heart to *love*.

Mama Vi Johnson
Senior Griot and Director
Carter/Johnson Library and Collection

Author Bios – Sort of!

(Who are these people? A.K.A. Is this book worth reading?)

This author bio section was written in the same way as the rest of the book: 30 minutes and done. Well, you'll see…

Who are Dan and dawn?
By Kevin

This is an interesting assignment. "Hey Kevin, write a whole bunch of stuff about your friends, in 30 minutes, with no warning, then read it out to them." At least with a eulogy the person you are talking about can't be offended or complain.

And you know, that is maybe the right place to start with this description. Dan and dawn represent the most free and egg-shell-less relationship I have ever had, beyond the one with Katie. I am able to speak to them authentically, and they have committed to allow that space. They are people who have the practiced ability (with each other) to listen with generosity and non-defensively. They understand that words are hard and that I care about them and wouldn't just randomly take shots at them. So one of the things that makes this assignment bearable is that if I say something that they find annoying, they will understand that was not my intention, and they will honestly express that annoyance, and we will chat about it. They don't play bullshit relationship games with Katie and I, in much the same way they don't play them with each other.

I really appreciate how similar yet vastly different we are. We all live the same relationship style, yet how it is expressed is different. Oddly enough, dawn and I are similar in our attention to annoying details and fretting about unexpected outcomes. Dan and Katie are similar in their relaxed approach and expectation that things will work out and nobody has to worry.

You know how a lot of couples have the "I don't know, what do you want to do?" cycle, with each one attempting to defer to the other, or invite the other to have a preference? As Authority Transfer couples we rarely have that problem when alone with our spouses, but when we are all four together it rears its head occasionally. Imagine two Followers waiting for two Leaders to out-defer to one another. Within a few seconds Dan gets bored of the process and decides how it will be decided. Usually that means he points to somebody and says "You decide. 5....4....3..." and if they splutter and stammer he points at somebody else.

Dan seeks adventure and new experiences. Last night I watched with my own eyes as he smeared artichoke dip all over a glorious ripe strawberry. Not all his adventures are wise. I watch as dawn forces herself to give up all her pre-conceived notions and adapt to the new direction of her Leader. Not that Dan is flighty and inconsistent, but he's not against changing lanes in a big fucking hurry if the drive gets monotonous. Dawn sort of pauses, reboots the computer, blinks a few times, and says "Yes Sir."

> They are the busiest, creating-est fuckers I've ever met.

They are the busiest, creating-est fuckers I've ever met. They always have a dozen irons in the fire—podcasts, classes, book writing, website tweaking, personal growth, RV adventures, full time job, health maintenance, etc. etc. I feel like I'm pretty busy each day until I realize that Dan accomplishes much more than I do while still working a full-time job. Dawn manages to be Dan's hyper-busy Follower, attending to details in his name, keeping their various projects afloat, and still manages to out-score me on our shared Wellness challenge.

We love to game together—board games or online games. Sometimes all four of us, sometimes three, often just Dan and I. Our personalities absolutely shine through. I'm back at the fort arranging chests and Dan is like "Huh. Wooow! Oooch. Oooch. Hey, I just triggered a boss fight." In whatever format and combination, they are always great sports. They win as often as they lose, and they are joyful the entire time, either outcome. You can learn a lot about someone from gaming with them.

We spend a lot of time with Dan and dawn just hanging out with barely any agenda. We will pull out little notecards or phone apps where we have recorded topics of interest. We just sit around and digest some interesting thing, or laugh at some recent experience, or hear some great story. Dan texted us from the bathroom a few days ago. "80," it said. A few hours later he said "I realize that spending $80 on a meal in a restaurant is not as enjoyable as spending a quarter of that and sharing a simple meal around the fire pit."

This isn't really who they are, I suppose. Except it is. I think I was supposed to talk about them individually, damn it. I need a great closer here though, time is nearly up. Dan and dawn are... robot cats? Meow!

[Author's note: Upon a second reading, I realize I may have answered "Describe your friendship" and didn't pay attention to the fact the question was probably actually asking something more like "Why should I read a book with them as authors?" In retrospect, I could have answered this much better and with the correct purpose in mind.]

Who are Dan and dawn?
By Katie

Dan and dawn are an Authority Transfer, 24/7 Inegalitarian couple who have done many things and been many places.

Kevin and I met them because they journeyed up to Northern Canada in the dead of winter to bravely teach at Lupercalia back in ... 2010? 2011? What they taught at that event were the first BDSM classes we had experienced that were not about play styles and toy skills. What a relief! We had waited for years to find like-minded people with information to share. We had some after class questions, some brief interactions through the event, and signed aboard to attend the first Power Exchange Summit they were launching that year.

> We don't want to fuck up the strawberry.

From that beginning grew a friendship that was intentional, thoughtful and brutally honest. We know them pretty darn well. Good enough that it is unnerving as we sit together and type about each other right now.

To answer the question that arises time and again when the four of us are together:

NO. The answer is no. We are not in a Polyamorous relationship with them, and neither do we fuck or play in the dungeon with them. They are treasured friends and we love the structure and connection we have created. Yesterday Dan took a juicy, ripe strawberry and dunked it into a garlic parmesan dressing I made. He thought it would be interesting and fun. It fucked up the strawberry. We don't want to fuck up the strawberry. (I share this here so that as you read this book, knowing we are not intertwined in this manner will be valuable.)

Dan and dawn, as a couple, are knowledgeable in many aspects of Polyamory and the BDSM subculture. They are compelled to share their knowledge and experiences—the Good, The Bad, And The Fucking Hot. A kinky movie yet to be made, but the script writers have been busy.

For years I have watched them pour their "free" time, their finances and their hearts into helping others find a way to be better people, better partners and better BDSM participants. So far, I have not seen the riches abound from this endeavor. If so, why didn't they buy me ice cream yesterday?

Now individually … Bwahahaha.

Dan is … gosh, this could be bizarre, poignant and fun. Like those parody songs that have a deep political message that wants you to ponder and cry a little, but you are laughing so much your brain doesn't realize it learned something. Dan is introspective and open. I see him time and again approach strangers to make a brief connection, share a kind word, invite them to join in when standing on the outskirts of a gathering. That generosity is real and something he consciously pursues.

Dan will put incredible effort into his passions and pursuits, but also has the balance and inner strength to step up and call something "done" if it doesn't serve the purpose or enhance his life. When he is suffering or struggling, he is at the same time bravely seeking solution and resolution. He is the Adventuring

Bard who sings and brings laughter while traveling and sharing information.

And dawn is so complex! But in a good way, not like you cannot figure her out. There are many aspects to what makes dawn. I love that she speaks her truth with me. If I ask if something is bothering her or she is having a bad day and she says, "No, I'm fine. Just too much coffee and I had to walk away from my last chapter of alien porn because I ran out of time." That is exactly the truth. I don't have to search my soul for some other reason she might be a bit off in her mood. I don't have to question her eight different ways for her to disclose the real answer.

Dawn is funny and fun-loving; her style is just not as flamboyant as Dan's. We have laughed for years together. She is open to lessons learned and sharing them even when it is deeply personal or still has some ouch in it.

Her spiritual path is essential to who she is and where she puts incredible effort into helping others. She is the Good Witch who casts her charms and healing energy about while traveling and adventuring alongside Dan.

Who are Dan and dawn?
By Dan and dawn, not on a timer.

Dan and dawn have been in a power exchange relationship since 2001. They are the authors of numerous other books, including *Hearts & Collars: Twenty Years in a Power Exchange Relationship* and *The Polyamory Toolkit.* They can be found at over a dozen events every year, presenting classes and workshops.

They are also the co-hosts of Erotic Awakening, the longest running power exchange & kink podcast on the net. They were part of the founders and directors team of the Columbus Space, an alternative community center; 2016 MAsT International Member's Choice Presenter of the Year Award winner; Great Lakes title holders 2010; creators of the Scarlet Sanctuary and Path of the Qadishti (sacred sexuality spaces); and are featured educators on both Kink Academy and Creative Sexuality, as well as mentioned in a number of books, articles, and other media.

They are currently traveling North America in an RV with their puppy Ginger as they search for new adventures. You can find everything Dan & dawn at *www.eroticawakening.com.*

Who are Kevin and Katie?
By Dan

Since Kevin and Katie are our co-authors, we clearly must think that they have something of value to say about authority transfer. Or maybe they have a lot of social media followers and we just want the likes?

We met Kevin & Katie at a conference in Canada where we were impressed by their easy nature—not just with each other, but in navigating the world around them. They embodied both confidence and humility in their authority transfer relationship.

Dawn and I have met literally hundreds of couples (if not more) that practice some form of authority transfer, but few that have the fortitude to make it through the trials of two decades living in the modern world and maintaining clarity in this style of relationship while still being both vulnerable and open-minded to whatever might come around the corner. The key aspect that makes Kevin and Katie worthy of not only examination but of emulation is the way they constantly push themselves and each other to grow. From simple things like good health routines (I am a bad influence on Kevin as I advise he eats this or that thing I found in a bakery) to deep internal reflection, they are never satisfied. From running authority transfer think tanks to local area munches that discuss Leader and follower dynamics, they continue to act as leaders in the AT community so they can be students of it.

It is hard to say a good thing about one of them which they don't both share as attributes. To a casual observer, Kevin is very intelligent and more keeping with a particular point, while Katie's

> From running authority transfer think tanks to local area munches that discuss Leader and follower dynamics, they continue to act as leaders in the AT community so they can be students of it.

sense of humor is singular and spectacular and goofy as fuck. Yet once you get to know them, you see Katie's wisdom and Kevin's dry wit.

Both are generous in giving of time and energy toward others. As soon as you mention something is broken, Kevin shows up with a hammer, ready to assist; while Katie is whipping up a treat in the kitchen and providing an offer to help in any way needed, mixed with comic relief.

Individually they are power houses as well. If not for what they are doing now, it is easy to picture Katie as a professional artist (her donations to various charities always bring huge windfall) or a caterer or any dozen things. Kevin could easily return to a career as a psychologist or instead become a handyman (or anything in between).

The one failing they have is that they continue to deny that they are polyamorous, not realizing that they are in a polyam relationship with dawn and myself—just one where we don't share spit.

Who are Kevin and Katie?
By dawn

Simply put, Kevin and katie are two of our bestest friends. Who else could we spend three weeks with, side by side in our RVs, and not get tired of? Spending each morning and evening writing and talking about our deepest selves, having deep or silly conversations with them and then spending more time checking out the area, playing board games or having dinner together? All of this and be our authentic Leader/follower selves?

Though their relationship vocabulary may be different than ours, and some of the specific things they do in their Leader/follower relationship may be different than ours, there are enough similarities that allow our relationships to work smoothly side by side. Watching their dynamic and their relationship in general is a joy. Katie is witty and silly and makes everyone laugh. Kevin is a bit academic and thinks he's the straight guy, but has his own sense of humor that bubbles to the top more often than not.

He enjoys katie's play on words and puns. "For fuck's sake, katie!" is a common phrase during the evening. But you can see it brings joy to them both and gets mixed in easily with "Get my coffee, girl."

If you spend any time with them, you can see how important their relationship, their relationship dynamic and their relationship with each other (yes that's a slightly different thing) is to them. It is the foundation of who they are, you might say. They support each other with a completeness that is hard to find. Their dynamic and love for each other is palpable even during hard moments that they've been through. Their gazes, their touches … They are each other's rock and anchor in this crazy world and they've turned it into a journey filled with joy. Life is an adventure for them.

> They support each other with a completeness that is hard to find. Their dynamic and love for each other is palpable even during hard moments that they've been through.

They are relationship hackers. If something doesn't work for them or something has shifted or changed, they discuss it. They come up with a plan of action or something to try. There is a lot of honesty and forthrightness in their conversations, a lot of self-reflection that is refreshing to see.

I look forward to spending more time with them. Kevin with his bullet points as he tries to get the perfect wording to a question. Katie with her silly references that sometimes I get, but sometimes it takes me a moment.

I could sum up this whole writing by saying, "They are good people that bring joy to my life, that I'm lucky to have as friends."

Who are Kevin and Katie?
By Kevin and Katie, not on a timer.

Kevin and Katie are a couple who have consciously evolved their relationship across the last two decades. As language, introspection, knowledge and experience revealed new possibilities, we adapted and changed.

We have called ourselves many things over the years. Most of the labels and titles sat upon us askew. The fit was not very comfortable. "Dominant and submissive" felt like we accidentally pulled our pants over our head and were looking for the head hole. "Master and slave" felt complete in the measure of pervasiveness and intensity of role, but the titles were a stone in our shoe. "Power Exchange" was a close fit but needed us to clarify that neither of us was taking nor giving power to the other. Today we are very clear and comfortable in who we are. Our pants are on our bottom half and we shook our shoes empty.

We identify as an Authority Transfer couple who enact the Executive Model. Kevin is the Chief Executive Officer (CEO), Katie is the Chief Operations Officer (COO) and the "company" is our relationship. We use the role titles of Leader and Follower because they are clear and noninflammatory. People rarely misunderstand the structure and intent of our relationship with our more precise and accurate use of language.

Kevin is a psychologist who retired early. He did this for a couple of reasons. We are not financially insatiable. We have a small nest-egg and live very carefully within our means. We want to wring as much wonderfulness out of life as we can. He wished to pursue research, writing and presenting about improving relationships.

Katie spent most of her adult life as an artist, both creating (she has a handful of published coloring books, for instance) and instructing (running successful art studios).

We have done many things within the BDSM subculture, teaching classes and intensives being the most predominant. We are not usually inclined to list off accomplishments like a DNA test at a Bukkake party. That said, you probably need a few bona fides to feel like we have something valuable to offer, so here are a few reasons we might be considered folks with worthwhile words about Authority Transfer:

❖ Won International Power Exchange title 2017

- ❖ Taught Authority Transfer and Personal Growth classes since 2009
- ❖ Ran Power Exchange Discussion Groups in numerous locations, learning from the struggles and successes of hundreds of participants.
- ❖ Legitimate research (and data collection) about Authority Transfer.
- ❖ An incredible twenty-year relationship that just keeps getting better.
- ❖ We bag our dog droppings, return shopping carts to the cart corral, never throw wrappers on the ground, shower daily and do yoga with a goal of autofellatio.

Section 1: Foundations

Each question we answered forms a chapter, with the chapters grouped into sections of similar topics. This section asks the following foundation questions:

1) What makes Authority Transfer relationships worth the effort?
2) What were the biggest hazards in the first couple of years of your relationship?
3) How important is sex, eroticism and intimacy in your relationship?
4) These roles are not the social norm. How do you have peace with them?

Chapter 1: Effort

To make it easier for the reader to follow the flow of these writings, the entire first half of the book will have an author order of Dan / dawn / Kevin / Katie.

What makes Authority Transfer relationships worth the effort?

Dan:
About a decade ago, our dog at the time had a medical issue that forced us to decide to either have her leg amputated and have the dog face chemotherapy (there was a specialized clinic in town for that) or to have her "put to sleep." At the time, dawn had mixed feelings, but really loved that dog. I did too … but I made the decision and was the one to tell the vet that having her put to sleep was the best course.

When the market collapsed and we could no longer afford our home, I said it was time to file bankruptcy. When one of the kids decided at eighteen he could do whatever he wanted, I forced the decision that he needed to move out or align with us. When bat (a poly partner) was dying, I had to be strong and clear-minded in what needed to happen—which included driving dawn to complete some very hard responsibilities bat left us with.

The effort I perceive in this question isn't in the above examples at all, but in the constant refinement and fine-tuning that gives us the foundation to do all of the above with consistency, bravery, and trust from my follower, so that when I say "It is decided, we are selling 90% of our stuff and moving into an RV, make it so," that they may be scared, but they say "Yes sir".

The question is ... well, faulty. It implies an alternative that is equal or nearly as good as. I've had two vanilla marriages and it just isn't what lets me be the fully engaged ... well, Dan that I am.

> The question is ... well, faulty. It implies an alternative that is equal or nearly as good as. I've had two vanilla marriages and it just isn't what lets me be the fully engaged ... well, Dan that I am.

Viewed from another way, what makes it worth it is dawn. Or to be more specific, the dawn of now versus the dawn of then. I have created an environment where she can grow to her full potential. I am providing a foundation where the dawn of the past is no longer needed and can finally rest as the authentic loving caring witchy happy slutty silly compassionate leader survivor mentor vibrant person that belongs in that body can form and breathe and be here. I didn't create it, but I'll take credit for an occasional nudge.

And this is true in other relationships where I have led: A spot to kick off from who you were to who you envision becoming, and the courage to do so. They had to do all the work, and some needed (or wanted) less than others, but I am providing some of my energy and effort and am pleased to see what comes from it.

Once more, the question implies that this is an option for who I am. I don't think it is anymore. I can't cure cancer, I can't save the whales, but I can help one person, via a power exchange modality, get beyond the crap the world has laid on them. And I can help a second person. And perhaps before I am done, a few more.

What makes Authority Transfer relationships worth the effort?

dawn:

All of my relationships have taken effort in one form or another—my good relationships, my bad relationships, my "I don't know how to label this relationship" relationships. This relationship with Dan, the hierarchical one, also takes effort. That's not a bad thing. People talk about "effort" like it's a chore, but this relationship is an important part of my life, so of course it takes effort, work, focus. I wouldn't want it any other way. This relationship has been the foundation for all the beautiful things *I* and *We* have accomplished over the last 20 years.

Part of the effort involved in this style of relationship is the fact that because it's so different from anything we'd actually seen before, we had to start from scratch. We went into it knowing we were designing something different. We looked at our "needs, wants and desires". I mean, who really does that? OK, I'm a little out of touch

> This relationship brings out my best self. Though I can create things on my own and lead things, it's much easier for me when I'm following a competent, confident Leader who expects the best from me.

with the younger generations, so maybe this is something they do, but it definitely wasn't something done in the generations I was familiar with. What I was brought up with was: You get married, have babies, and stay with that person for the rest of your life. I tried that. Now you want to talk about effort and work? That was effort and work.

Dan and I had both tried that scenario in the past, and found ourselves super unhappy. So when we got together, we decided to create something new, just for us. Each of us individually and together. It was a lot of work—a lot of discovering who we were and are. This self-awareness and self-discovery doesn't stop. With each new shift in our relationship, more self-reflection, more communication, more everything, happens. We don't allow ourselves or our relationship to become stagnant.

Because of all this work, we truly have built a relationship just for us. Dan is the Leader, I'm the follower, yes. But, it has looked different at different times through the last twenty years. There was "Building Foundation Year", "High Protocol Year", "Slut Year", "Slut Year #2", "Slut Year #3", etc., "Produce Event #1 Year", "Poly Years" … I could go on and on and on listing the experiences that we've had that have shifted our relationship but not our roles. *All* of this requires effort.

But the question is, what makes it worth the effort.

Well, I can talk more about the relationship … the trust, and transparency, and the other amazing things we've accomplished, and I do so elsewhere in the book. But I'd also like to describe how it's benefitted me personally.

This relationship brings out my best self. Though I can create things on my own and lead things, it's much easier for me when I'm following a competent, confident Leader who expects the best from me. This means I'm constantly working on myself—my reactions to him, my reactions to me, my reactions to the world. I'm constantly looking at what brings me happiness, what brings him happiness and what brings us happiness.

We have a sense of adventure. We try new things. I can share absolutely everything with him including my darkness, and did so once again yesterday morning. If I get stuck in a spiral, I have someone that says, "Fix me a cup of coffee," to pull me out of the spiral.

We have created something delicious and adventurous and so very healthy.

What makes Authority Transfer relationships worth the effort?

Kevin:

Having a Katie in my life makes everything worth it! For you other unlucky folks, who don't get to own Katie, I dunno.

Jokes aside, my relationship is built on a foundation of Authority Transfer. It isn't a weekend thrill; it is the core of how we manage our lives, face trials and make mindful progress. At its most basic, the existence of this relationship makes doing the stuff to maintain the relationship entirely worth it.

I think this question is about the benefits of AT?

The devotion of my girl. She is completely on my team, in the way that no other person can be. She accepts my choices as her own. I can 100% count on the fact that Katie is free from manipulation and subterfuge, and that she is giving everything she has to be an amazing partner. There is no part she reserves. I am certain that her intention is always to serve and love fully. That devotion, that certainty, is worth any price.

The endless sex. That's pretty great too. A free use hottie is pretty valuable.

The clarity of our roles is a massive benefit. I love knowing that we have a structure, a toolbox, that allows us to know what our job is. I know I have to (or at least can) make the final decisions on everything. I know that the tasks I assign to each of us will be done. Pure, simple clarity.

The way this relationship quiets the little accountant in our heads is valuable. We are able to disentangle "fair" from "equal." I no longer worry about whether my work pumping out the RV sewer tanks is equal to Katie doing the dishes every evening. I no longer keep track of how many times each of us has walked the dog. This relationship is not equal—Katie is my Follower and I use her as I see fit. But it is fair—we both benefit greatly, and we both do the things we agree to do. In many ways this "zero scorecard" relationship is a powerful trust builder—I can trust that everything will be fair, even if, in the moment, I'm working and Katie is surfing social media.

> The devotion of my girl. She is completely on my team, in the way that no other person can be.

This relationship fosters our personal growth. I am a better person in a hundred different ways than when I first met Katie. I strive to be my best, to make her proud, to have her want to fall to her knees. I want her to see me as the absolute best partner she could have, and I do that by trying to make myself as amazing as I can (not by undermining her own sense of worth!). My physical health is better. I am more disciplined. I am a better Leader. I am a better lover. I am a better partner. I am more considerate. I am a better public speaker.

For fuck's sake! Only three minutes left to this writing period and my thoughts are a tumble and I've only scratched the surface. What makes it worth it, Kevin? The look in Katie's eyes as she adores and worships me, as we laugh and fuck our way into the anniversary marking two decades of a glorious relationship.

What makes Authority Transfer relationships worth the effort?

Katie:

There's probably some meme somewhere with a raging penis image that says Hard Things are Great Things.

This relationship is demanding. It requires me to be introspective. It requires me to be disciplined—not by Kevin, but from within. Why is it worth all that effort? The rewards, the pragmatic benefits, the ease and flow of what we have created.

I think of an athlete spending years dedicated to a skill. Taking the tumbles, the aching, the failures, the tears. Putting the hours into fine tuning their craft. The reward is being exceptional at what they do. But even when they attain that level of skill they cannot take it easy. They must continue to practice, keep toned, and find new aspects to sharpen.

What makes it worth the effort, katie? Answer the fucking question!

I crave order. I know this doesn't sound hot. I love knowing my role, what is expected of me. I know Kevin's role—what his responsibilities are. It is such a luxury to be certain of who we individually are, what we are to each other, and what our priorities are. I feel secure that we have the methods in place for navigating disagreements, for making big decisions, for having difficult conversations.

> We have a life intertwined with laughter, sex, eroticism, and joy.

Being this conscientious has us twenty years down the road without a whole bunch of ugly crap behind us that we have to forget we said or did to each other. Yes, we have had fuckups and hurt each other, but those incidents are rare. We resolved and healed from them with absolute devotion to each other and sorrow for the suffering we stepped into.

I know if I am hurt by something Kevin says or does, all I need to do is transparently share that with him, and he will immediately attend to rewording what he said so that I hear him the way he meant it, or reroute a path we wandered down that has me suffering. We are just as conscious about attending to the fun and good times as we are the rough spots. It is critical that as a couple we have joyful interactions and pleasures together. We do not want to just survive this life, we want to thrive. This means we have a life intertwined with laughter, sex, eroticism and joy.

Kevin's leadership and oversight helps us to keep the vision of where we are headed and what is essential to our well-being and growth. My support and following him gives incredible energy to our endeavors and impetus to getting goals met. He is my CEO, and I am his COO, and our company is the relationship. We have an incredibly successful stock that has had very few dips in its valuation over the years but overall consistent growth with amazing dividends paid out regularly.

Chapter 2: Initial Hazards

What were the biggest hazards in the first few years of your relationship?

Dan:

When we first got started, it was actually great. The energy of that new relationship, the discovery that someone was as kinky as you, the realization that power exchange—regardless of the lack of terminology or tools—was feeling very much like we found a missing part of ourselves. And it was great for us that we were both "newbs"—our expectations of each other was appropriate as we both knew we were just getting started and doing our best. We often say we didn't have great teachers—power exchange in our area was way less common than kink, and the internet was a fledgling community of bulletin boards strewn out across a google-less land. But we did a lot of things right. We took a lot of time to really think about what we were doing, wrote it out, talked endlessly, and found that one or two other PE couples in the area to learn from (and sometimes that learning was about what we did not want to do).

Fortunately, we never heard the advice I hear a lot today: If power exchange is too hard, take a break and be vanilla for a bit. Instead, we stayed on course and figured things out.

> We are both of a mindset that challenges are to be solved. Not that I welcome them with open arms—often it was with a sarcastic, "Oh, another opportunity."

OK, sounds like we had it easy. But of course we had some bumps. One of my goals in our relationship was to protect dawn. And that led me to avoid some hard topics or make some choices that denied who I was for "the good of the relationship". But overall—and maybe dawn's writing will remind me of some dreadful moments—I don't recall a lot of hassles that any new couple would not have faced. Kids, bills, jobs, all that was just part of our life and we faced them as best we could.

I suppose the biggest hazard was fighting against the habits or tools that we had for non-power exchange relationships. Because for me, they were not only unhealthy but the opposite of what we needed.

Skills like hiding the uncomfortable, avoiding conflict, and knowing what not to say—these did not serve us in PE and had to be unlearned.

Energy management was a hard one for me. Being the Leader, 24/7, and seeing some unrealistic examples of "great" Leaders, led me to hit burn-out more than once. But that has to be balanced with the hazard that lack of consistency is the death of many such relationships. So allowing myself to have a break, to be alone or just "on call", gave me a chance to re-energize.

See, the problem in this writing for me is that we didn't have a lot of hazards per se because we don't view things that way. We had a lot of challenges. And we are both of a mindset that challenges are to be solved. Not to say I welcome them with open arms—often it was with a sarcastic "Oh, another opportunity."

We set a ground rule when we got started that power exchange was who we really were. But a higher priority than that was that we would not interfere with either of our searches for self-discovery and internal exploration. Said in a less convoluted way, our foundation is power exchange, but if something comes along that feels like it needs to be part of the authentic self—for me, monk training, changing my language, exploring polyamory with vanilla folk—then that is added to who we are as a power exchange couple instead of being in opposition to it. This allows us to avoid thinking of things like this as hazards to our power exchange but instead of new aspects of it.

What were the biggest hazards in the first few years of your relationship?
dawn:

When you've been together this long and try to remember the beginning, it can be a little difficult. While we were setting up the timers for this writing, I asked what was meant by "hazards". Does it mean challenges? Does it mean "nuclear" hazard? Well, the rules are, we aren't to discuss the question before the writing. But it struck me that it could mean exactly that ... nuclear, toxic, flammable. Those are things you would see on hazard signs on the side of a truck.

When we first got together, I had this beautiful idea of creating something from a fantasy novel. I'd give of my heart and self without hesitation to the man I trusted more than anything. He would cherish me and see my strengths and use them. He would see my inner slut and help me embrace it and we'd have years of sexy fun and stability. Everything would be super easy once we accepted and embraced our roles.

Well, that didn't exactly happen. Not with the ease I had dreamed of.

> The hazard signs I wore on the side of me like an 18-wheeler rolling down the highway carrying toxic sludge. Toxic. Nuclear. Flammable.

Maybe if we'd met someone beforehand who had done this before and could have given us some warnings or at least someone to talk to, it wouldn't have been such a hard adjustment. It was easy on the weekends when we sent the kids to their dad's, used our code words to state we were in Dom/sub mode for the time they were gone and enjoyed the sexual escapades. That was easy. We learned more and more about our D/s selves and how it fed us and how it became harder and harder to turn off, until one day we decided not to turn it off and to bring it into our whole relationship as "D/s Lite".

But that was mostly sexual play. Even getting his peanut butter sandwich was part of the sexy play while we were in our D/s weekend mode. That was easy. That was hot. I've come to figure out that that is a need of mine that was being fulfilled.

Then we started stretching our D/s beyond the sexual. Once it became hard to turn that switch off after the weekend of play and we started rolling it into our relationship, that's when the struggle began, at least for me as the submissive. Submissive in sex play, absolutely. Submissive in the relationship? Much harder than I thought it would be. Why? Because of the hazard signs I wore on the side of me like an 18-wheeler rolling down the highway carrying toxic sludge. Toxic, Nuclear, Flammable.

Dan had known me for years and these shouldn't have come as a surprise, but maybe they did. We were building a conscious relationship with him leading and me following. It should have been easy. But we figured out the hard way that those signs I was wearing weren't just for show, they were there for a reason.

Let's start with flammable. Anger. Anger was the emotional lens I experienced the world through. As a woman with a traumatic childhood, having to fight for everything I wanted from childhood through my first marriage, making it through years with a husband that never supported me in any of my growth opportunities, constantly feeling like I was having to fight my way to the top of the pond and breaking through thick ice to take a breath and all the other things I could list but won't, anger was (and still is some days), the emotion that forms my baseline in everything. And it did in this relationship as well. That was a huge hazard that we had to work with, sometimes on a daily basis. And it needed work. Anger is something that Dan doesn't take to very well. He's a much calmer person and will not have his follower responding in anger, perceived justified anger, or rudeness. He needs me to be a calmer person that doesn't take things personally or feel like they have to fight in all situations. This took some work.

And anger causes me to respond in toxic ways, our next sign, mainly in the mode of passive-aggressive. Passive-aggressiveness is a huge one, but at least I recognized it, and he recognized it. It's a form of manipulation that he and I absolutely didn't want in our relationship. This is one we could talk about and point out to each other as not allowed. My time in therapy actually helped a lot with this. Once I was able to talk to someone about the toxicity of my childhood that could help, this toxic way of dealing with life became more noticeable and fixable.

Then, there is nuclear. You wouldn't think this is a hazard sign that would be involved. But, yes, in my toxic way of dealing with life, nuclear was there. And it popped out without warning once at the beginning when Dan said he wanted me to do something—I don't even remember what it was—and I tore off the collar and left it on the bed, saying "I'm done, I can't do this!" and left. That is one of the reasons we have a clause in our contract saying steps have to be taken for either of us to leave the relationship. We can't be walking around giving our all and our best to the relationship if we are constantly wondering if one of us is just going to tear the collar off one day and say "Nope, I'm done." Though that could happen, we've put things in place to make it harder and give each other a chance to breathe before making a nuclear decision.

Thankfully, these signs don't live on the side of me anymore. I've done so much work and Dan has been my "remover of hazard signs", so that we can now travel through the tunnels without worrying about blowing everything up.

Instead of a huge 18-wheeler with barrels of toxic sludge, I'm more of a hippie van full of flowers, healing and light. The sludge has been neutralized and the light can shine through. And if any sludge is left behind and works its way through, we are much more able to deal with it.

What were the biggest hazards in the first few years of your relationship?
Kevin:

This question instantly provokes a lot of content for me. It obviously brings to mind all the early hazards, which also makes me contemplate what hazards we are facing now, but will only really understand in the fullness of time.

The biggest early hazard would probably be assumptions and fantasies. Neither of us knew much about being in an Authority Transfer relationship, but we had some exposure to people being "Master/slave" in online chat rooms, a few popular press examples (*Secretary* and the Gor books), one kink book (*The Loving Dominant*) and, for me, the hierarchical relationships shown in some of Robert Heinlein's books. We, like many couples, built our relationship based on the fantasy and assumptions that we brought into the relationship—and that was super dangerous to the success and longevity of our relationship. We had to figure out that all the wank-fodder and fictional worlds don't translate perfectly to the real world. We had to be willing to be relationship nerds—designing, experimenting, testing, learning, adapting, evaluating. I believe that many of the failures of this relationship style are in those couples unable to free themselves from their assumptions and fantasies, and instead create a relationship that is pragmatic and functional (but still smoking hot).

The second hazard might have been laziness. It was good to be King. Some of my early beliefs about being a Leader, plus my natural inclination to be lazy, made it easy to slack off on doing my role, maintaining my end of the deal, taking care of my shit—the list of places my laziness had to be noticed and corrected is almost a book on its own. Not being attentive and effortful means that the relationship could have coasted into failure.

Lack of self-awareness, coupled with a poor understanding of Katie, was a hazard. It was easy to make decisions and guide us based on my superficial understanding of what I thought we should be doing. But I hadn't really come to explore my own priorities, Katie's priorities, and what those meant to the priorities of the relationship as a whole. Decisions were driven by interest, or my attraction, or by inclination and whim, not by a rock-solid reference to what was critical to us. Said another way, my Leadership was influenced by our wants, not by our needs. Beyond that, not understanding my Follower made it easy to imagine a fantasy version of her, then be surprised when the Real Katie didn't behave like the girl in my head. Learning about Katie allowed me to understand the amazing creature I own and make full use of her, while still respecting and honoring who she is, and her individuality.

> I believe that many of the failures of this relationship style are in those couples unable to free themselves from their assumptions and fantasies, and instead create a relationship that is pragmatic and functional (but still smoking hot).

Related to the other ideas, my own lack of self-discipline was a huge early hazard. For example, if I wanted to play games all day, I did. Lazy. Neglectful of my responsibilities. Dismissive of the value of time with Katie. I still love gaming, but I have honed my self-discipline such that I am more mindful, present, and engaged in our lives. I do my jobs. I prioritize time with Katie. I rarely sink so deep into a game that I ignore the world around me.

I suppose the final hazard that comes to mind are the handful of terrible decisions I made that hurt Katie or undermined her ability to trust me, and my ability to lead. I acted selfishly, or pushed her to do things that were not good for her, or punished her when it was unnecessary because I believed I "should", or made decisions for our livelihood that were financially destructive. Terrible dumb stuff that was a real hazard to our surviving as a couple. The solution to this one was not effort and attention—it was taking responsibility for the fucking mess, doing everything I could to fix it, promising to learn from the experience, and then gaining the forgiveness of my girl.

What were the biggest hazards in the first few years of your relationship?
Katie:

Hot domination. Soft submission. Sex and scenes and gracious service at any moment. A quiet mind releasing authority and attachment. Ahhh, the fantasy!

The fantasy version is hot. The book versions are clear and concise, like reading an owner's manual for a La-Z-Boy chair.

The reality vs the concept was my biggest hazard. As the songify video says, "Reality hits you hard, bro." (Google time!)

In the first couple of years, I was continually faced with the surety that I was doing it wrong. My daily interactions with Kevin were nothing like "The Right Way" I pictured in my head. This left me continually measuring myself as a failure. Worse yet, instead of seeing improvement, I saw myself wandering further from the fantasy with each step. Within the first six months I wondered if I had offered Kevin something that I could not deliver on. I was tormented by my false advertising. I was not meek, not instantly compliant, not quiet in my head. My personality and natural inclinations boiled up through my attempts to be otherwise.

I am a Gitterdun Girl.™ Super driven. I love organizing *myself* and my surroundings. I thrive with delegation of duties rather than supervision. I struggle with pride and an inclination towards fragile self-confidence. That's a super bad combo, but it remains an issue even today. This means sharp correction, harsh micromanagement, and a lack of autonomy slides me into a dark place. These were all aspects of me as Kevin's follower that we both needed to learn and I needed to accept.

The turning point was a moment when I was crying on the couch saying once again, "I'm no good at this. I think the wrong things, say the wrong things, and do the wrong things."

Kevin was holding me and he said the perfect statement to start me towards serving with acceptance of myself. He said, "You are who I chose. You serve me the way that pleases. If you weren't, I'd let you know and we would fix it. I am the one to judge if you are doing a good job."

There was such appreciation from him and recognition of my style of service. There was such relief to become aware that I did not have to change my personality for this relationship style, I just needed to be used in a way where I flourished and felt valued.

> I was crying on the couch saying once again, "I'm no good at this. I think the wrong things, say the wrong things, and do the wrong things."

Those first couple of years are rocky for anyone in any relationship. Settling in, fitting the pieces together. Authority Transfer adds the benefits of structure and being intentional, but also the higher demands of those aspects. The first years are going to be about incredible growth, or crash and burn. We didn't crash, but we certainly banged into a lot of shit. We didn't burn, but we treaded close to ignition a few times.

I believe that the humility of Kevin as a leader was essential to navigating that part of our journey. He was able to hear my struggles not as criticism of his leadership, but as a problem the CEO of the company needed to resolve. When a hazard arose, he would slow down, hear me out, clarify the information and together we would find our way towards solutions.

The most important part was that we then attended to our solution and were mindful of fixing the issues. It's easier to have a conversation than it is to do what you say is important. Like an exercise plan, it takes discipline beyond the initial agreement to do what is healthy and improves your life.

Chapter 3: Eroticism and Intimacy

How important is sex, eroticism, and intimacy in your relationship?
Dan:

To quote John Cleese, "Now, sex. Sex, sex, sex. Have we gotten as far as the penis entering the vagina?"

This is actually a very challenging question. I like sex. I enjoy sex and sexuality. I enjoy sex with dawn as well as with other people. I have fond memories of my first one-night-stand (which happened a few weeks ago, over the course of two dates, and we are still in touch—I am not very good at one night stands, it appears).

I am reflecting, is it that what is important is not sex or eroticism, but instead an acceptance of them? If eroticism is sexual desire ... blah, blah. I am too much in my head here This is sex! Fun, exciting, messy, adventurous, enjoyable. Fucking and sucking feels good! Orgasms are awesome; sometimes not having one is also awesome.

> Eroticism though, if it is the acceptance of sexual desire, is important. Very much so.

Here is a new thing; I am more inclined than ever before in my life to have a bisexual experience because ... well, why the hell not? When I see erotic images that include boy parts I don't ignore them as much but instead say "Huh, that isn't so scary." (Just for fun as I share this in our group writing session I'm going to stop and give Kevin a flirty leer).

The question in all this has not been answered, and I am not really sure I can. Because "how important is food" is easy for a man with a full refrigerator to answer. If I want sex, I get sex. If I can't sex dawn, I sex others. And often ... I don't want sex. Got other things to do. I've gone through significant amounts of time without. Not really a big deal to me. So, take my answer with a grain of salt. Or saltpeter.

Eroticism though, if it is the acceptance of sexual desire, is important. Very much so. Although we have played around with sexual power exchange, I don't currently limit dawn in any of her sexual right to fuck or masturbate or explore sexual stuff. If anything, the opposite. She is turned on by things I don't dig sometimes. But I don't reject any of it, I just don't participate.

Intimacy—from cuddles to boob grabs to loving looks to spooning in bed to simply being present for each other—is important. Compared to sex and eroticism, intimacy is the most important. When we lose intimacy, we start to lose each other. Sex can be a great communication tool, but intimacy is one of the foundational aspects of who we are to each other.

How important is sex, eroticism, and intimacy in your relationship?
dawn:

So in another writing we talked about BDSM and how important that is in our relationship, and I pretty much said that we don't have the scenes like we used to. We like it, but it's not super important to keep our dynamic going.

But sex? Eroticism? And intimacy? Super important. I actually feel this is one of our superpowers that we use to stay connected. This is part of what makes this relationship so joyful. Especially the intimacy. There may come a day that BDSM and sex may not even be possible for us … I hope not, but it could happen. Thank goodness I see others in their 80s that are still sceneing in the dungeons … they are my role models and my hope for our future. But if it happens that sex and BDSM are no longer on the table, it doesn't mean the relationship has to peter out. (See what I did there?)

Don't get me wrong, I love sex. I love sex with Dan. I love how we connect and after 20 years can still turn each other on, finding new likes and interesting things to do to make it hot and sexy. Remembering things we used to like and had forgotten about, now trying again. New positions that work better in an RV, those overhead cabinets for the win.

But more importantly to me, we embrace eroticism and intimacy. We have those moments in the morning where Dan gets up before me and when I step the two feet from the bed to the dining room table where he is sitting, I kiss his forehead. As I'm fixing my coffee another two feet away, he may lean over and pinch my ass, or come up behind me and wrap his arms around me, whispering in my ear or just hugging me tight.

Love and ownership taps in the form of karate chops or arm punches with weird noises and smiles happen all the time with us. Ask Kevin and katie.

> But sex? Eroticism? And intimacy? ... I actually feel this is one of our superpowers that we use to stay connected.

Just the other morning, a hug turned into a dance. Sometimes we just sway or step to whatever music is playing on the radio or is in our hearts. There is still a lot of hand holding and leg rubbing. All these moments of just saying, "Hey, I love you", or "I'm glad you are in my life", or "You're special to me", with a touch and a smile or gaze. Letting the other know that we are thinking about them. Sometimes with a wiggle of an eyebrow or a gleam in the eye to let the other know we are "thinking" about them.

We really make a point to share our feelings through touch. The light touch "hello" up to the rough grab of "you're mine". OK, Dan does that with me, I don't rough grab him. I don't karate chop him either, though I did punch his leg the other day for fun. That took us both by surprise. Not something I usually do.

All of these touches and dances and whispers, make me feel cherished. There are times I share that I need to be cherished in a relationship. This is one way that this happens.

So, sex. Important. Intimacy, super important. What about eroticism? Fuck yes.

For me, eroticism is how this all started and is still important to me today. I'm an erotic, sexual person. I like sharing naughty stories and pictures with Dan, sharing what I like as my tastes in erotica change. Sharing my naughty fantasies with him and then asking, "Is that too slutty?". All I have to do is to look down to get the answer to that question. Is he sporting a woody? I like being able to share that part of me with someone that gets it. Someone that embraces it. Someone that waters that garden, helping it grow.

So we may not have a lot of the traditional BDSM scenes, and sometimes not even a lot of sex. But that's OK because we have all the other stuff, all the other ways of showing each other how important we are to each other.

Remember we talked about what a crappy day looks like elsewhere in the book? A crappy day is when this sort of connection isn't happening. Every other day it does. This is our mode of operation which makes every day a good day. We are cherished, we are loved, and life is hot and sexy.

How important is sex, eroticism, and intimacy in your relationship?
Kevin:

Super-duper important, although if sex suddenly went away, we treasure and value this relationship enough that we would find ways to still foster intimacy.

Katie and I have built a relationship with sex, eroticism, and intimacy woven through our daily experiences. In part this is because we find the power play and transfer of authority sexy—so when she says "Sir" or when she kneels in front of me it is an intoxicating erotic experience. When Katie takes the time to nuzzle against me in a sweetly submissive way, it is immediately arousing. We have the amazing benefit that we have found a highly pragmatic relationship style that also happens to be really fucking hot in the way it is executed. We accidentally get eroticism simply as sparks in our ordinary daily interactions.

I sexualize a great deal of our ordinary interactions. Often when Katie is on her hands and knees washing the floor, or when she is bent over to reach something in a lower cupboard, I ask her whether she is intentionally flirting with me. And in fact, Katie is often intentionally flirting with me. She enjoys attracting my lusty attention.

We include a huge amount of touching and caressing in our daily life, even without it progressing to more overt sex. As we drive in the car I will often have a hand on Katie's arm, but gently lifting and nudging her boob with the back of my hand. She will stand close to me while we wait in line in a store, pressing her boob against the back of my arm in a way that is erotic. As we navigate around our home there are frequent squeezes and caresses. Katie will often walk directly at me, as if she intends to walk right through me, then stop and look up at me with adoring eyes—almost always leading to hugs or sweet kisses.

Am I writing porn here? Sorry. I'm not sure if I'm answering the question or just mentally masturbating.

Simple intimacy is also pervasive. We hold hands most of the time we are running errands together. When we sit side-by-side, usually we are very close. Even in public spaces Katie will often rest a hand (non-sexually) on my arm or thigh. We love physical contact and closeness, and we believe it is one of the many tools that keeps our relationship vital and exciting.

Sex ebbs and flows. We have had times where actual sex happened once every week or two. We also have times where twice per day is not unusual. By that I mean more of a "meal" of sex, rather than just a tease or treat or sample. The thing I most like about the "sex" part of our life is that we don't see a need to take sex to orgasm, particularly for me. Since Katie is ... orgasmically talented ... she is allowed to have orgasms whenever I haven't

> We have the amazing benefit that we have found a highly pragmatic relationship style that happens to be really fucking hot in the way it was executed.

denied them for her. So "sex" can often be a super erotic middle-ground for us, between a fondle/tease and a full sexual meal. Sex can be a five-minute interruption to our day where Katie gets on her knees and nuzzles and kisses my cock, gets me raging hard and crazy with desire—then we stop and go about our previous jobs. Sex for us is often a ten-minute fuck, and then we both pull up our pants, and try to get back to other tasks—but feeling freshly loved and intimate.

In part this manner of engaging with each other is just part of our kinks. I think her orgasms are sexy, so I want all of them, any time. I think having sex but not orgasming is super hot since it leaves me a horny, distracted, wreck. We both have a bit of a "free use" kink—meaning that Katie is available any time in any way for me to pleasure myself. Katie has an objectification kink, so having me (sometimes) uninterested in foreplay or her pleasure and just using her to enjoy myself is hot to her.

This way of relating is soul affirming. We constantly communicate that we adore each other. We communicate that the other will not be rejected. We communicate that touch is welcome and that we feel loved and loving.

How important is sex, eroticism, and intimacy in your relationship?
Katie:

"Let's talk about sex, baby,
Let's talk about you and me.
Let's talk about all the good things,
Boobs, butts and dingalings."

Sex and intimacy are a crucial part of who Kevin and I are. Not just the fun and orgasms, but the interactions that highlight our dynamic. I start to slump if there is a significant break in our sexual interactions. Kevin voices dissatisfaction with our days if we lose focus on it.

Intimacy

We are deeply intimate. Often it is through affection and tenderness during the day. Kissing and touching, being open and available to each other. I cannot remember a time that I stood in front of Kevin and he did not reach to embrace me. Nor a time that I pushed away his touch.

There is vulnerability and intimacy when I kneel and put my head in his lap. It is as sexy as fuck—no, literally, it is as sexy as fuck. It also highlights that I am devoted to him.

> Sometimes sex is Kevin using me as a cumdumpster for instant gratification.

The intimacy of kissing his feet. Gah! My pride still scuttles along a bit on this one. It used to be near impossible for me to do this when commanded. Instant raging bone sword for Kevin, though. That response helps me get there. Being in the right headspace also makes me more gracious about it. Sometimes feet-kissing intimacy is a tool Kevin uses when we are out of alignment with our roles.

There is intimacy in sharing our kinks and desires without fear of judgment or "ewww". In fact, we can pretty much count on each other to help explore those desires.

Eroticism

I'm really trying to tease apart the aspects of this question without hitting the dictionary definitions and getting too Data about it. There is so much eroticism in our days. We make intentional, conscious effort to be hot with each other, to arouse and tease each other. Subtly in public, blatantly while driving about or at home.

Kevin transforms before my eyes when he charges up the dominant energy towards me. The intensity of his gaze. His manner of holding me. His powerful stature with all muscles engaged. I dissolve in the eroticism of how hot he is.

I am erotic for Kevin by choosing my clothing to please him. Sometimes the focus is to merely look attractive for him. Sometimes it is about thin shirts without bras and happy nipples. When at home, my clothing is often about easy access. Tops with loose necklines or armholes. Skirts without panties underneath. Pants that drop easily. We are erotic in our flirting back and forth and with other people. We both have a Sharing Kink and find it extremely exciting to see each other be sexy with others.

Sex

Sex can be in all of the above. Sex is often of varied durations. Sometimes one of us has an orgasm, sometimes both, sometimes just me over and over again because that is Kevin's biggest kink.

We do not define sex as:
- ❖ Do things with the parts that need washing the most.
- ❖ Have orgasm.

Our sexual interactions can be a few strokes. A blowjob long enough to get him fired up. An intense makeout against the wall. Kevin is not focused on his orgasms most of the time. This allows the luxury of many interactions throughout the day.

Sometimes sex is Kevin using me as a cumdumpster for instant gratification. Yum.

Probably by now it is obvious that intimacy, eroticism and sex are incredibly important to us and an extremely entertaining way to highlight our dynamic.

Chapter 4: Outside the Norm

These roles are not the social norm. How do you have peace with them?

Dan:

If this question was about the labels we use, that would be trickier. After all, dominant and master are charged words and my journey of claiming both (and then retiring them) is deep and introspective. But this is a different question, so you'll have to read about that, if you are interested, elsewhere. Also, I'll note this question requires my one and only rant in this book, and it is a rant about politics and religion. If that is not your jam, feel free to flip over to the one of the sexy questions, lots of sweet stuff there. The following is not sweet, but instead, bitter.

> ...grown from who she was (someone who needed someone like me to help lead the way) to who she is now (someone who is here only because she wants to be and would be just fine without me.)

Let's look at the role and how I am OK with it. I understand the question; let me push through a bit of a ramble to get there. To start with, here is my probably incomplete and inaccurate version of history. Pardon me for a binary gender perspective. *Ahem.* In the old days, women gave birth to life, so they were clearly the more important gender. Then religion came along and said "You know, a woman's place is in the home, and they are too delicate to vote and too dumb to have real jobs so they should not be allowed to own property or have inheritance. Also, men not being able to have a bit of self-control when they are near a pair of tits should be solved by making women wear too many clothes at the beach". And other similar bullshit.

Now, at least in America (all I can speak of), some people have broken free from that stereotype and consider men and women equal. Further, they suggest men that lord over women just because they are men are douche-nozzles. But don't get too enthusiastic yet, because religion is making a comeback, buying politicians and pushing laws to remind us of the good old days where uteruses have less rights than rapists. Rant over, but you asked the question, not me. And to be honest, that was a pretty mild reflection of how I feel about it.

I feel that and have seen that women make just as good Leaders as men; I have followed many women in different roles in my life. With all this in mind, let's answer the actual question. I am at peace with my male Leader/female follower role because I am, at the end of the day, empowering dawn.

Let's restate. By taking away dawn's power, making her do what I say, correcting her when she was less than pleasing, making her fuck and suck when I want and it being about my pleasure … she has grown from who she was (someone that needed someone like me to help lead the way) to who she is (someone who is here only because she wants to be, and would be just fine without me).

Two other aspects. One: no one outside of our relationship except our friends and the alternative community know we are a Male Lead/female follower couple. And two: when we teach power exchange, we make a point of making it clear that although we are who we are, we know and respect and look up to many great Leader-follower couples who have Female Lead and other combinations.

Finally, the part that I am a bit avoiding because it sounds … well, you'll see. I know that what we have works. As annoyed as I am to type it, "Yes, I know that what we are doing perpetuates the fucked-up social norm, but we're different!" Yet, in my heart, I feel that is true, I see dawn being more powerful and complete than she was. I do not feel I have any rights to anything because I have a dangling wiener.

These roles are not the social norm. How do you have peace with them?
dawn:

At this point in my life, I don't particularly care what people think. I turn 55 today and I'm going to start wearing red hats (maybe purple) and telling people to get the fuck off my lawn. I'm happy. We are happy. This is consensual and what feeds us. We are sitting in our seats of power and I have no problem with telling people to mind their own business.

But at the beginning, I struggled a bit more with this. Well, a lot more. Was it because I was a woman desiring someone to take control?

Was it because of my past baggage and I was trying to relive the past? My ex certainly thought so. I tried to find people to talk to about this, but couldn't find anyone.

I remember stressing about it and talking to Dan. His reply was that it was consensual and wasn't hurting anyone else. But of course he would say that. He's a guy and wanted me to submit to him. Though, in reality he wanted it because I wanted it. We were feeding off of each other. Which is what made it so much sweeter.

Wow. I just had a memory. I was still in contact with one of Dan's ex-wives at the time. I shared with her what was going on. She had the same sort of background as me, and basically told me to tell anyone that had a problem with it to fuck off. She had actually explored power dynamics and felt that she deserved to do whatever made her happy, and if anyone had a problem with it, it was none of their business. She had come to peace with it. Oddly enough, talking with his ex helped soothe some of the doubt I was going through.

Then, along comes the intervention that I'm sure I've talked about elsewhere in this book or the podcast or something. Dan and I were in our second year of being collared. This was after a year and a half of designing our contract and playing at D/s Lite. We met a powerful couple in the spiritual community who were hosting a drumming circle at their house. It was the High Protocol year of our relationship and even though we tried not to be obvious about it, since this was a spiritual gathering and not a kink or Leather group, I entered the backyard behind Dan, holding a gift for the hosts. Dan had his hand on my belly, a soothing gesture for us.

"You're a femininst, right?" She nods. "Well, so am I, and that means I get to decide what I want to do as a woman. I get to decide what to do with my life. THIS makes me happy."

The couple didn't show it, but took offense at me walking behind Dan with his hand on my power spot. They'd done a lot of work with groups about empowering women and it struck them as wrong. It wasn't much later that the wife invited me out for tea, stating she wanted to talk to me about what's going on with me and Dan. This was a rescue mission for her.

I showed up to the house with a folder of information. (I don't even remember what was in it at this point.) I'm trying to explain to her how it's a valid relationship style. How I'm doing fine and it's consensual and …. I babbled for 3 hours. She was trying to figure out how I could allow a man to be in charge. These were the years of fighting back against the oppression of women. *[Added—which are still happening!]* I get it. I see what it looks like from the outside, but damn it, I'm happy! I finally get so frustrated at myself for not having a clear answer that will satisfy her that I almost yell ... "You're a feminist, right?" She nods. "Well, so am I and that means I get to do what I want as a woman. I get to decide what to do with my life. THIS makes me happy. THIS is consensual and I trust him with all of me. THIS is what I want. I'm sorry you don't understand, but I don't NEED YOU to understand." She sat back with that. "Well, if you'd said that at the beginning, we'd have saved 3 hours." Over the next year, she and her husband started exploring themselves and then became the producers of one of the biggest kink groups around. If it wasn't for the pandemic (Covid-19), it would still be going strong.

So I had those experiences, but I had a third that really helped me out. My therapist. I had been seeing her during my divorce and during the beginning of my healing path. I actually saw her for almost a decade, but the important part of the story is here at the beginning. I was seeing her during the time when Dan and I got together and when Dan collared me. I'd been wearing my day collar for a few weeks when she asked me if I was going to tell her about it. She knew what it was and had hoped that I would bring it up.

I didn't want to be judged by someone that I highly respected and I thought would try to talk me out of it. But she brought it up and had me talk about what it meant to me. No judgment. Instead, she asked if she could meet Dan. He came in, they had a chat, she was satisfied and we moved on with my therapy that had nothing to do with my choice of relationship style.

Then, Dan and I started hanging out at events, running our own power exchange group and creating events. I met so many people in power exchange relationships. Gender didn't matter. There were so many combinations. I was supported in my belief that I'm not the submissive just because I'm a woman.

Years go by. I'm pretty stable with my beliefs and embracing this life we've built. We are now into today. I will admit that when this question was first pulled out of the box a couple of weeks ago, fire flew into me. I wouldn't have been able to answer that question without a lot of "Fuck the world! And what's going on in it!" instead of a real answer. So I asked that we wait 'til I had calmed down enough to look at my progress over the years.

Because of the current political situation of the government trying to take away women's rights and the old men in office trying to change laws and turn back time to suit them, I've had to look at my role again and have wondered what people think about me being the follower in my relationship with a man as a leader.

I could worry about what others think and walk away. Oddly enough, this is the first time in the weeks of me being upset at the situation that I even thought of that. Instead, I lean into our relationship and my role with even more conviction that it's the right way for me to exist. I'm powerful and no one better doubt that, regardless of my role as follower or that I'm a woman. Dan is powerful not because he's a man, or in the Leader role but because he's Dan. Our dynamic works not because of being man and woman and who is in charge, but because of who we are as people, what we've consensually designed and our perseverance to make this relationship work.

So, the world that has an issue with it, can fuck off. I'm the happiest I've ever been.

These roles are not the social norm. How do you have peace with them?
Kevin:

I suppose I'm going to poke at this a couple of ways. A few bullet points later ... and I'm ready to rock!

Society looking at me
The first issue that comes to mind is that folks might look at my relationship with a variety of energies—interest, disgust, curiosity,

arousal, etc. They might look at me personally with some concern about being abusive or controlling. They might look at Katie with admiration, disgust, lust, or rescuer energy.

We avoid almost all of that by keeping our relationship pretty quiet. We don't want Mrs. Grundy peeking through her blinds into our life and having an opinion about what makes us happy. We can be authentically us, showing our love and joy to the folks we encounter publicly, and I can make Katie be my mindless toy behind closed doors.

I recall that at one point we made friends with a couple who we originally met as simply friends-of-friends. We were totally out to them about our Authority Transfer because they were swingers and we figured we were all kinky fuckers, so it was OK. About a year into our friendship with them we had a nice dinner on the town and they admitted to us that they were really freaked out by our relationship, initially. They were really worried for Katie and thought that I was a domineering asshole. Except they never found any evidence of that while watching us. They only saw joy and respect. They saw caretaking and admiration. They eventually had to give up their "societal norm" first impression because they took the time to see us authentically. Society is rarely so gracious.

> I accept that my weirdness in the eyes of society is because I am an adventurer, exploring the places other people fantasize about.

[Note: They now explore all kinds of BDSM and Dom/sub experiences, but that started long after we moved away. Not our fault!]

Me feeling weird

If I am outside the norm, I face the internal challenge of not fitting in or being an outcast. Humans are built, through thousands of years of evolution, to viscerally avoid being outcast. We are (on the whole) inclined to want to be included and accepted. So having a condition or making a choice that puts us as outsiders can be painful. I have a few ways I manage this. One is that I keep my other-ness hidden. I look like a great husband. Another is that I consider Authority Transfer an improvement on the relationship models that I have been exposed to in society. It is sexier. It is pragmatically superior. So I accept that my weirdness in the eyes of society is because I am an adventurer, exploring the places other people fantasize about. The general public thinks hopping a steamship into the depths of the Amazon is weird, while the explorer thinks sitting in a tiny flat in the cesspool of London is weird. Potato Po-tah-to.

My influence on society

As an explorer, I have the opportunity to say "Hey! You fuckers that are starving to death in your cave? Yeah, you. There's actually a buffet just over that hill right there." Katie and I teach, in part, because we believe this relationship choice is a great match for some people. We would love to teach to non-kink crowds and will likely make an effort in that direction in the years after the COVID peak.

I've written elsewhere about the worry Katie and I have about worsening the situation in society, or reinforcing the belief that having a vagina means you are inferior, or should be controlled. We don't want our carefully constructed hierarchy to reinforce the use of power-over on women in particular.

We justify ourselves in a couple of ways—first, we keep our relationship so down-low that nobody can take it as an example of control and use it to bolster their own shitty opinions. Second, we believe we have the right to live our authentic and joyful lives, and that compromising what brings us joy simply to keep some nameless faceless "society" outside our door happy—is not acceptable. Fuck that.

The norm is a disaster

Let's pretend you are from a society where clitoral mutilation is the norm. Or where firing 1000 babies out into space as an offering to Space God happens every New Years. Or Hunger Games are in your district too. Sometimes it is appropriate to say "Hey, you know what? What is normal around here really isn't very great."

We look at all the terrible things people do to each other in egalitarian relationships. We look at the subjugation of women (in particular) in much of the world. We look at the work ethic, the repression of sexuality, the cancerous growth of humanity, the violence to each other … on and on. Society has very little room to judge my loving perverted delicious life.

[Once the time ran out, a couple of people needed 2 minutes to wrap up. I couldn't figure out where to profitably spend that 2 minutes on this writing, so I spent it being goofy instead. You're welcome?]

A few limericks:

There once was a lady from Ryde
Who ate a green apple and died.
The apple fermented
Inside the lamented
And made cider inside her inside.

There once was a lady from Bryte
Whose speed was much faster than light
She set out one day
In a relative way
And returned the previous night.

These roles are not the social norm. How do you have peace with them?
Katie:

I have played piano enough in my life that my middle finger works with ease.

Actually, I do not approach societal impressions with disregard. But let's start with self-acceptance.

Self-acceptance

I approach this as a series of internal questions. I will list as many as I can regurgitate quickly like a seagull with a belly full of Sea Bass.

Am I loved?

Am I joyful?

Do I find myself content with the person I am, as well as eager to improve and grow?

Do I feel empowered and competent?

Have I chosen a Leader wisely to ensure that all of the above values are supported?

The answer is absolutely. I am healthier, happier and more loved than almost every other person I have met in any relationship. That sounds egotistical and maybe even arrogant.

If you don't know what you have,
How do you recognize that you have what you want?

I don't know if that is a real quote from someone somewhere or I just became Homer Allen Poe. I'll look it up when the clock isn't ticking.

I know the value of what I have in my life, my role, and in Kevin as my partner. If I can't find self-acceptance in this amazing life with such an incredible person, it isn't likely to ever happen for me.

I do not view the follower role as an inferior position. We are a team. We are aligned. The business model we use as a touchstone supports this acceptance in my mind. I got hired on to be the COO of a company that has grown and improved for twenty years. My CEO is the best boss I can imagine. The employee perks are incredible. I get *down* time often. I do not feel less.

> If I can't find self-acceptance in this amazing life with such an incredible person, it isn't likely to ever happen for me.

I have shared elsewhere that there is an inclination in my brain that easily slides towards being sad and beating the shit out of myself with internal dialogue. I *know* it has nothing to do with Kevin or his regard for me. Sometimes it gets activated by my brain chemicals being askew, sometimes by stress, sometimes the universe just tilts my CPU on its side and I do not compute well.

Self-acceptance takes a beating for this period of time. A day, a week, at one point it lasted a few months. Kevin and I are hyper-aware of this situation and we go into repair mode. I work hard at my internal dialogue. He supports that with words of direction, appreciation and love. I do not lash out and look for him to be my punching bag or cause of the sadness. He does not get frustrated with me as I do the hard work.

I have not shared this with many people, but here it is. Ah well. Maybe that totally balances the above statements that seemed egotistical and arrogant. I mostly want folks to know that self-acceptance isn't all sunshine up your speculum. Self-acceptance has ebb and flow to it. It takes mental discipline to keep it in place, but also patience when it wanes.

Social Norms

I feel more for Kevin than myself in this topic.

We are in a male-led relationship. The vagina carriers have been stomped upon since their hair was long enough to be a handle to get them into a cave. Kevin is cautious to be very subtle in his role in public. We know who we are, we do not want folks angry or worried for me because they don't understand. I do not struggle with social norms beyond being concerned that Kevin may be cast in a poor light—and so undeservedly.

We present at Human Sexuality classes for universities. We talk about consensual, inegalitarian relationships and how they can be successful. Kevin grants me the floor for an excessive amount of time so that students can hear that I am happy, joyful, funny, successful, competent, financially secure on my own, able to manage my daily life. I need to knock down all the stereotypes of the subjugated woman—I cannot imagine how difficult this is for male followers! These classes with up to 80 university students get a clear window into who I am, how successful this relationship is for us, and how loving and caring Kevin is.

Social norms can either free people to be who they want to be in life, or restrict people into what others want them to be.

I choose freedom.

Section 2: Interactions

The questions in this section explore some of the specific details around our interactions with our Authority Transfer partners.

5) What actions/tools do you use to maintain the dynamic on a daily basis?
6) Is your relationship goal and growth driven? How do you attend to that?
7) Can and do you inspire your partner into their role?
8) How do you give feedback to your partner?
9) How do you encourage and support open communication?
10) What is your experience with leading as the Follower, and following as the Leader?
11) How do you attend to "reaction" and "resistance" in your relationship?
12) How do you interact in public? Talk about the subtleties of your role.
13) How important is BDSM play and scenes in your dynamic?

Chapter 5: Daily Tools

What actions/tools do you use to maintain the dynamic on a daily basis?

Dan:

This should be an easy one to answer; dawn and I are all about tools. We have two previous books that are basically that—we tell some stories and then share the tools that assisted us in getting us through them. (From the department of self-promotion, those books being *The Polyamory Toolkit* and *Hearts and Collars*—buy two of each, have one more than you need!)

When it comes to daily action, though, this is a bit different. Some daily actions/tools are the ones that keep things focused and remind you of the style of relationship you are in. For example, dawn getting my meds at night. There is no logistical reason for this—I can get them and do a good job of remembering them. The only reason she does it is because she is mine and I will it to be so. Other actions have included having coffee for me when I wake up, packing my lunch in secret (this way it is a pleasant surprise when I open it), preparing my clothes for the next day, and many others. Some of these are simple tasks and others are part of more complex rituals. In this conversation, I'll define the difference as my level of interaction with it. For example, dawn brings me coffee, held in a certain way, waits for me to acknowledge it. I do so, she hands me the cup, I smell it or sip it, and look up at her and tell her it is good, or thank you, or correct some small thing. This is a simple connecting ritual. As a task, the only part that has to happen is coffee into a cup, then a cup into my hands or placed on the table. I might look up from whatever I am doing (and normally would and say thank you) but I might not.

As either a ritual or task, these little items dawn does for me throughout the day keep us connected.

> As either a ritual or task, these little items dawn does for me throughout the day keep us connected.

Other daily actions we have seem way more conventional. When we eat dinner, we often do so in front of the TV. Yes, I know, but don't get all judgy-judgy yet, let me finish the paragraph. We have two modes of eating dinner in our home, first the fully-engaged-with-the-food mode (which we do via a raclette sometimes, or by going out, or by just enjoying eating on the picnic table). The second is every other time we eat; then it is part of our ritual of going from both of us working our asses off (me at my 9-5 job, dawn with her million bits she does every day) to sitting with each other and transitioning to the rest of our evening. The show we watch will be short, light-hearted, and funny. Just something to give the mind a break so we can switch gears. (TV shows for us that meet this criteria include *Scrubs*, *Kim's Convenience*, *Ghost* on BBC, or *Would I Lie To You*, a quiz show.) Regardless, what this actually does is a tool that allows us to not only make the aforementioned shift from work, but makes sure we laugh daily. We normally laugh a lot regardless, but it is not to be overstated that laughter is a great daily tool we benefit from.

In another part of the book we talked about intimacy, so I won't repeat that here but that is both an action and a tool that is of huge value to us. An example of that is when I go to bed every night, dawn comes over and covers me up. She then climbs into bed and snuggles, whether she is going to bed yet or not. We talked in that same other section about sex, so again, no need to cover it again, beyond I'll mention sex can be a great tool as well. I won't suggest we have sex daily … but if you'd like to imagine we do, and what it is like, please feel free (and send me any erotic fiction it inspires).

Other daily tools I'll quickly point out that maintain our dynamic because they maintain my being a somewhat balanced human being include meditation, journaling, exercise, eating mostly well, and staying creative.

I will say this about a long-term relationship. We've practiced the tools enough at this point that I feel like many have become second nature. When the huge issues arise, they don't feel so huge because we maintain a foundation of who we are.

What actions/tools do you use to maintain the dynamic on a daily basis?
dawn:

I'm having a hard time with this one.

Part of me wanted to jump in with this writing and start talking about rituals and protocols and other things that we advise others to do when they are first starting out or who are trying to re-engage in this style of dynamic. I mean, rituals are a great way to shift that energy from egalitarian to hierarchical.

But now that we are full-time RVers, we don't use a lot of rituals or protocols in our daily life. We've become much more casual and nothing like that seems to be needed at this point. Though, we have gone a couple months where I was staying up a couple hours later than Dan, which meant that he was getting up a couple hours earlier than me. So, he had me make his coffee before I went to bed. Until that wasn't what he wanted anymore and now I don't. I also get his meds at night as a form of service. But that's about it for ritual.

"Use me, use me, I'm not your average groupie."

What we do have is ongoing power exchange with a pretty solid foundation, where we enjoy being in our roles. Dan just sent me over to our RV to get him a drink, after a little clarity, and it was "Yes, Sir". I like being a tool for him. I like being of service. I like making his life easier. I think that's one of our biggest tools. Reminds me of the song *Baby Got Back*: "Use me, use me, I'm not your average groupie." And he likes using me. Luckily for things more than fetching him a drink, of which I'm sure I'll mention at some point.

I do most of the domestic stuff in the RV. Is that because I like being in service to him, though, or because he works a full-time job and I don't? Well, it's a little of both. I have a lot of work to do that isn't domestic, but I like taking care of him and doing the cleaning, cooking, laundry and other such mundane things, which is literally in service to him. I don't like doing these things for just anyone. This is a way of staying in my role that we both take advantage of.

Another tool is simply his tone of voice or the words he uses when he tells me to do something. Especially if we've been silly and casual most of the day. Those are simple things that help maintain the dynamic.

We also use moments of intimacy and karate chops and arm punches, sex and all the hot stuff as tools as well. When he grabs my hair or pulls me into a hug or grabs me from behind when I'm bending over in the kitchen or pinches a nipple out of the blue. Those are all quickie moments that remind us who is in charge. They are the fun moments that get mixed in with our normal day.

Sometimes he'll come up with a new order just to shake things up a bit and just because he can. Sometimes it's a "flex" moment, sometimes not. Recently, he's given me two orders that I'm still adjusting to. One has to do with changing an honorific and another has to do with our daily/weekly health routine that we are both working on and trying to figure out. These are things that I don't particularly want to change, but will with some adjusting on my part.

So, even though I will always recommend rituals and protocols as a way for maintaining a dynamic, there are so many other options that we are currently figuring out and enjoying.

What actions/tools do you use to maintain the dynamic on a daily basis?

Kevin:

One of the first actions that comes to mind feels like it might be ... I dunno, less lofty and valuable than I would want as my opener. But fuck that, timer's ticking, boyo.

Katie's status as a free-use sex toy is one of the ways we are frequently aware of the AT dynamic through the day. While she is always a willing partner to touch and other shenanigans, the fact that I can use her at my will, with no regard for what task or condition she's currently in—that simple truth communicates "ownership" to each of us. But my ability to grab a tit whenever doesn't feel like it should be the best tool at my disposal.

On a daily basis we talk about our schedules and task lists. In particular, Katie comes to me with a list of jobs she would like to accomplish. We review the jobs that I have on my list, and how her list will be influenced by my needs and preferences. Sometimes I decide that some project on my list will be enhanced by her participation, and that means something on her list gets delayed. Sometimes she has errands on her list and that means that unless I want to wipe with printer paper, I make the command decision to make sure that task gets prioritized. In this way I can, as the Leader, make best use of our time, be aware of her schedule, ensure that our priorities are being attended to, and find places for fun/recreation/health pursuits, etc. If I let Katie make her own schedule she would simply work until she falls over.

> The way Katie asks questions, or provides input to me—heck, her communication style in all ways—is a reinforcement and tool used to highlight our AT dynamic.

Katie will, throughout the day, bring me decisions to make. The vast majority of these decisions are simple daily activities or choices that she could easily manage on her own. In fact, she would be significantly more efficient if she didn't slow down to get my approval and simply did the thing as she saw fit. She forces herself to not make all those simple decisions because it reinforces our roles for each of us. Why is she asking me—again—whether I'd like her to put her hair into a ponytail? Because in asking me she is highlighting for both of us that I have control over her life. Why is she asking me—again—whether I want her to buy bananas? Because even though I have said "yes" the last fifteen times, she wants to help each of us remain mindful of our roles. She doesn't do this robotically, unable to make decisions or function without my approval. She does it thoughtfully and strategically, to provide the little touchstone to our dynamic.

Katie spends a great deal more time anticipating my needs and seeking after my comfort than vice versa. I want to care for her and adore her, but I rarely offer to go to the fridge and find her a little snack. Her effort to make my day joyful and comfortable are constant reminders that we have a special relationship dynamic.

The way Katie asks questions, or provides input to me—heck, her communication style in all ways, really—is a reinforcement and tool used to highlight our AT dynamic. She never says a judgmental or unkind word. She carefully gives feedback in a way that is respectful even if in disagreement. Her very method of communication is a minute-by-minute tool that keeps our hierarchical roles foremost in our minds.

Well, so far it looks like Katie does all the great stuff to maintain the dynamic. That's interesting. I ... let her do that stuff? Kevin—think, man!

Huh ... I guess I've mentioned a fairly frequent action that highlights and maintains the dynamic. I tell Katie "no" a lot. She wants to wash the dog, or scrub the roof of the RV, or ride her bike with her yoga mat and laundry basket on her head for maximum efficiency of her trip—and I don't allow it. Her not getting her way because I impose my preference happens pretty regularly. So I suppose the Leader action that I do to maintain the dynamic is give direction and have expectations, which she must accommodate. Having to follow seems to remind her that she is a Follower, eh?

And I often impose my will on her clothing choices. Left to her own devices—pretty outfits. With my lordly oversight? Side boob. Under boob. Sheer. Tight. Loose. Pretty much make a list of what Katie would never wear otherwise, and that is her current wardrobe. Pretty sure that is a constant reminder of our dynamic as she tries to get her boob back into the barely existent "shirt" I've "requested" for the day.

[Kevin-the-reader ruefully notes that I started with sex-toy Katie and closed with side-boob Katie. I swear I don't really have a one-fuck-mind. Track. One-track-mind.]

What actions/tools do you use to maintain the dynamic on a daily basis?
Katie:

Have you ever done a bootcamp? First day sucks and everything is exhausting. It takes incredible concentration and determination. No coordination to the exercises. Aching. Suffering. Then the first day is over and you realize you have to take all that exhaustion and lessons into the next day and do more. And then another day.

You have to push. You need tremendous self-discipline. You feel like you are perhaps doing worse instead of better. Two weeks of this consensual body and mind torture passes. Suddenly you realize that you go to the gym to work out and whoa, that was smooth, I think I will add five pounds to this exercise, have I already done 40 pushups? I can still breathe, didn't this start with me grinding through every exercise with determination and scrambling along to keep up?

That's Authority Transfer for me.

At the start, the daily interactions were grindingly hard. New ways to think, to communicate, to problem solve, to fuck, to love someone. Day after day, until habits began to form, it began to feel like natural interactions. Building on that basis of relationship fitness we added more expectations, fine tuning the relationship.

Kevin is likely to turn a hug into a throat hug, with his penis, from the inside.

Kevin and I have consciously put tremendous effort into learning how to speak to each other in a way that maintains the dynamic. Not only in normal conversation, but also very aware of kicking our conversation into a more demanding level of our roles. When this happens, Kevin's requests and direction are more precise and commanding. My manner of addressing him is more respectful and honoring.

Daily we address each other in our Authority Transfer "dialect" with habit and grace. It is easy. At any time one of us may step into a more intense level of communication. Highlighting that he is my Leader and I follow.

Instead of "katie, please get me a coffee," it might be "Girl? Go get me a coffee." I might approach him with Sir at the beginning of my sentence.

The way we express affection and touch each other is also supportive of the dynamic on a daily basis. (There's another question in this book with all the fuck details.) We are very intimate with each other throughout the day. The dynamic is highlighted and supported by me showing affection in a soft, but ravenous manner. Kevin is likely to turn a hug into a throat hug, with his penis, from the inside. (No, seriously.) He will hold my neck in a way that says, "Mine." He will grind against me. I am literally free-use to him. Not like those Reddit porn girls who pose with their library books while getting fucked. Literally. Drop that vacuum right now and bend over, stop digging in the garden and show me your boobs kinda free use.

Our routines and daily expectations support the dynamic. Part of what we treasure in this Authority Transfer relationship is improving ourselves in many aspects. We literally have daily expectations that we both meet to ensure our well-being and attend to that commitment. For years now we have daily measured our exercise, diet, hydration, sleep, creativity, satisfaction and more. This has us very mindful of who we are for ourselves and each other.

Intentionality is the word that most sums up the way we continue to be just as fresh in this relationship as we were years ago—perhaps more so even. We are hyper-aware that what we choose to say and do either supports and deepens the relationship or undermines it.

The Bootcamp finished a long time ago and most of the brutal suffering of growth and improvement is behind us. We have a level of Relationship Fitness™ that is mostly maintained by regular routine and attention. We also push it for intensity and growth from time to time so we do not become lazy and complacent.

We have worked this hard to be Relationship Athletes™ and we do not want that muscle turning to flab. Maybe I have taken this metaphor too far.

Kevin has a big cock and a long tongue. I want him to keep using them on me. So I do nice things for him every day.

Chapter 6: Growth Driven

Is your relationship goal and growth driven? How do you attend to that?
Dan:

This is actually a fun question for me and I can answer for my primary relationship (dawn) as well as other power exchange relationships I've had. But first, let's talk about non-hierarchical relationships for a moment.

> It is like going to a personal trainer and saying, "I want to lose ten pounds," and they say "OK, here is the plan." Except in this case, after a few weeks you start skipping cardio and they show up at your door and demand you do better.

I've had a couple of relationships which are not like the "transfer of authority" that I've been in the past twenty years. One, with Karen, lasted twelve years. The other, with Kat, is at seven at the point of this writing and continues on. These are not per se growth based but love based. But growth happens. Organically and naturally; not due to anyone driving that outcome. This is great and enjoyable and I have nothing bad to say about it. I enjoy them. Check the years I mentioned above; good stuff. And yay polyamory.

But when it comes to power exchange relationships, these are always for me growth based. More specifically, you (the follower) will experience growth as a result of my Leadership. And if that doesn't happen, it means I am not doing a good job. Love may also happen. Normally so.

To put it another way, I identify as a Leader. So where are we going? Where am I leading you to?

The answer is to lead you to you. Less bullshit, less internal lies; more courage to be you, more clearly stated desires. If you are in a power exchange relationship with me, that is part of it and that must be understood. I don't want a static fuck toy or a changeless servant. I want us to start at A and work our way toward … well, we shall see. More on that below.

If you agree to PE with me, you are agreeing that you are ready to look in the mirror, determine what you really want, and make the effort to get there. It is like going to a personal trainer and saying "I want to lose ten pounds," and they say "OK, here is the plan". Except in this case, after a few weeks you start skipping cardio and they show up at your door and demand you do better.

The fun part of this is, to continue the above analogy, that losing ten pounds isn't the goal sometimes. Sometimes you work with the trainer and realize what you really wanted was to be more fit or feel sexy or be more confident. Or you get a twist that the trainer says you are not going to lose weight; instead, we are going to work on your body acceptance.

I realize that we may not know what the goal is in some areas when we start.

"The destination isn't the goal, the journey is." And thus, there is an adventurous element to growth. And we both have to be on board with that. This has been true for every single power exchange relationship I've been in. We start with "I want to learn about Leather" or "I just want to be a sex slave" and it takes a turn along the way and ends up somewhere new. Which is ... well, it is what it is. It is the way of things. I go into every one of these with a plan and a goal and knowing that our trip to Pittsburgh may end up with a stop in Cleveland we hadn't planned on.

Part two of this question is "how" and I have not left myself enough time to explain that in any valuable way. I'll instead point out two things.

First, the secondary impact of driving a follower to grow is that we as a relationship grow as well as I, as a Dan, grows.

Second, the big key to "how" is that I keep growing, striving, pushing and cajoling me to grow. I have to have a set of tools to share and the experience behind them. I can't advise you to embrace your sexuality if I don't. I won't have trustworthy tools around self-love unless I have tried them out.

I'll point out that this is the first book I've been a part of where I haven't said something like "This is what works for me, but if you are doing something else, that's fine, I'm OK, you're OK", etc. In this case, if you identify as a Leader and you are not Leading your follower in growth, then I'm a Leader, and you're a cucumber.

Is your relationship goal and growth driven? How do you attend to that?

dawn:

Well, the simple answer to the first part of the question is, yes. Our relationship is goal and growth driven. This is simply because Dan and I are both built that way. I would probably describe us as .... well. I am Goal and Growth driven and Dan is Adventure and Growth driven. The only difference between these two is that I have a couple different lists of goals that I want to accomplish over the next three years, vanilla goals and naughty goals. Dan doesn't actually have a written list of goals like I do, but does have a theme of experiencing life which leads to growth.

Over the years, each of us has also been known to shake things up on purpose for growth opportunities if things feel like they are getting stagnant or stale or boring.

How do we attend to this? Besides lists, and shaking things up on purpose, and starting new adventures, and being self-aware, and going through years of therapy and somatic therapy on my part, and all the new things we get involved in, producing events, teaching classes, writing books?

It almost sounds like a trick question ... how can you be in a relationship like this and not be growth or goal oriented?

Well, I guess I just answered my own question .... this is how we do it. If we feel a little stuck, we come up with a new class to teach. If we come up with a new class to teach it's because we want to bring something into focus. Maybe it's something new we've learned and want to share, or it's something we want to pick apart that has become important to us. What better way than to write a class about it? Designing the outline and building the terminology to be used and then gathering the meat of what to talk about?

Or we build a new event to produce. And then figure out how to keep our dynamic in place as we build something new and learn new skills like negotiating contracts [with hotels] and figuring out our staff for each event. Or we write a new book so that we can look at various topics. Like this one.

Writing this book and answering these questions is definitely a growth opportunity. It's a whole new way of writing that is absolutely out of my comfort zone. Pull a number to a question on a spreadsheet, state the question, type the question, set a timer for 25 minutes, and then a second timer for 30 minutes. Go! No time to write an outline to make sure I cover what I think is important. Instead it's free flowing thought which will actually break through most walls I've built up around the subject ... which becomes free flow writing. I learn something about myself. I learn something about Dan. Growth.

And I just mentioned something else that we do regularly, or I should say that Dan has me do regularly .... step out of my comfort zone. Those are amazing growth opportunities once I work past the resistance.

As for goals, at least my personal goals, I'm very self driven with that. Dan doesn't need to push most of the time as goals are very important to me. But, if he sees me not attending to something that he knows is important for me to accomplish, he'll bring it up. And either we discuss a plan of action or he makes a plan of action and tells me what is going to happen.

This is one of the major benefits I see in this style of relationship. We are here to support each other and help each other be the best people we can be. If one is feeling a little stale but doesn't have the motivation to move forward, the other can embrace their role and help push. Part of me feels that it's easier for Dan to push. And I think it is. If he sees something isn't getting done, or that we need a little shake up, he has the power to make it happen.

If I see it, I have ways of bringing it to his attention or by embracing what he expects of me and continuing to do the expectations to help motivate him.

The danger zone is when we both fall into a slump. And though we work hard not to let that happen, it has. And we struggle to figure out how to pull ourselves up by our bootstraps and get moving again. We look at each other, me at Dan hoping he will pick up the leadership again, Dan at me hoping I'll do something that motivates him. The longer we stay in the slump the harder it can be to pull ourselves out of it. Thank goodness one of us will get frustrated enough to call bullshit and do what needs to be done to pull us out of the hole we've dug.

It almost feels like a trick question....how can you be in a relationship like this and not be growth or goal oriented? I guess it's possible, but I'm not sure how.

Admitting you want this style of relationship and putting the work into it; looking at your needs, wants and desires, how could this be anything but about growth, in yourself as a person and in your relationship? I'm sure someone will let me know.

Is your relationship goal and growth driven? How do you attend to that?
Kevin:

You betcha it is—and much more so than any other relationship in my life has ever been. Growth is a priority we invest a lot of time in - for ourselves, for each other, and for the relationship. Even this book writing exercise is a huge opportunity for reflection and growth.

Even though it isn't part of the question, I want to take just a second to explore why we make it a priority. Partially we do so because we want to avoid stagnation. A clean flowing river rather than a smelly swamp. We also recognize that change is inevitable. We are going to evolve into different people as time passes and our relationship is going to alter over time—so we might as well accept that truth and intentionally take an active hand in designing and guiding that change. We believe we should do that which is in our power to ensure that the change is positive, rather than a slip, decline or roll of the dice.

How do we do that? Depends on the piece of life we are trying to address!

We set goals in order to have a target in the future. The goals can be aspirational—like being more open to adventure. The goals can be concrete—like learning to play the harmonica. We share and discuss our goals, and we support each other in working toward those goals.

We also have the goal (the conscious intention) to manage our health and aging to the best of our ability. We want to attend to that which is within our control in order to maintain our health and function for as long as possible.

We attend to our eating habits. We sometimes decide to be more strict with our eating plan (like a few months of ketosis) or we do a 24 hour fast as a digestion reset. Usually we just aim for being healthy and avoiding unhealthy food options. Very little restaurant food. Very little packaged and processed food. I'm currently doing an 18/6 intermittent fasting schedule.

We attend to healthy choices. No smoking. No drinking or drugs. Wearing seatbelts, masks, bike helmets. That isn't about growth so much as preventing early death, but it still speaks to our commitment to take care of ourselves, I suppose.

We attend to our health choices and our intention of both maintenance and improvement (growth) through a goal-tracking spreadsheet. We monitor on a daily basis whether we are getting exercise, getting sufficient hydration, getting sufficient sleep. Our current commitment includes 20-30 minutes of yoga each day and 30 minutes of walking/biking/hiking. We are not perfect at that, but we have a daily check on whether we are on task and attending to our goals.

For relationship growth we often rely on discussions. We discuss with each other and commit to taking lessons and applying them to improve our relationship. We also sometimes have discussion groups with peers and use that as an opportunity to discuss Authority Transfer topics and learn how others see a particular issue or problem. We also have more intense periods of introspection, like this retreat and writing project with Dan and dawn. We are digging into how each of us sees AT, how we manage our roles, how we connect to our partners. This helps us not only monitor where we currently are, but also set goals and aspirations for improvement.

> We believe we should do that which is in our power to ensure that change is positive, rather than a slip, decline, or roll of the dice.

Katie is exceptionally growth-oriented as a person. She wants to learn new skills, take on new projects, and have interesting new experiences. I am much less so. She bravely tackles things way outside her comfort zone—I cautiously tiptoe into growth opportunities. I am all about supporting her growth, and guiding us toward shared physical and relationship health, but I am probably pretty lazy about my own growth. That seems to be an unfortunate theme of this book. My own battle with laziness. Huh. I guess the fact it keeps popping up might mean I need to process it some more. And that is an example of how we manage and prioritize growth, I suppose. That topic seems to be near the surface of my consciousness, so I will discuss it in depth with Katie and we will together help me discover and then act.

We attend to growth by making it a shared priority, then putting action to that priority in the ways we are able.

Is your relationship goal and growth driven? How do you attend to that?
Katie:

Our relationship is intensely about being the best we can and improving ourselves and each other.

Kevin and I did not start that way. At least, not with the self-awareness that it would become a focus. We never had an initial conversation that stated, "I want to focus on health and wellness. I want to fine tune our relationship to be amazing. Growth and Personal Development are absolute Needs to me." Today, that would be part of the initial conversation for certain.

First our foundation was laid. How our dynamic looked. What our style of leadership and following was. How we communicated and interacted. Those basic pieces of growth and goals. From that foundation we found ourselves keen to continue to improve ourselves and our relationship. How do we attend to it?

- ❖ Deciding long and short term goals.
- ❖ Being aware of our values and priorities.
- ❖ Being willing to make change—sometimes drastic change to fix a problem or get our asses back in the saddle.
- ❖ Openly share where we feel we are lacking or if we have stopped attending to what is important.
- ❖ A commitment to pouring energy into the wellness of us and our relationship.

It is an incredible relief and comfort to me that I can read that list and answer, "Yes. Yes, we actually do all of that and have done so for many, many years."

Decide upon long and short term goals.

Kevin and I have frequent conversations about daily goals, weekly goals, long term things we want to achieve. Not merely stating the goals, but breaking it down to how we are going to get there. Making sure they are attainable. Making sure that it is going to enhance our life.

Being aware of our values and priorities.

As we discuss those goals we always reach back to the touchstone of our values. It is easy to end up off-course if we do not make sure that our efforts are aligned with what we value.

Sometimes we do this poorly. Allow me to address that with an example:

Being willing to make change—sometimes drastic change to fix a problem or get our asses back in the saddle

Kevin and I decided that we would contribute on a larger scale to the BDSM subculture by becoming involved in creating a public space for classes and events. We signed aboard with our intellect, with our bank account and with our physical energy. As time went on, we realized we were no longer aligned with our values, and our priorities were completely fucked up. The sacrifice of time, of physical labor and suffering was too great. We were doing so much for others that we were no longer attending to our health, our diet, our household … fuck, the dog hardly knew us any more.

When we find ourselves off track to this level of extreme, the fixing is ugly and painful. We had to be willing to make amends where we could. Throw money and apologies at the situation. Resign from the position we had signed on to. Then we faced the long road back to doing what we valued the most.

> Growth and personal development are absolute Needs to me.

Openly share where we feel we are lacking or if we have stopped attending to what is important.

Staying with the above example, at some point in this endeavor Kevin and I were sitting at a Jimmy Johns sandwich chain, totally exhausted, covered in drywall and paint, trying to eat so we could go back to work. I looked at Kevin and started to silently cry. Kevin held my hands and said, "I know baby. I know." And from there we started to figure out the hard shit we needed to do to get back to us.

When we have strayed from what our values and priorities are, we have to let each other know. Even if it is embarrassing: "I'm not eating right. I'm not happy with my body. I need to fix this problem and be more disciplined." Even when it is the other person: "You are speaking to me with less respect and regard." "I'm worried that you have been sedentary for days and not doing the right thing for your body."

Transparency and vulnerability support correction and improvement.

A commitment to pouring energy into the wellness of us and our relationship.

We have a commitment in this relationship to attain goals—to be the best we can be. We do this for ourselves and each other.

If you are green, you are growing. If you are ripe, you are rotten.

Chapter 7: Inspiration

Can and do you inspire your partner into their role?
Dan:

Well … of course. Maybe the question is different than what I am hearing, but cultivating my follower to be a follower is one of the primary things I do. I find out the best way to get the results I want, modify if needed or drive them the way I want in the name of "because I am the Leader". This is where I am different from some dominants that I've met both in real time and online. I am tempted to say that is the difference between a good one and a bad one, but that only applies to me and my home. My role as a Leader is to lead, to create opportunities for my follower's growth; to come up with a plan if they don't have one or to support the one they have. Actually, I would not have a follower that doesn't have a direction they want to grow. They may have a vague idea of where they want to be, but my followers have all had a common thread of "today I am this, but my heart or desire or passion or calling is to grow into that". Some would say you should be satisfied with the way things are—even my own delving into Buddhism suggests that always reaching for something you don't have is a path of suffering. Well, with all due respect to Siddhartha Gautama, fuck that shit. It is great to take an occasional breath and sit on your laurels, sure, but the truth is we have limited time on this planet so a) you should not rest until you are fully grown into the greatest human you can be and b) you will never be the greatest human you can be (and that is totally OK).

> The best way to inspire (these) is to practice it myself.

Is this a perk of Leadership? I not only inspire my partner into their role, I sometimes create it. I create the following to align with what I want and need. Learn to shine boots, prepare my coffee just so, give a great blow job. And although we pretend this is just about me, and in a way it is, it also is not. It is about that follower being fed by being in service.

The key is to find the baseline. "My follower is about service or administration." "My followers are invested emotionally or they are here to gain specific skills." "My follower is a romantic partner or a sexual explorer that I am leading through slutty fantasies come to life." Or a combination of those. Knowing this is the key to good Leadership. Forcing a sex slave to be good at writing letters of appreciation or forcing an administrative-minded follower to the fine art of pegging my ass is not necessarily going to inspire anyone.

The question does not ask how I do this, but I'll answer it. For a sex toy, service slut, admin assistant, etc. the key is vulnerability. Show me your inner workings so I can help motivate you to be the best follower you can be. We both gain—you in your maturation, me in receiving the agreed-upon service.

I believe I inspire my follower via my actions as well. I want to inspire dawn to be calm when challenged, balanced when someone argues, courageous when scared. The best way to inspire these is to practice it myself. I clearly remember her saying, some 30 years ago, that she saw me doing the work to change and realized she could do it as well. So I keep doing it.

This is where we move into indirect inspiration vs direct. Direct is easy—do the thing. Indirect is harder but more impactful. "See what I do; you can do it too". And it ends up being of benefit to me in reverse. I tell dawn the benefits of meditation. I meditate. She starts mediation—not because of an order, but because she is inspired. Time goes by and I stop meditating but she—in the most recent case, just minutes before we started this writing—says that she should meditate. I realize how long it has been since I have.

You are allowed to Lead your follower any way you want. I don't have all the answers and don't have a lot of attachment to what an internet stranger does. And who cares if I respect your Leadership skill or think that you are no more a Master than I am a cucumber or think that your submissive telling me that they think my desire to use honorifics is because I have an ego problem is a direct reflection of you and your skill?

But if you ask me "Is being an inspiration to my follower a requirement of being a good leader?" I would answer it is a very clear and definitive "Yes", and then ask you what you are doing to be a Leader other than tossing around random orders and demands for oral sex?

Can and do you inspire your partner into their role?
dawn:

I've had this conversation with other long-term followers and have found that it seems to be a theme with us. I thought it was just something I did and wasn't so sure how I felt about it at first. I mean, it could be taken as manipulative. So, I was super excited when a friend spoke up and said that's what his goal for the day had been. His Leader was in a heavy headspace and he was trying to help her out of it. It was affecting their power exchange and he'd learned that instead of moping about it, he could do something about it. So, yay, it's not just me and the way he talked about it seemed so right and loving and helpful and devoted.

So ... my short answer to this question is Yes. Yes, I try to inspire my Leader into their role. Or at least I try to remember to do so. I didn't even know that was a thing I could do when we first got together. Dan was in charge. Dan liked being in charge. We had talked about this and if that was the case, I figured it should be easy for him. I found out over time that that is not always the case. I thought my struggle as a submissive was what was causing the struggle at the beginning. I did not realize that he was having a struggle as well. He always seemed so confident. Hell, that was part of what drew me to him. Years later he told me that he went through a lot of "fake it 'til you make it".

> Being his devoted follower and his steady rock, and being the best follower I can be each day, inspires him to be the best Leader he can be.

Not only do I wish I had known this— or at least I think I do— but I wish I had had the skills I've learned since then to have helped him out ... to inspire him into his role.

What does this mean? And what does it look like?

What it means is, instead of waiting for him to get back on track during a lull in our power exchange, by just standing to the side and waiting, instead I continue to be his follower. That can be a little hard for me, because I don't want to be seen as pushy. But this relationship style is what we agreed to, and this is part of me fulfilling my role.

And I'll admit, I've also purposefully stroked his ego as a Leader. I've been vocal with how much I trust him or when he's figured something out that feeds me as a submissive or makes it easier for me to surrender. I let him know when things make me happy. I make sure to tell him that I'm proud of him. I've found that the more successes he experiences, the more confidence he has. And its confidence that helps him sit in his seat of power.

Sometimes this means I need to reassure him about a decision he's made. In the fantasy world, it doesn't seem like that would be needed. The Leaders in the books I've read are in charge all the time without any doubts. But, in reality, and as humans, everyone goes through doubts. It can be healthy to not believe you have all the answers all the time, whether for yourself or for someone you are leading in a relationship.

I want Dan to know that I have his back in everything. That skill took some time to cultivate. As a person that doesn't trust easily, it took some time to build up that trust to such a degree that I can legitimately say that I've got his back in everything … OK, almost everything. 98% of everything. And even that 2%, I'll be there for him if he needs me. I'm the rock waiting for him at home as he explores the world around him.

Being his devoted follower and his steady rock and being the best follower I can be each day, inspires him to be the best Leader he can be. And that's one of the goals, isn't it? Each of us sitting in our seat of power. Supported, growing, being our authentic selves.

Can and do you inspire your partner into their role?
Kevin:

Fuck, I hope so!

This is an interesting topic to me, and one that I absolutely did not endorse for including in the book. Katie used her golden buzzer to get it here … and now I'm stumped trying to decide whether I'm actually doing my job as Leader.

Katie can inspire me to my role. A look, a phrase—she can inspire me to remember I'm supposed to be Leading, she can inspire me to take control of her, she can inspire me to smoosh her back into place. But … how do I do that for her?

I suppose there are the simple and obvious things: I remind her to shift into her role by saying "Girl…" in the right tone of voice. I sometimes grab her by the throat or by the tit as she is making a salad and nip an ear and whisper sweet porn into her ear. I think that might be an example of reminding her she is mine.

But it feels like this question isn't about just a fast reminder about her remaining gracious in her speech to me, or a demand that she hand me the chocolate cookie in a sexy subservient way instead of simply setting it on my desk and walking away. I can move her into a submissive state through gestures or demands … but is that inspiring her?

I think I inspire her into her role in a number of ways, many of which I should take a hard look at and perhaps try to intentionally foster. I probably inspire her to follow through exuding confidence. If I act with surety and don't faff about endlessly regarding decisions, that likely helps her see me as a valuable Leader. If I'm endlessly deliberating and can't make up my mind, that's not very inspiring, or attractive.

> I seek to be predictable, but that also means I'm stable. She knows where she stands (kneels?).

Interestingly, there is a list of traits that might make it possible to follow me, trustworthiness, or humility … but I don't know that seeing those makes her want to fall to her knees in awe or worship. I don't know that those make her crave my guiding hand.

Similar to confidence, I probably inspire her to follow through exuding (and providing) clarity. If I am clear—knowing what I want, clearing expressing needs, giving clear expectations of her—that inspires her to follow. I think I probably inspire her to follow simply through my own efforts on myself. I'm striving to do my role well. I'm striving to be loving and appreciative. I'm striving to grow and improve. Those things likely inspire her to take action within her role to be the best she can be for me.

I maybe inspire her through appreciation and recognition. Being sure she knows how pleasurable her following is to me. Expressing gratitude for service, for sexiness, for the thousand ways she enhances my life - not simply as a partner, but as a Follower. Hopefully my appreciation communicates that it isn't simply her loving care that is pleasurable, but the care that comes through her devotion.

I think I inspire her through consistency over time. I tend to be predictable, but that also means I'm stable. She knows where she stands (kneels?). She knows I will make the effort, walk the mile, face the struggle ... she knows I'm solid and she has evidence of that over 2 decades. So probably the passage of time has in some way provided some inspiration to her—she feels the anchor of my presence and knows that I have her, I contain her, I keep her close and safe.

I still struggle as the time ticks down on this writing. I want to have a clear answer within myself what I do (or could do) that makes her feel soft, vulnerable, submissive. What makes her feel in awe and worshipful. Not simply what makes her want to follow, because some of those aspects are simply the benefits of the relationship—the pragmatic value of following. But what are the things that put her best into that space of feeling my power, and wanting to feel the weight of it on her? What makes her heart beat faster and her knees weak and her cunt slippery?

[Editing Kevin notes this essay was written while we were traveling full-time in an RV and having a pretty shitty experience doing it. In a different time and place, my answer would have been very different.]

Can and do you inspire your partner into their role?
Katie:

Whoa, this is an intricate question to answer in a snap without rewrites.

I certainly do my utmost to inspire Kevin into leadership. That sounds egotistical, as if he does not have the impetus on his own. Let me explain ... no, there is too much. Let me sum up. My demeanor towards him, my manner of speaking and attending to him has the ability to lift him up and highlight his role in the relationship. When a wave of humanity bows in awe before a Leader, that person is elevated. That person has a heightened awareness of their position. Likewise, when I speak to Kevin with deep respect and regard, he knows that I am doing my utmost to support this dynamic and our agreed upon roles. This in turn causes him to be aware of his interactions and manner of speaking to me.

That sounds like I have control over him—that I can manipulate him. Manipulation and coercion are never my intent. That would break trust and undermine all we have created. Instead, my focus is on making sure he feels appreciated in his role.

I adore that he takes charge, makes decisions and has the ultimate responsibility for us. I recognize that it is often a heavy task, not just blowjobs on command. Just as I can undermine his joy in Leadership by being cranky and critical, so too I can enhance his role by support and respect. My words of appreciation and encouragement are important to his confidence and surety. My words of comfort and acceptance are important to salve wounds on hard days.

There are times that I try to inspire him by falling to my knees and burying my face in his lap. I become "smaller" so that he is elevated. It feels sexy. His power and authority are being emphasized. I feel my own power and the confidence to put myself in a vulnerable position. Doing this act when we are upset or have a stressful situation keeps us both mindful of who we are to each other and what our responsibilities are.

> Just as I can undermine his role by being cranky and critical, so too I can enhance his role by support and respect.

There has been a time in the past when we had someone else with authority in our life—someone I had not agreed to follow. I found it necessary to encourage Kevin to step above that person and take the lead—even if it meant they were no longer around. I said to him, "I agreed to follow you. I need you to be in charge of this situation. I don't trust them to have my best interests as a priority." At the time Kevin was very new to this, and those quiet words were all he needed to know that I trusted him deeply and would support and follow.

Reinforcing his leadership and encouraging him can be as simple as honorifics. It's like the ear nibble that makes a clit twitch. Pathways to make our relationship vibrant and stay fresh.

As a leader he can easily instigate those interactions and moments. As his follower I instead seek to support and make space for them.

Chapter 8: Feedback

How do you give feedback to your partner?
Dan:

When we first started, I made a point to demand constant feedback from dawn. First was the BDSM aspect—I was doing things to her that were new to both of us. Sure, we had fantasies about flogging and orgasm denial, but as we translated them into real life I needed to know that it was a yummy thing we were doing, regardless of dawn's noises.

> Intuition +
> positive
> feedback
> inspires
> confidence.

I will note that dawn gives great verbal feedback during both scenes and sex. But sometimes there is a fine line between the sound of "that feels so great, never stop" and "that is so owwie, who thought this was a good idea?" I tend to push into the noises regardless. The point being, if you get a chance to use dawn sexually or in a scene, you should; she gives great feedback. Now then, where was I?

When it comes to the power exchange aspect, my need for reassurance was even more significant, as we went from talking about me controlling her and, since we have a punishment dynamic, making her pay a price when she did not. That feedback was essential after pushing her to do a thing she did not want to or correcting her when it was not to standard. The feedback comes after the fact (you would not want to check in in the middle of discipline) but would need to happen. For a while at least—intuition + positive feedback inspires confidence. Once you are confident, the feedback is less required.

Now, to return to the actual question, how do I give feedback? The first thing I have to do is to pay attention (observer). This is the simple understanding that part of the exchange in me telling dawn to make the bed is that I noticed if it has happened or not. Then, once you know something has transpired (or not happened) you can acknowledge it.

Once more, back to specifically how I do that. I keep thinking there must be more to it, but it is really just speaking up. "The bed looks nice," or "I'd prefer my coffee less hot," or "I need more focus on this task," or "Oh god that feels good."

Some feedback is more, shall we say, direct. I may order dawn to first stop doing what she is doing and pay attention to me; perhaps stand up and come to me. Some less pleasant feedback starts with me telling her to kneel, but some pleasant feedback starts that way as well.

I give feedback primary verbally as noted above, both good and bad, to reinforce we are moving in the appropriate direction. I give feedback in the physical form very rarely. We say that we have a punishment dynamic, but I have not used a physical punishment in— yep, I literally cannot recall. I will caveat that with that I do employ a quick pinch or hair tug if there is a lack of paying attention.

Feedback is for both guidance and reward. Be generous with praise and concise in correction. Ask for feedback on your feedback when appropriate (does that make sense, do you understand why, etc). You need to be aware if you are giving more negative feedback than positive. And you need to make a change so that isn't the case.

Finally, to steal something that dawn often tells me, don't walk on eggshells. When dawn requires negative feedback, I need to have the fortitude to speak up and, if needed, change something. She is not fragile and signed up for this because I push her. If she wanted to be coddled, she had other choices. Not to say that at times I might pause on saying something if we are in the midst of some crisis or such; but it will get said and I will get a "thank you, sir" after giving that feedback. This helps her trust that when I say "I am proud of you" that I truly mean it.

How do you give feedback to your partner?
dawn:

When it comes to feedback, I usually think of negative feedback and one of my main goals is not to be passive-aggressive or manipulative with how I present information. If something needs feedback, I try my best to warn him it's coming first. On great days, I let him know that I need to talk about something and then we have a conversation. But we grew into that over time.

At the beginning, it was so hard to give any sort of feedback, including the positive feedback. The negative was almost impossible for me. It felt confrontational, which I don't do unless I've tipped the point of how much anger I can hold on to, while trying to work on it. It felt judgy and I didn't want to hurt his feelings. Usually, because I didn't know how to express it, it would bottle up to the point of anger. A place I didn't want to go. Fortunately, we worked through that completely enough that I can't even think of examples at this point.

What I remember is floundering, not knowing how or if I should speak up. Feeling like everything going wrong was my fault, etc. Many followers know what I'm saying here. I remember admitting that to Dan and that I didn't know if I should speak up, because it seemed to be my problem, whatever it was going on.

> Positive feedback can be just as hard to hear as negative feedback some days.

Dan convinced me I should share it all, but it was how I did it that mattered. If I started the sentence with, "Master, with all due respect," I was allowed to say almost anything. That it was more difficult for him to master me if he was guessing how I was reacting to something, or not having a clue that something was wrong, or even right for that matter, unless I spoke up. He's not a mind reader. Of course, at first I didn't believe him. My feedback for someone or something had never been taken positively, so why should Dan be any different?

But I tried it. I also made sure to give him positive feedback, not just negative. And it worked. He listened. And I didn't get punished with a cold shoulder or such. It was kind of clunky at first and has slowly smoothed out as we've learned other tools over time.

We do our best to make it a positive experience, regardless of what the feedback is. And though the question doesn't ask this, I'd like to add that how feedback is received is just as important as how it's given. When Dan gives me feedback, I do my best not to take it as a personal attack and get on the defensive. I have an issue with rejection, so I try not to fall into that dark pit. I stay present, I listen. I listen to see if a course correction is coming up or if it's something positive that I should be thanking him for. That takes concentration on my part sometimes depending on what kind of head space I'm in. If I'm flighty and it's something positive, sometimes he has to slow me down, make me make eye contact and hear what he is saying. Positive feedback can be just as hard to hear as negative feedback some days.

Today, I'd like to believe I give much more positive feedback than negative. And the negative I've learned how to give in a calm manner. We are new RVers, learning how to live in a tiny house that moves every 2 to 3 weeks, and learning how to develop a language for backing the trailer into tight spaces. Sometimes it takes a lot of energy and concentration to remember to have these conversations with right-effort and right-speech. But it's so much easier now than it's ever been, because we've developed tools to make it so. And if we hurt someone's feelings, we know how to talk about that as well. Feedback is needed or this relationship isn't going to be what either of us wanted or that is satisfying to us both.

How do you give feedback to your partner?
Kevin:

Everyone around the writing circle is sighing with relief at the ease of this question. "Finally," they say. I'm looking at this one with some hesitation. Obviously giving positive and appreciative feedback is not a confusing process (mostly). I am lavish with my praise and gratitude. I give feedback that I find things attractive, that I value a service, that her humor is appreciated, that her devotion is noticed. There is rarely a reason not to give positive feedback, as it helps reward and provide guidance for correct and pleasing action.

Giving corrective feedback is a delicate, deliberate, thoughtful process. Good communication requires a lot of things to be successfully in place, particularly when the topic is challenging.

I must be clear on what I want to tell Katie.

I don't want to just give Katie random correction or direction. Do I want to tell her she failed? Is the mistake serious enough that I want her to hear I am disappointed or does she simply need to hear that something different should occur in the future? Do I want to communicate that she made a mistake, or that I made a mistake that led to her failing—if I said "Go do the errands," and I wanted her to be back in under two hours but failed to say so, then I may need to give the feedback that "I expected you home before noon and now my plans need to be shifted. If errands are going to take more than a few hours, I need an updated ETA." This isn't a case of her fucking up, it is a case of my direction being insufficient—but she might still need feedback to avoid the same problem in the future.

I must be in the right mental and emotional place.

I want the things I say to be clear and unblemished by emotional garbage. I want Katie to be able to hear the feedback with as little defensiveness as possible. I never want to issue a correction to Katie while I am in the midst of turbulent emotion. I want to be centered and reasonable when I begin to provide potentially upsetting feedback.

Is the time and place right for this feedback?

I have no interest in catching Katie when she is distracted or busy or overwhelmed. If she is in the middle of doing a chore, or is freshly frustrated due to spilling the soup all over, it isn't the time to have her successfully hear and internalize feedback.

I must consider the aim of the feedback.

Is this feedback to complain about something that has recently occurred, or is it to simply state a preference for things to be managed differently in the future? If my goal for the feedback is simply to express dissatisfaction, that is a completely different set of feedback than defining a problem and giving direction for a satisfactory solution to that problem.

Once I determine that I am centered and have clarity, and that Katie is likely to be in a position to be ready, willing, and able to hear the feedback, then I will typically give Katie some useful preliminary information, especially if the feedback is heavy. Things like "I'm troubled by the way that interaction went with Egbert. We need to sit down and discuss it." She knows that I am speaking to her from my position of Authority, not as a casual conversation. And I suppose that is a good thing to mention— sometimes feedback is a less formal process, similar to what egalitarian

> I never want to issue a correction to Katie when I am in the midst of turbulent emotion.

couples might do. "Hey, honey, you left hair in the sink." I don't need to pull on my mantle of ownership to mention she accidentally left the cabinet door open. But conversational correction, even as a one-off comment, still carries a great deal of weight, simply because of my position of authority. I need to even be mindful of lightweight feedback—given as a quick comment as we pass in the hallway— because I am the Leader and my words have impact and weight. An incautious feedback from me can have lasting effects because Katie strives to be pleasing and correct in her actions.

F F F … time! So much more to say!

How do you give feedback to your partner?
Katie:

How do you give feedback to your partner? I sing really close to the speakers. Rockstar!

I think of giving feedback to Kevin as supplying information. Not as complaining, nagging, or pointing out his failures.

Again, the business model helps me keep the right methods and perspective in place. He is my CEO. I am his valued employee. Kevin has assured me that he values my thoughts. He leads with a level of humility and grace. If my boss needs more information, I can do that in a respectful manner without volatility. Feedback is not a struggle unless I do it in a disrespectful manner. Then the feedback isn't the problem—me stepping out of my role and treating him without proper regard is.

If he is making a big decision, Kevin takes the time to hear any knowledge I have that could help. We lived different lives for quite a while before being together. I offer him wisdom from those experiences.

If I am struggling with some kind of upset, it is my responsibility to openly share that with him.

Example, katie!

I have an overwhelming day of tasks ahead of me. Kevin is doing his own stuff and not aware. Perhaps I am overwhelmed because of a headache, or the jobs have piled up. Maybe I am just having a sad day. I MUST share this information with him! It is not the ultimate service to be silent and suffer.

I will say something like, "I am really overwhelmed today," or "I'm feeling pretty low and ineffective today," or "I am crushed with my deadlines and tasks right now."

None of those statements are an attack on Kevin. "Why don't you do more? I have so much more on my list than you! You hurt my feelings and now I can't accomplish anything."

Once I give him the heads-up that I'm struggling, Kevin always steps into leadership and has solutions. "Let me see that list," or "Let's work alongside each other for a while and love each other," or hugs, comfort and a plan.

> If my approach is too far off the mark, then I ask for a Mulligan. "Please, forget that. Here, let me say that the way I really meant."

If I am worried or upset about something relationship-wise, my feedback is essential. I will ask for the time and attention necessary to address the issue. No flyby shots of frustration. Most often I will have taken the time to think through what the issue is and how best to present it without attack. My goal is to seek relationship improvement or adjustment. My words, my manner of speaking must support that goal.

Even with all that intentional care, sometimes what I say, or more often what Kevin hears, is not accurate to what I meant. We address that issue with slow conversation. Kevin will let me know what he thinks I am saying. I will reword if necessary or agree. If my approach is too far off the mark, then I ask for a Mulligan. "Please, forget that. Here, let me say that the way I really meant." And I work hard at supplying him with a more precise account of my struggle or concern.

This relationship is pragmatic and effective. An essential part of that being true is me being willing to give thoughtful feedback and Kevin being open to hearing it.

Chapter 9: Communication

How do you encourage and support open communication?
Dan:

I think of the "original dawn"—from when we were just friends, and barely that—and how she communicated. Her yelling and door slamming and crying when no one was watching and passive-aggressiveness was all based on fear. Fear of the past, fear of the future, fear of being found out and found lacking and found unworthy of love.

That dawn, as she agreed to surrender some power to me, was ready for change. She was really good at being angry, so much so that we, the people around her, had strategies to avoid it. So how to take a lifetime of skills that, although they had a negative impact on her, worked so well at (in her view) keeping her safe? And not only get her to change, but to help her drive the process for giving them up?

On a quick aside, writing this now, I am reminded of that previous dawn, and I wonder what I saw that made me—who had neither the background nor even the right to think I could help—decide to engage and open myself to … well, what we've become. It is very rare that I speak of "a higher power at work" but I'll be damned if I have a rational explanation. But I digress.

And that I am still Dan, still the Leader, still striving, because those things I think are anchors are only temporary. Via time, energy, tools and intent, they lose power over me until they rust away.

So the solution I found was simply open communication. Not just "you can say anything" but "you can safely reveal your innermost beliefs, fears, desires, self-hatred, depression, silly songs, sluttyness, and the battle scars you've hidden so long." And that I, as a listener, will simply listen. And accept you. And not reply with anything but acceptance. Never anger, never pity, never ignoring it.

In a power exchange setting, I created that container for communication via compassionate discipline. When you speak, I will hear you. When you don't speak, I will remind you that you are required to. I will order you to tell me everything. And I will make you engage other resources—from counselors to doctors—who have the skills I don't.

I will make it a practice to speak about myself as well. The time I was impotent, the time I was assaulted, the time I failed at—well, there is a list of things. And that I am still Dan, still the Leader, still striving, because those things I think are anchors are only temporary. Via time, energy, tools, and intent, they lose power over me until they rust away.

Another aside—time does allow some wisdom. Did you know that when I was a young man of 17 and I tried to fuck and my dick said "nah", I thought that was a huge fucking deal that might mean something the rest of my life? Now, as a man many years later, and whose cowboy has not shown up for the rodeo a few times, I realize that it just isn't that big a deal and I should avoid caffeine before playtime? Again, I digress.

So, you thought this question was about open communication around the little things? It is. Once you have revealed the big bad, the deep and dark, it then becomes way less challenging to share "I pissed on the floor" or "I think I'm hot for your girlfriend". You trust your partner will react, but that won't need to be an argument or huge deal.

Not to suggest it is always easy. In either direction. But we have gotten to this—to be honest, kind of weird space—where I am asking dawn for help creating a contract for a new follower or telling her I want to watch her get porked by some random from OKC or that I am worried about some unlikely event and she just openly—and fearlessly—engages. Or reminds me to laugh at myself and not take it all so seriously. And she sets an example—she smiles so much more than that dawn of 20 years back.

How do you encourage and support open communication?
dawn:

Dan and I went into this new relationship with little to no communication skills. We knew we wanted something different, but if you haven't seen what you wish for being modeled, how do you figure out how to do it? When you want open, transparent communication but you've been taught to keep things to yourself or you pay the price for the result, how do you break through that?

How did we break through that?

Before Dan, I had a long-term marriage. I learned early on to keep secrets from him. He was not on board with my feelings, my memories, my struggles. Then, near the end of our relationship, he wanted me to open up, but it was too late then. All the secrets and "me" that I needed to share with him at the beginning were buried so far down that I couldn't let them see the light, just for him.

Before that marriage I had a long-term boyfriend. Again, I wanted to share all of me with him and I wanted to know his thoughts. Instead, he had been taught to keep secrets so that he wouldn't have to pay a price if he was caught doing something.

Good grief, all the way back to my childhood. Secrets, secrets, secrets. Open communication was something that happened in a fantasy world or in the romance books my mom used to read. This wasn't real. But I need it to be real.

Luckily, my and Dan's relationship started with the story I told of the workshop in the bookstore, elsewhere in the book, with me dumping so much stuff at his feet and him not walking away. We both needed the ability to do this and decided that was going to be a foundation of our relationship.

Open communication, transparency, share all the things, embrace the truth and emotions ... decision made, so it should be simple right? Well, like a lot of changes, it was not simple or easy. My belief is fear made it harder than it needed to be. I have a strong emotion, or a whatever emotion or thought, and I instantly share it and am supported, right? Not necessarily. We have both come from relationships where things like this were used as manipulation or the knowledge was used against you.

> Perseverance. We NEED open communication in our relationship and worked hard to make it happen.

We had to build that trust in each other and it wasn't something that happened instantly. I would not want to share something because I didn't want to seem high maintenance. Or I wouldn't know how to share something and stay in my role.

And it wasn't just me needing/wanting to share all about me ... I needed Dan to share about him. I needed to know ... and need to know ... what's going on in his head. Shit, I knew him when he was a junkie. I needed to know what was going on in his head to make sure that he wasn't falling into old secretive habits.

But early on, I was very emotionally reactive. I did not make it easy for him to share things with me, especially if it was criticism of me or us or even himself. My reactions could be extreme and then he'd have to deal with it. How crappy is that? Every time he brought up something new or something that didn't involve me, I'd go from being calm and listening to the edge of a breakdown. Instead of him sharing something and us talking about it, it would be him sharing something and then all energy turns to dawn to help her figure out how to handle it.

That was so much work at the beginning and took a lot of determination and fortitude to get through. But open communication was so important for us as a foundational thing that we put in the years of work to resolve this so that we wouldn't fall back into the easier old habits of keeping everything to ourselves and not causing waves ... or in my case, tsunamis.

Little by little, we learned the tools we needed. We continued to state that we wanted transparency and how important it was to each of us and our relationship, and then something would shift. We'd come across a tool to try and a person would show up in our life with a tool that we would try. I could list them out here, but I only have a half hour to write and they are listed in a couple of other books we've written.

One of the biggest tools I learned doesn't actually show up anywhere else and I'm going to call it "Be the Witness". Step back, don't take anything personally, and just listen. This was very hard for me because everything involves me, but it doesn't. For Dan to be able to be open and honest with me, he needs to be able to share without thinking of the cost of that sharing or the work that may be involved to help me work through whatever emotion might spring up.

Unfortunately, it took time and work to get to this point of our fantasy and make it a reality. It's so much easier to have this open communication we've worked so hard to incorporate into our lives. I can tell Dan anything. Have always been able to. He tells me anything ... and even now, steps back and waits for the fallout, but usually there isn't any anymore. I'm the witness to whatever is going on with him and after he shares, he lets me know if he needs my opinion or advice on the matter.

Perseverance. We NEED open communication in our relationship and worked hard to make it happen. I'm sure it's much easier for many couples, but when you come in with baggage of past and past relationships, it can definitely be a challenge, especially if one of you is an internal processor and one of you is an external processor. But that's a whole other topic to write about.

How do you encourage and support open communication?
Kevin:

One of the best tools to get Katie to open up and share difficult issues is my own self-control. I want her to be certain that whatever she brings to me, I will hear calmly and generously, to the best of my ability.

If I react to her topic in anger, whether at her, or at some external source, it is likely to impact her willingness to bring those topics to me in the future. If I react with sadness or injury, it will make it harder for her to broach topics that probably are really valuable for me to hear (and maybe suck a lot to hear). If I react with judgment, it will make it harder for her to bring to me things about which she feels vulnerable or shy. If I react defensively, and immediately launch into justifications and explanations, then she will know that I'm not hearing her with a desire to understand and help, but with my shields up.

"What do you need from me in this conversation?"

We usually broach difficult topics with caution and deliberation. If we realize a topic could be a challenge we set aside time to address it. Katie will say some yellow-flag warning phrase like "When we can set aside some time, I have something I need to discuss..." We also try to give some up-front information that helps the other understand the basic layout of the situation and where the landmines might be—Katie might say something like: "I'm hurt and sad right now, but it isn't about us. My daughter has been rude and I'm trying to figure out how I want to manage it." By creating the expectation that we provide clarifying structure and information, it makes it easier to be present in the way our partner needs.

Relatedly, because I am the Leader and my inclination is to protect and save my girl, I try to remember to ask, "What do you need from me in this conversation?" Sometimes Katie comes to me to help her solve a problem, but sometimes she just wants to have help exploring an issue to seek clarity but not a solution. Sometimes she wants me to simply hear some uncomfortable feedback about a time or way that I've goofed up. Sometimes she warns me that she has some revolutionary idea bubbling in her head, and she wants help either getting excited about it or stomping it out, depending on whether I'm on-board. My task in all this is to not only remember to ask my role in the conversation, but also to do my best to actually do the task that has been requested of me. If I'm supposed to help her find clarity, but instead I jump in with how I would solve the issue, or how I order her to move forward ... that isn't great. And it shuts down future conversations where she hopes to get my help to find clarity.

I try to communicate to Katie that, while I expect her to bring me topics calmly and rationally, I'm also willing to sit with her when her thoughts are disorganized and messy. If her issue is an ugly jumble with lots of tears, I will listen calmly and generously while we work to figure out what's troubling her and what we need to do to move forward. She's allowed to bring me poorly formed and goopy situations, and I'll try to help her find the heart of the problem. The underlying message, though, is that I don't expect a dump and run. She isn't supposed to just vomit a bunch of heartache or frustration, then clam up. If she brings a topic, the expectation is that we are going to wrestle with it and try to find some peace.

On the other hand, I also communicate to Katie that solutions are rarely clean and easy. Hard topics are rarely one-and-done. I give her permission to share an issue, then after we finish to percolate and contemplate—and then realize there are more aspects that she needs to discuss that we didn't address the first time.

Gah—I think I've still got a list of things to say, and two minutes left!

We usually touch while addressing hard topics. This is a method to communicate that we are a Team facing a challenge, but also that we love each other and are aligned. We even verbalize that fact - this topic, whatever it is, doesn't change our dynamic or love.

[A thing I didn't have time to add but feels important enough to add afterward is our agreement that if necessary we can "Mulligan" a sentence or entire conversation. Sometimes we say something that isn't precisely what we meant, or the phrasing is such that it leads to a misunderstanding. We will occasionally say "I'd like to retract that. I'm going to back up and try that again. I said that poorly and would like to try to do a better job."]

How do you encourage and support open communication?
Katie:

Kevin is going to be so proud of me as I utilize bullet points!

There are three main skills I use to support and encourage open communication:

- ❖ Not being defensive and reactive when Kevin has a discussion with me.
- ❖ Asking questions that are not accusatory or disrespectful.
- ❖ Seeking clarity rather than jumping to conclusions.
- ❖ Viewing our level of openness as an essential part of our relationship.
- ❖ Good counting! Paying attention is a communication skill too! You get a point!

Not being defensive and reactive when Kevin has a conversation with me.

Why is it our natural inclination to get all butthurt and try to shift responsibility and be defensive with someone who loves us? How ridiculous is that?

I focus on listening completely when he addresses an issue, rather than get all whirled around in my head about what I am going to say back. Of course, I don't enjoy hearing that things have gone sideways! But I **need** to hear that. I need to understand what he is seeing and his perspective. My ability to listen without rapid-fire retaliation supports ongoing communications.

Asking questions that are not accusatory or disrespectful.

When I ask questions in a discussion with Kevin, I am careful about wording. Words wound. I have many words at my disposal—I can take the time to pick the ones that are closest to my intentions. Yesterday we had a short discussion about how the word *annoyed* felt yuckier than *confused.* "That confuses me," vs "That's annoying." Taking the time to get the wording right saves much misunderstanding.

Seeking clarity rather than jumping to conclusions.

Ah, jumping to conclusions. You know in a game show where the host is asking a question and the contestant hits the buzzer before the question is fully asked? That's a loser move. I do loser moves ... My answer will immediately show that I have jumped off the wrong saloon roof and there is no horse waiting to be straddled. I just splat in our chat. Presuming I know the issue does nothing to support or encourage open communication. This inclination has me all in my head instead of seeking what is in his.

Seeking clarity. Slowing the fuck down. Upsets are inclined to be fast and intense. Upsets between Kevin and I are slow and cautious. I ask as many questions as needed to be sure of what I am hearing. I will say things like, "You said tired, but I think I hear frustrated." Or "Are you saying that you feel I'm not attending to being sexy enough or are you saying you just wish we had more sex in our day?" Those kinds of questions encourage him to share more information and clarify what he wants to say.

> My answer will immediately show that I have jumped off the wrong saloon roof and there is no horse waiting to be straddled.

Viewing our level of openness as an essential part of our relationship.

The ability to talk about *anything* with each other is an incredible boon in our relationship. We can share struggles. We can share kinks. We can talk about the ugly and the delicious. It is essential that I attend to my responses and openness to hear Kevin so that communication walks through an open door.

[Edit to add: Both Dan and I wrote about cowboys. How weird is that?]

Chapter 10: Rigidity of Roles?

What is your experience with leading as the Follower, and following as the Leader?
Dan:

When I follow dawn, even though my relationship with her is I am the Leader, it is … no big deal. Doesn't bother me a bit. I'll go a bit further to say it feels like a mini-vacation. Someone else is leading the charge, stepping up front, making decisions, taking chances that a path will lead to success. So I get to follow along, make sure they have what they need, and give my mind a break as I fantasize about how I would have re-written that movie scene where Kirk and Picard first met…

Let me clarify here in case I am getting glares from some of my co-authors that I do not believe following is easy. Instead, I am portraying that movie where the King gives his crown to a similar looking commoner so they can go fuck off for a day. Or when another King did that in Bubba Ho-Tep (obscure reference, let's just keep going).

Following has no impact on my ego; I don't believe dawn will see me as "less than" just because she is more competent in an area and I get out of the way. Areas like research (which she is good at), cooking (which I secretly wish I cared enough about to learn but don't), social media (thumbs up this book on Facebook!) and many other areas.

As a couple, turning the reins over to dawn to lead is no big deal assuming it starts with me saying "You are in charge of this thing." I like to say dawn is my service "fire and forget missile". Meaning I set her upon a task and I can dismiss it from my mind because I know it will get done. So this includes "You are in charge of packing up the condo and getting everything to either storage, market, or a donation center." It does get more challenging for me when it is a task that takes lots of time and isn't an area where either of us are experts. The "packing the condo" is a great example of that as I have opinions about the best way to do that. Actually, that isn't true—I don't care about the best way, at least in this example, but I was focused on the "get it done now" way. Which is why I put dawn in charge in the first place. I would have simply called some charity group and told them they could have everything in the place, just come get it. That would have been a terrible idea on many levels and I would have had only one pair of underwear to my name.

Following as a Leader for me is easy if I let it be. Once I've said "You are in charge," I then get the fuck out of the way. I offer advice or counsel when it is asked of me. Help with bits when asked to help.

My personal biggest challenge in this area is where I leave it to dawn to lead because she feels like she needs to be safe. It is easiest for me to say "Fine, you lead this," instead of dealing with whatever does not feel safe to her. It is not an appropriate response or good for our relationship. I don't always step up here, I'll admit. Why apply the time and energy to this small bit when I can let dawn have her way and we are both at ease? Because ... I am not really at ease. I am giving up. It is a tiny little give-up, but a path toward complacency, which is the death of power exchange relationships. Instead, I need to direct energy toward the fear, make the decision, walk us both through it, and review what we learned. Had we followed the path of fear, we might still be in a condo in Columbus, thinking "One day we will try RV living." Or any number of smaller things. This is not a slight against dawn, by the way; she has mastered so many of her fears in the past 20 years it is surprising when they show up now.

> Following has no impact on my ego; I don't believe dawn will see me as "less than" just because she is more competent in an area and I get out of the way.

After dawn has been the leader of a thing and it is completed, I never feel the need to "push her down" or put her in her place. She doesn't come out of these situations wanting to lead more; I quickly lose comfort in following. We are both happy to be back in our proper seats.

What is your experience with leading as the Follower, and following as the Leader?
dawn:

I have agreed to be the Follower of Dan. That's my role. That's what I do. And ultimately that is our relationship design. Dan leads. I follow. But there are moments within our dynamic where I need to lead or Dan needs to follow for a moment of time. This doesn't mean we are switches. Not at all, and it doesn't affect our ultimate dynamic and foundation.

But there are layers that I'm not sure how to describe here and it's slowing me down. The foundation is Dan leads, I follow … but sometimes there is another layer on top of that which requires something else.

For example, when I became clergy, that put me in a leadership position. When I work with the couples to design their ritual or when I'm actually officiating, the couple and attendees need someone to be in charge. It's not valuable to anyone for me to also be in service to Dan. I'm ultimately his, but also in charge of this situation. I need to walk into the environment in charge, exuding confidence, to put everyone at ease on such a nerve-wracking day. Dan expects this of me as well.

> I'm ultimately his, but also in charge of this situation. I need to walk into the environment in charge, exuding confidence, to put everyone at ease on such a nerve-wracking day.

The first wedding I did was in someone's home. I walked in first, Dan brought my table and stuff. And as they pointed me to where the wedding was going to take place, I led the way and Dan helped me set up. Then, as I'm setting up the altar and the little nibblibits that need to be in place for the ceremony, Dan lets me know that he's going to go get me some food. What? That was one of my first hiccups. Get me some food? Should be the other way around, or I'll get my own. It feels so weird for him to say he'll get me something to eat. He explains that's his way of taking care of me, and I get it, but for some reason that made me really stumble and I felt like I was failing as his Follower. It's odd how something so simple like that could trip me up. But he let me know that he wanted my focus on what I was doing. It's a wedding, I'm in charge, he's there for support and part of that support was making sure I was fed since I hadn't had time to eat dinner before this evening event. Yes Sir.

The wedding was fantastic and I've done hundreds more since then. Some with his help, some without. It's much easier now to let him know how he can help the most in these situations. I can tell it's hard for him sometimes if I have a bigger wedding with a lot of moving parts. He wants to let me know how he would do it. And sometimes he does, but in this situation, ultimately it's my responsibility and my decision. There has been a time or two when he's done this and I've fallen into a 'Yes, Sir'. We both realize that we've fallen into foundational roles instead of the current moment role and we step back and let me be in charge of the moment again. It's my job and my responsibility. I flip and look at how his service can be the most beneficial in the moment. Sometimes it's keeping the grandmother occupied while I lay out the stuff on the altar, sometimes it's standing in back of the attendees ready to give me a hand signal to let me know I need to raise my voice to be heard in the back during the ceremony. This flip-flop has gotten much easier.

The harder moments are when I'm put in charge of something that's not necessarily mine; unlike the weddings or my spiritual groups I've run, or the submissive roundtable I facilitate or the submissive intensive I've created, which are mine. There are some things where I'm only mostly in charge, like with the events we produce or such. This happens a lot. I'm put in charge of a piece of producing something and it's mine, until it's not. Those are harder for me. "Dawn, you are in charge of this thing, make it happen." "Yes, Sir." I go forth and make the thing happen. I showed it to Dan. He wants it tweaked. Maybe I don't. But that's one of those moments where it only looks like I was in charge of a thing. In actuality, I was an extension of his will. There is a difference, and I have to know which is which. Am I in charge of the moment? If so, I have to flip flop my brain and expectations of each of us. Am I an extension of his will?

Recently, when we needed to get the condo packed up quickly because we were putting it on the market with only a couple of weeks' notice, I asked Dan if he could leave me in charge of doing it my way. I needed him to step back, concentrate on his day job and let me just do it my way. We have such different ways of doing things that it was going to slow me down to constantly have to change how I was doing something. I did the things that needed to be done, but then there was a day that I'd saved everything to do at once that I needed his help with. Mainly physical labor stuff. But I needed him to just do what I needed done and not come in and change all my plans. My brain was working one way and needed to continue to do so. That was a hard request for me, but I decided to speak it. I could tell it was hard for him to not come in and take charge and flip what I'd been doing so that he could see the progress. But he came in and did what I needed. And to keep from taking charge, he would just sit and wait for orders. Kinda funny when we talk about it now, but every time he sat down and waited for an order from me, or direction I should say, it reminded me that he was keeping to his word and I didn't have to fall back waiting for him to tell me what to do. It was a hard situation though to stick to my guns and be in charge enough to make the day be as productive as I needed it to be. We lightheartedly call this "Follower Day".

What is your experience with leading as the Follower, and following as the Leader?
Kevin:

I actually think Katie is probably the better Leader in many ways—and I do have an inclination to serve and be found pleasurable—so I'm not fundamentally opposed to the roles being "switched" for a particular task or experience. That said, even when I am doing more following than leading, I'm still the person in charge. I still have ultimate authority and responsibility.

I can give a great example: One week after winning our International Power Exchange title we were booked to cater a VIP dinner for Dan and Dawn at their Power Exchange Summit (PXS) event. Katie has a great deal of catering experience because we dabbled with it as a business a decade ago—300 person weddings being the spot where we Peter Principled and decided to quit before we got any more successful. Anyhow, Katie knows how

> Maybe the primary reason we are in our selected roles is because the Follower role is harder and requires a better person.

to make the timeline flow exactly to get a perfect, delicious meal in front of hundreds of people. I do not. My job as Leader in that situation was 1) to agree to do the catering for the event, 2) to put Katie in charge of the catering, 3) to follow Katie's leadership to the best of my ability, without questioning or slowing her down with my need to be in charge.

We sometimes try to dissect how we came to be in the roles we occupy. If Katie is super competent, why is she not the Leader? Is it simply misogyny and enacting cultural norms? Giving ourselves the benefit of the doubt, we don't think that gender roles have forced us into our male/Leader and female/Follower arrangement. We've talked about whether it is "need for control." I tend to feel more need to manage the events in my life. I don't much like being the passenger in another person's vehicle, even when it is their job (like a shuttle driver at the airport) to convey me safely. And it isn't that I think I could do their job better, or even as well—I'm certain I could not. It is more about preferring to have caused my own accident than being the helpless victim in an accident caused by someone else.

We then speculated that perhaps it is the person with the greatest attachment to stuff that becomes the Leader. The Follower is the person that is best able to become unattached. Followers give up the right to have things their way, or have the outcomes they prefer. So maybe I'm the Leader simply because I have a harder time cultivating non-attachment. I'm maybe way more invested in having the world conform itself to my view. Katie is maybe better at letting the world flow, and accept that what is, is.

Katie has offered a different insight and theory: the Leader is the person who has the hardest time trusting. I sort of hate the idea that my inability to trust is the rationale for me being in the Leader role, but it makes sense. I don't trust that everything will be OK unless I (very arrogantly, I recognize) have my fingers in the process. I don't trust the shuttle driver to move me safely even when it is their job. I don't trust that the tradesperson will repair the plumbing correctly, so I linger over them while they work.

I've done a fair amount of "following" and "service" in my life as an employee and as a provider of mental health services. I take care of people and help them find comfort and growth. I listen to my boss and do as I'm told, or even anticipate problems and try to resolve them in advance.

I can follow and serve. I actually, as I said before, do pretty well at it and enjoy it. And Katie has all the skills to be a Leader. For limited durations she has been in charge of me, and has done a great (although very cautious and a little uncomfortable) job of guiding and instructing me on the tasks she needed accomplished.

In summary then: although we never swap roles, we have occasionally had times we swapped roles, right? And maybe the primary reasons we are in our selected roles is because the Follower role is harder and requires a better person. My personal struggles with need for control, attachment, and trust prevent me from being able to take the Follower role.

[As I read this out loud to the rest of the group, I said: "Somewhere around here I took a left turn and stayed with it to the bitter end." I feel like this is a really good writing about something. This is me successfully shooting the guy with the apple on his head directly in the heart. Great shot. Wrong target.]

What is your experience with leading as the Follower, and following as the Leader?
Katie:

Flexible and Adaptable. Kevin and I consider this one of our superpowers for success.

We are dedicated to the *structure of our relationship.* Neither of us are rigid in what *acts* we do in our roles. It is extremely common for people to get locked into what Leading and Following *looks* like. Good luck with that.

Often, with a quick, superficial glance, it can look like Kevin and I are in opposite roles. Example, katie:

There's the silent auction we were helping with. Kevin arrived after me and said, "OK, what can I help with?" I answered, "Please set up the table and chairs and put these items on them, starting at smallest and gradually going to largest." The person running the auction asked me which one of us was in charge. Thing is, I was serving, not leading. I

> Instead of looking at this as who is Boss, we view it as who is the Lead Person ... like on a business endeavor. *[Also, I really want to say Plodding Possum again.]*

helped him dodge getting assigned cellophane-wrapping baskets and tying bows. Kevin was humble enough not to stride into a situation and tell himself what was needed. We were again encountering a superficial misconception. It is pervasive enough that we are quite comfortable with getting misinterpreted.

Back to being flexible and adaptable. Instead of looking at this as who is Boss, we view it as who is the Lead Person ... like on a business endeavor. The Boss is still there, but one of the employees might have been hired on with a special skill. The Boss puts that person as Lead on the project. Often the CEO could be viewed as serving or following the direction of their COO. That's a surface read.

When we are catering a meal for a large group of people, Kevin assigns me Lead to the project and helps as much as he can.

When we are redecorating a home, I am Lead.

When we are organizing our living space, again, my strong spot, my Lead.

Kevin will pitch in, ask for direction and clarity of my vision. Often he will have many suggestions and sometimes even step in to make a decision of redirection. Mostly Kevin focuses on supporting me. This is an endeavor he has assigned to me with conscious intent. He put me in front for a reason.

He "serves" the situation and endeavor, not me. I Lead the project, not him.

It's an action, not a role. Say it again. Action not role. These are not conjoined twins. Unless you are rigid and don't adapt.

Perspective. Again and again. So much about this relationship style working well is in perspective.

Also, the manner of interacting can support or undermine this fluidity of acts. If I am bossy and bitchy in my way of addressing him or requesting assistance, that is when I am stepping out of my role. My directions to him are polite and respectful.

I might say, "Please put these trays diagonally at the far end of the buffet table, potatoes first, we are behind schedule." Instead of "Get these out there! Diagonal. Potatoes first. Step it up—your pace sucks! Hurry, you Plodding Possum!"

To summarize:

- ❖ Skills and training should be utilized.
- ❖ Watch your language.
- ❖ Helping out does not melt your Mastercard.
- ❖ Acts are not roles.
- ❖ Perspective is key.

Chapter 11: Reaction vs. Resistance

[NOTE: This chapter was written prior to the start of the actual book, as an experiment in whether this would be a fun project. The time limit was the same. The "no discussion in advance" was the same. The biggest difference is that this writing didn't have the "journal out your soul" intention, so ended up somewhat more like class notes. I suppose a few of our current writings may stray in that direction, but this one may stand out to the careful reader as slightly different in tone.]

How do you attend to "reaction" and "resistance" in your relationship?

Dan:

Sometimes I get "a look". I will give an order to my follower and they give me a response that I read as pushing back. It might be because it is making them do something they see as unpleasant, or it may be because it brings a fear to the forefront. When I see that visual indicator (the look), I need to be able to determine if it is simply a) a reaction—shock, surprise, disgust even; or b) resistance, as in "Nuh-uh, that ain't happening." Now, either way, I can be unyielding and ignore the response and say "Do it," and be done. I have that right. But it isn't the most healthy or positive option all the time.

In either case—reaction or resistance—I first pause and give them time to internally process. For dawn, when her response is some level of negative reaction, this is easier to manage, as once you've been together for a significant amount of time and continued to prove your skill as a leader, your follower develops first trust, then faith. And as dawn has faith in my abilities, she will drive herself past reaction with a breath and obey. Prior to that time where faith has developed, I would add a few verbal (keys) to help her get to the place of following: "Do you trust me?" "Do you have confidence in

> Resistance is an emotional response that I want to understand—is it based on fear, selfishness, lack of confidence—because it is of value to me (and of course her) to not be tied to those emotional states. In other words, serve me regardless of fear.

me?" or "Are you ready to serve me?" are all ways to reinforce the dynamic and help her just "do".

This same technique works for resistance as well, except I might seek to understand the resistance first. Resistance is an emotional response that I want to understand—is it based on fear, selfishness, lack of confidence –because it is of value to me (and of course her) to not be tied to those emotional states. In other words, serve me regardless of fear. Serve me regardless of selfish desire. But prior to having her obey, we might discuss those. As an example, if I say "dawn, reach out to my other submissive Joe and invite him to come on vacation with us,", I might see dawn respond with resistance to that idea based on her desire to have that time alone with me. Or that she doesn't really like Joe's presence and being stuck with him for a week might be unpleasant. It behooves me to see that resistance and take it out and look at it. Sometimes management of that resistance is me (and thus her) going after that center of resistance and working on it. Sometimes it is me saying "I've noted your resistance; it is happening anyway," and working on it after the command has been obeyed. And other times, in all honesty, I've changed a command. It is very important to remember your limits as a leader; you can't order a submissive "Don't be jealous." You can say the words, but it doesn't change an emotional state. So if you want a change, it is up to you to work on it with your submissive. Be a leader. And some things—in the example above, where I've invited Joe to an existing vacation—that might be more impactful on dawn than I realized. So the command gets modified (perhaps Joe joins us for the last few days, giving dawn and I some alone time) or I have a separate vacation later with Joe.

Either way, you'll notice I lean toward 'manage/guidance' vs discipline. I require willingness. And actually having a follower have a negative reaction or initial resistance and saying 'do it anyway' *and* having them obey is a powerful (thing) for both of you.

How do you attend to "reaction" and "resistance" in your relationship?
dawn:

When we first started our power exchange relationship over 20 years ago, I was also just starting my healing path. I was going through a divorce and trying to bring a fantasy life into reality with no role models. There were a lot of moments that were scary for me. I had been responsible for my safety since being an adult and now I was depending on someone else for a lot of things, including my safety. Purposefully. And this someone likes to help me push through my fears and judgements. Which can feel unsafe to my inner self. And when I feel unsafe, I can resist moving forward. But being stagnant or not moving forward in this relationship is not an option. Which means I needed to learn how to spot my negative reactions to something new, so that I wouldn't resist and would obey with a sense of trust and faith.

Physically, I learned how to recognize my negative reactions that were because I was uncomfortable and those that were actual triggers based on past baggage. Triggers manifest in my body as huge, tight knots in my stomach. A heavy weight. Over time I've named these "WAM" moments—"What About Me?" Whereas uncomfortable moments are just ... uncomfortable.

"WAM" moments cause me to emotionally spin out of control. My safety feels threatened. The feeling of scarcity clutches at me. These are the feelings that cause me to resist an idea or a command. It took us a long time to put a word to that feeling. But now that I have the language, if I say "I'm having a WAM moment", Dan knows this is something that has to be treated a little differently than a full out resistance issue. My trigger has me screaming "No" in my head. Luckily, after a lot of time, I can now say that I'm having a "WAM" moment and he knows that this may take a little bit of work to get through.

> But being stagnant or not moving forward in this relationship is not an option.

This is how "porchtime" was developed. We did not know how to handle these emotions that I was going through. I had spent a large portion of my life staying away from actions and places that would cause this type of emotional response. With this relationship we were pushing this on purpose. "Porchtime" allowed us to step away from our power exchange dynamic and work through these feelings, sometimes very loudly. We didn't have other communication tools and this worked for us. But we made sure not to use it too much as we learned other communication tools. All in all, we may have used this communication tool 6 times in the last 20 years.

Since then, I've done a lot of work on myself and my reactions, along with learning to meditate. This has allowed my reaction time to slow down so that I can catch the reactions and label it so that Dan doesn't assume it's a flat-out resistance. I have the tools now to work on these reactions. Most of the time I just let him know it's a "WAM" moment and I need a little time to breathe through this, remind myself that I'm safe and ask for his assistance in working through it, if needed.

This is different from feeling uncomfortable. "Uncomfortable" isn't that out of control feeling. It's lower key than that. And what I've figured out over time is that uncomfortable doesn't mean that something is wrong. Dan hasn't told me to do a wrong thing. Dan isn't wrong. Time and time again, Dan has proved that he's trustworthy and now I have faith in him. Resistance doesn't happen that often, and when it does it's usually over something logistical. At that point, he usually listens to me, but if he wants to do it his way, he says so. Once he says it's getting done his way, I flip my thinking from listing pros and cons, to figuring out how to do it his way.

There are moments where he'll say we are going to do it a certain way, and I'll get a look on my face. When he looks at me funny, I make sure to speak up and let him know that I've just popped into logistical mode. I'm sure the look on my face looks like I'm about to say "no" or something else that is in essence a "no". That's not the case. I'm trying to think of the most efficient way of making it happen.

How do you attend to "reaction" and "resistance" in your relationship?
Kevin:

When either the Leader or Follower has an immediate unfiltered reaction, I don't expect them to be able to completely hide it or manage it. Katie might be annoyed by something I've requested and have a flash of emotion across her face. I allow that as a natural human occurrence. However, I expect her to do the right mental work to recognize, analyze and correct any knee-jerk emotions and bring them into line with our priorities and agreements.

Similarly, I might find myself having a knee-jerk reaction to something Katie says simply because, for example, it reminds me of some bad experience in my past. I have an obligation to notice my irritation, figure out what is going on, and correct my behavior before letting it impact the relationship.

However, Followers are expected to, well ... follow. If they are suddenly digging in their heels, or standing in the way of the Leader's directive, that is a more serious matter, needing immediate attention and correction.

At this point, I think that I would add a third component: reluctance. Is the Follower simply hesitating? Are they reluctant to proceed, and if so, why? What is their reluctance to comply? Are they struggling with a need to be right? Are they struggling with a need to be heard and acknowledged? If something is standing in the way of their ability to joyfully follow, then this is an opportunity to explore and understand that reluctance. Where is the couple out of alignment?

If the reluctance continues, then there is active, willful resistance to the direction of the Leader. In our relationship that would indicate a need to stop all other plans or discussions and deal with that resistance. Katie is allowed to voice her opinion. She is allowed to be temporarily frustrated. She is allowed to be concerned about the wisdom of a choice and express her concerns. She is not allowed to actively refuse, interfere, or undermine a decision. She is obligated by our relationship to work to her very best to follow and support. Resistance would indicate that something has gone fundamentally wrong.

> I have total trust that if Katie appears to be resisting my direction that I am simply mistaking the situation, or we are having a miscommunication.

So how do I know if Katie is giving me some sort of pushback or resistance? How do I know, for instance, if when she says she won't have sex on a ladder with me, whether she is experiencing a "can't" or a "won't"?

The answer is two-fold: trust and intent. I know that Katie is a joyful and willing Follower. I have never seen her take any action that was not her best effort for me and the relationship. I have total trust that if Katie appears to be resisting my direction that I am simply mistaking the situation, or we are having a miscommunication. It is inconceivable to me that she would be intentionally opposing my will. Said another way, I know that her absolute intent is to follow, to serve, to enhance, to align, to prioritize. If I have trust in her and I know she is of pure intent, then when it appears she is resisting my will, my only conclusion is that something is goofed up in the process.

So I deal with apparent resistance by investigating where the process has failed. Was my order unclear or unrealistic? Am I asking her to do something about which she is afraid? Would my order cause some calamity that she is (by my explicit orders) obligated to refuse? *[She isn't allowed to do things that endanger her, for instance.]* If she appears to be resisting, I can be almost certain the failure is in the communication or the order itself, not in Katie's willingness to follow.

Now ... in a relationship that does not have that long-term surety, I believe the answer is nearly the same: investigate! In many (the majority?) Authority Transfer relationships the Follower has agreed to follow without resistance. If resistance appears, then a core agreement, and therefore the foundation of the relationship is at risk. Immediately stopping all other pursuits is necessary. Don't ignore it. Don't joke about it. Don't let it slide. Don't save it for later. Right then stop and very pointedly say "You appear to be in violation of the terms of our agreement. If you have a problem or concern, I need to hear it now so that I can understand it, take it seriously, and address it. I need some explanation for why as my Follower, you are choosing not to follow."

It is scary, because true resistance means the relationship is at risk. True resistance means things are fundamentally out of alignment and that the core of the agreements is crumbling. Reactions and reluctance are the normal parts of being human and should be noticed and supported to transcend. Resistance should be immediately addressed with all the focus and intention one can bring to bear—but still in the spirit of loving investigation, not punishment or discipline.

How do you attend to "reaction" and "resistance" in your relationship?

Katie:

Sometimes orders, changes of plan, and correction of direction come at me in an unexpected manner.

So far I am not Robotgirl or Spockslut. So reactions may occur. Reaction for me is the initial – sometimes unfiltered response I have to fear, frustration, and confusion. Kevin will see it in my facial expression, body language and sometimes words.

Let me give you an example:

I am working outside in the yard and have a sequence and plan in place. I am going to leaf-blow-out the flower beds, sweep the decks, then mow the lawn and the gathered debris into some manner of piles for disposal. Kevin comes outside and sees me full of energy and focus on our yard. He signals that I turn off the leaf blower and says, "Don't worry about that, I want you to cut back the hedge and focus on getting the mowing done today." POOF!! My eyes get big, my shoulders slump, I am silent in response and I stand there a moment.

That's my reaction. Not, "Yes Sir, right away Sir!" Not a smile of delighted compliance with the change of direction. I am unsettled. I am—yes— even frustrated. I had a great plan. His plan is great too. The hedge looks dreadful and we only have so much daylight to get work done outside.

Now I am faced with the choice of whether my reaction moves into resistance and ongoing struggle for both of us. This is where I often do some quick accounting in my head. I ask myself a set of questions that zip through quicker than that fourth helping of gooseberry pie.

> What is the best thing for me to do right now that attends to my priority of having an incredible relationship with Kevin?

The questions are somewhere in this following list:

❖ Is my plan and way important?

❖ Is there information I should give him that he doesn't have?

❖ Even if my way might be the better one, does it have to be THE way things are done today?

❖ How much joy will I get out of accomplishing what he wishes to have done today, and how much satisfaction will he have of me cheerfully working alongside him in his service?

❖ What is the best thing for me to do right now that attends to my priority of having an incredible relationship with Kevin?

So often the answer is, "It is not important, it is merely my inclination or preference." What is important is that I honor our dynamic. He has accepted the responsibility of final-decision-making and accountability for those decisions. My part is to support and believe in him.

Reaction is often almost a primal thing. No matter the temperance and self-discipline one might have, reactions can seep out and be tangible.

Resistance is Futile, so says the T-Shirt. Not because Kevin crushes my soul into compliance. Resistance is a sliding path to disagreement and discord. Seeking to win. To be right. To have my own way.

Let's break that down:

I dig in my toes, get sullen and cranky. I tell him in a moody way that I already had a plan to work on the yard and make it amazing. Then I drag my feet over to the damned hedge and start chopping away with grumpy toddler face on. Do I end up with a joyful afternoon outdoors working alongside my Leader whom I adore? Do I build him up in his role to have more confidence and trust in me? Do I lift my self-esteem and feeling of value?

It's an absolute loss if I allow reaction to be sustained and move into resistance. There is no win—for either of us. And the biggest loser is the serenity of our relationship.

But what if it is super important that I finish the leaf blowing? If that is the case I will respectfully share information with him, while adjusting my mind set and keeping in mind that I want to problem-solve, not win. I might say, "Yes, the hedge looks horrible. I was just thinking that it is going to rain tomorrow and it will be so hard to do the leaf blowing for a few days with them wet. But we could trim the hedge those days. What do you think?" There. I have given my information and concerns over to him. He always hears me, considers my input, and then once again takes on the responsibility of making a decision.

I manage reaction and resistance by *always* keeping in the forefront of my thoughts that my priority is a wonderful life and an amazing relationship. That removes so much of the struggles and poor choices when we are not aligned in the moment.

Chapter 12: Public Interactions and Subtleties

How do you interact in public? Talk about the subtleties of your role.
Dan:

When we go out in public, I try to do the courtesy of having the leash I have on her to match her shoes. OK, I was being facetious. Dawn isn't allowed to wear shoes.

To get to an actual answer. We do not interact in public much differently than anywhere else. She doesn't use honorifics. And we don't have random sex. Beyond that, is there any difference? If I think of any others, I'll come back to this.

> When we go out in public, I try to do the courtesy of having the leash I have on her to match her shoes. OK, I was being facetious. Dawn isn't allowed to wear shoes.

The things we continue to do in public are the ones that people don't see (or at least don't see as a result of power exchange roles). We have a foundation of respect for each other, we never argue in public, and if a decision needs to be made I get final say.

The subtleties of this role ... I hear my co-authors furiously typing away at their keyboards and wondering what I am missing. My influence and decision making and other leadership aspects; dawns calm confidence and self-assurance in her actions as she follows, either because of a direct task assigned or her internal radar of "What would Dan do?" These things are neither overt nor subtle to me.

I'm sure after we all share what we wrote I'll kick myself for not adding more to this one. But at this moment in time, there is no "aha" moment, we are simply who we are.

How do you interact in public? Talk about the subtleties of your role.
dawn:

Paying the dinner bill at the cashier station in a buffet restaurant, telling the cashier that the chain around his wife's throat means she'll do anything for him and then commanding her to kneel in front of everyone, her doing so in a presenting Gorean position in a short skirt, is NOT how we interact in public. We don't need to be preening peacocks on display with neon signs over our heads, "Hey look at us!"

Though, we were with the couple that did decide to show off in this manner. It was embarrassing to watch. We kind of separated from them, quietly paid our bill after they left, and then met up with them outside. They were all excited about how they had shocked people with their display of dominance and submission. We were not impressed with their display and didn't go out to dinner with them again.

Funny enough, we had also "interacted" as Dom/sub during the whole evening, but I'm betting this couple didn't even notice because it wasn't something super large and in your face. For example, it was a buffet. Which means I could serve Dan's drink. I would keep an eye on the level of his water and before it got below halfway, get him some more. Sometime during the evening I had to go to the bathroom. I lean over and ask him quietly if I may. That's not something that needs to be asked out loud for everyone to know, just so that everyone knows. It doesn't need to be a display for it to be connecting for us. There was a moment where I went to jump into the conversation and he squeezed my leg to let me know that my input could wait. Our dynamic is about and for us, not everyone else.

> We don't need to be preening peacocks on display with neon signs over our heads, "Hey, look at us!"

We just don't need the displays of "Hey, look at us, we are Dom and sub! Aren't you impressed? Or shocked? Or envious?" Which, in my opinion, are enacted by those with large egos or low self-esteem. They want to be seen for validation.

We are much more subtle. For one, no one else there asked to be witness to that display at the restaurant. Consent is huge for us, even in moments like that. Grandma and little Billy didn't need to witness that while eating their dinner.

Not to say we don't do sexy power exchange interactions while out and about. We just don't make it a grandiose event. The subtleties and doing things undercover is big for us. One night we took a walk in the park. I like wearing leashes. It was cold out so I was wearing a winter coat. Dan clicked a leash into place, snaked it down my coat sleeve and held the leash, walking me in the park. That was hot. Or he's had me kneel in the grocery store by making me get something from the bottom shelf without bending over. Things like this are possible without screaming to the world that they are witnessing D/s. We just don't need that.

Hells, I can even remember being punished in public and no one but Dan and I, and a Master friend knew what was going on. Dan is so creative and it leaks out during these types of moments. My hand in a cup of ice on its side with the (whispered) order of "Don't cry," while we are having lunch with this Master. A quiet, not dramatic, not "Hey look at me being a Master," moment. Effective. Us.

Not to say that big displays of dominance and submission aren't fun. I love when Dan grabs my hair and makes me kneel in front of people. Or takes me up on a stage and makes me kneel, or bends me over in the middle of the dungeon, demanding I bark like a dog, or … OK, you get the picture. It's just that we save those moments for kink events, dungeons and play spaces where it can still shock some people but at least it's an environment of consent.

For me, in public, subtle is sexy and hot.

How do you interact in public? Talk about the subtleties of your role.

Kevin:

This is one of the things that I fret about, honestly. Not just the subtleties in public, but the subtleties in general. Like anything you have practiced mindfully for twenty years, some things become natural and easy.

Katie and I now flow in our Authority Transfer. Our roles are rarely confusing to us. We have shorthand ways of communicating (which I might address in this essay, if time permits). We are attuned to the fluctuating conditions in our partner, in ourselves and in the world around us—and how those impact the expression of our Authority Transfer.

In other essays we've hinted at the fact that early years in the relationship were challenging. Challenging due to life circumstances at the time, but also because we had old relationship habits, and unrealistic fantasies about how we were supposed to do these roles. This means that much of our AT interactions were more blatant. If I wanted obedience, I might put Katie on her knees and take on my Domly visage and lower my voice a menacing octave "Katie, go get me a fork from the kitchen!!" Right? Way more overt power than necessary getting squirted around like cum from a mustard bottle. (Katie does these bizarre statements much better than me, apparently.)

Now everything is more subtle. The overt use of power is reserved for special occasions. Dan calls a momentary use of power, particularly when not really necessary, a "flex". Such a great term—and a useful practice that I probably need to incorporate more.

I say I should consider more flexing because of the worry I started this writing mentioning. Is it possible for the Authority Transfer to be so natural and easy that it just melds into the background and disappears? Dr. Bob Rubel uses the term "vanilla drift" and I think he means it to refer to getting less intentional and mindful about your Authority Transfer until it sort of fades. If that is what is happening—not great. But what if some "vanilla drift" is simply two people so synchronized and so harmonious in their AT dance that the flow of power is never obvious?

> Our overriding rule is that we don't want anyone concerned for Katie's safety or happiness.

Aww, for fuck's sake Kevin, did you read the question? Damn it.

All that, I suppose, leads to the answer. Our interactions in public are always role appropriate and enhancing of our roles, but likely entirely unnoticeable to the common person. Sometimes when Katie and I hold hands, I adjust enough that I am holding onto her wrist instead for a few paces—enough for her to recognize that I'm the owner with my property, not (just) her sweet boyfriend.

I speak to her in the same respectful way I speak to her at home, but that means that she interprets my gentle requests just like at home—as directives. As we go into our separate bathrooms in a public place I will almost always point at some spot nearby, often without saying a word. Katie knows that is where I expect to find her when she is done. If she is done first she goes there and waits. If I am done first I do whatever I want for a couple of minutes, then go there to collect my girl from where I parked her. This allows me to know she is done and I know where to find her, rather than hang around the bathroom like a pervert watching the women's room door for 10 minutes while she has already left before me and is out filling the grocery cart.

When we separate while shopping, I will text her "??" and she will text me her location. If the location changes before I find her, she will text me her new location. I'll be damned if I'll wander the store like a lost child while my girl roams around willy-nilly.

Our overriding rule is that we don't want to have anyone be concerned for Katie's safety or happiness. We will never behave in a way, in public, that looks like a use of power over her, because people might worry for her. Beyond that, we are unwilling to have me use my consensually obtained authority, flex my power, and subtly reinforce fucked-up societal norms regarding men's non-consensual use of power. Since we can't explain to folks that "Yeah, but my being a bossy-pants is because we have negotiations and consent..." we do our best not to let our personal lifestyle choices worsen the social norms regarding women.

We probably put a bit of effort into explicitly adoring one another. We don't want to offend or shock with public displays of affection (although I do have a kink for exhibiting Katie, it doesn't show up in this way). So we don't make out on a park bench, but Katie does stand affectionately close as we wait in line to check out. She stands in front of me, with her ass gently brushing me and my hands on her shoulders. Or she stands beside me and rests her head on my shoulder. Like "normal" people who adore each other, but respect the situation and the people around them.

How do you interact in public? Talk about the subtleties of your role.
Katie:

Kevin and I were holding hands, walking into a Canadian Tire one day. We happened across a lady from our hometown. She greeted us by saying, "Are you two on a date?" First of all—it's Canadian Tire! We did a quick check of what we were doing that seemed date-like. All we could come up with is the hand holding and laughing together.

That is both sad in general, but also highlights how naturally we move into public connection with each other.

That has fuck all to do with our relationship style though, right? It doesn't unless it does.

Does the gaze have an eyebrow raised? Are the quiet words fun because he is saying something a bit naughty about owning me? Does his hand holding slide up to holding my wrist for a moment as a sign of his dominant energy?

Subtleties are not difficult at all. *Keeping them in use and being aware of them is the hard part.* Mindfulness. Conscious, intentional mindfulness. I know, I've said this before. It is that important.

The first time I met Kevin in person was at an airport. As he approached me, I suddenly came up with the idea of tying my shoe. I was able to drop to one knee briefly, right there at the airport. We both knew my shoe was tied. Nobody gave an extra glance or care to our interaction, but it was profound for us.

Over the years we have added many ways to interact in public that have other meanings to us. Hell, you could touch your partner's earlobe, tell them the next time you did that they needed to remember being bent over the table, spanked and begging to cum. Touch that earlobe from then until eternity and it has meaning.

If Kevin does a short stroke of my arm or leg while visiting folks it usually means stop talking soon. A squeeze means be careful of the topic.

If I bring him a drink or serve him in some way at a gathering of family or colleagues, I will most often put the item in place and then gently touch his shoulder. That means, "Here you go, Sir."

When Kevin and I first got together I had my teenage children with me, plus a child we both adopted. We had sixteen years ahead of us with other humans underfoot. For us, we did not wish the details of the relationship to be obvious and influential to the children. No disclaimer, katie! We wished to behave before them the way we would in public. That meant we had to find a way that felt responsible and a positive influence to them, but also allowed us to grow our dynamic. Subtleties abounded.

> Subtleties are not hard at all. Keeping them in use and being aware of them is the hard part.

The children—well, they are grown and have their own wonderful relationships now—see us as a compatible couple. They have never witnessed a harsh word or fight between us. They are aware that I will seek out Kevin for input before making a decision, though that is usually, "Hold on, let me make sure there is no conflict in schedule. I'll ask Kevin about the calendar." A smooth way to convey that Kevin and I are a team that work compatibility and with consideration of each other.

Before Kevin retired as a psychologist there were many instances of us interacting with caution and regard for his colleagues. Not because we were embarrassed about who we are—we love who we are. Instead out of respect for who they are. It was a professional environment. We did not want people to misunderstand the consensual, joyful relationship we have. We were careful not to have misunderstandings of our relationship cast a shadow or limit Kevin's ability to do his profession.

Other subtleties would be that Kevin will take what would usually be an order at home, "Sit down, girl, you've done enough," and change the wording to, "katie, why don't you take a break. I'll go get that box from the car." People hear it exactly as it sounds. I hear that I have been given a command that I do not disregard or push back on. The answer would be a generous smile and "Thank you!"

There was a group of friends we hung with for years that were not in the BDSM subculture. We would have meals, play games, and watch movies together. As comfort grew, I'm sure it became obvious that I attended to Kevin. I heard as soon as he spoke. We didn't bicker like other couples did. Kevin's care and loving words were noticeable to them. I would often just drop on the floor at his feet while watching a movie. Other folks were sprawled on the floor as well, mine just had meaning.

All of this writing is about being intentional about actions and words. Having a blast with finding ways to be subtle. Keeping it fresh and … buzz….

Chapter 13: BDSM

How important is BDSM play and scenes in your dynamic?
Dan:

I don't do rope. I tried for a while but never really felt like it was something I had any inclination for. I am good at spanking, flogging, and predicament play. Not so much at fire play, yet pretty handy with canes.

What I'm really good at is power exchange BDSM. This is not the power exchange relationship where you have a commitment, mutual growth, and expected results. This is a scene where I am clearly in charge and although we have negotiated what we are going to do, a lot of what happens is because I drive a person to submit to the scene. Impact play is great for these, as is sensuality.

If you are wondering what question I'm actually answering, you'd be right to suggest I've gone off topic and am talking about what kind of BDSM I enjoy instead of the actual question. Well, mostly. Because my initial answer to "How important is BDSM to your power exchange dynamic?" would be "Not at all". But that isn't really true. It is not essential or on the same list as open communication, trustworthiness, or consistency. But it is a tool in the box.

> Sceneing for me includes primal power exchange—hair grabbing, forcing, demanding, pushing. It brings my focus totally to the person I am playing with and the world starts and stops at this scene, this moment.

Because sometimes all those other tools are too cerebral. Or you just don't know what is wrong. Or maybe nothing is wrong, just kinda … blah. A good physical intense scene might be just what we need to reconnect.

A good scene requires engagement and connection. Sceneing for me includes primal power exchange—hair grabbing, forcing, demanding, pushing. It brings my focus totally to the person I am playing with and the world starts and stops at this scene, this moment. And regardless of if the scene ends up in tears, massive orgasms, or just happy looks in the mirror at a new set of bruises, they end with the intimacy of after care. For a random scene, that is a conclusion. But for my power exchange partner, that results in a deepening connection.

How important is BDSM play and scenes in your dynamic?
dawn:

I'm having a lot of resistance to answering this question, and I'm not sure why. BDSM and sceneing are super important to me. I love it. Kink is my fetish. Actually, power exchange is my kink and kink is my fetish. Without a doubt, I need it in my life. That's my personal need.

How important is it to our relationship? Well, at the beginning, our relationship was all about the hot, kinky, slutty sex. I found this whole world of kink while surfing porn on this new thing called the 'internet' and then wanted to make that part of my life. Dan was totally on board with the idea. We would slip out at lunchtime from work, find a secluded spot, talk naughty with Dan whispering in my ear how he wanted to take me, or me whispering how I wanted to beg for him ... or Dan would take out his bag of neckties he'd collected and tie me to my seat in the car and do naughty things with me. Or we had to a favorite section of woods where he'd tie my hands to trees, spreading me wide and fucking me with a dildo, with the command of staying quiet. .... all of that super fucking hot. D/s play was what it was all about at the beginning.

> Kink is my fetish. Actually, power exchange is my kink and kink is my fetish.

I placed so much importance on it that if we weren't playing regularly, I felt something was truly wrong with our relationship. If we went to an event and didn't play, it's because something was wrong with me or us. I had intricately wound our play around our relationship.

Who wouldn't? It's hot and sexy and honestly, if I got on my high horse or had difficulty in submitting or getting into that headspace, a good take down scene would be the best fix for that. Bam. Back into headspace.

The weird thing is that over time I started separating the play from the dynamic. Don't get me wrong, I love to play. I love playing with Dan. I love all the toys … or just his hands and teeth … and him taking me. I have a need to submit. It's juicy and hot and feeds my slutty side. But I didn't want our lack of play at times to affect our relationship dynamic, so I think I've separated them. Plus, getting his peanut butter sandwich in service had become just as hot to me.

Maybe that's why I started out with resistance to answering this question. I want to say, we have hot BDSM all the time! It's super important to our relationship! We make sure to have play as a focus whenever we can … but honestly, we don't have a lot of big scenes. We have a lot of smaller, instantaneous intimate moments. Dan likes to karate chop me out of the blue. He likes to pinch me for no reason at all. If I bend over in the kitchen, he might take that as an opportunity to either smack my ass or fuck me with a couple strokes, leaving me begging for more. But it's rare that we pull out the toy bag and have *the* big scene. And now that we are in the RV instead of in a house with our spanking bench and liberator, it's even more rare.

Wait, is that true? I remember that poor spanking bench getting dusty from lack of use even when we had it set up in our basement, unless we brought someone home to play with.

So, BDSM and scenes are super important to me. Like I said, it is part of my kink, part of my fetish. It's fun and super connecting for Dan and me. As a tool, it builds trust and taps into his dominance and my submission. We have learned to make a point to use it as a tool, and have scenes every now and then to feed this connection.

But thank goodness that even though our relationship really started around naughty, fun play, it shifted and it's not so important now. There will most likely come a time that we are not able to physically play, at least like we used to. And when that happens, our relationship will be OK. Just like when sex fades out, though I hope it doesn't, it is possible … our dynamic will not crash and burn because of the shift.

How important is BDSM play and scenes in your dynamic?
Kevin:

Dan just said "This topic seems pretty easy," as we started writing. Oddly, I was just thinking that this has the potential to be a little complex for Katie and I.

For starters, I don't believe that all Leaders are Tops, or Sadists. Some Leaders prefer to bottom in scenes. As a Leader I am barely interested in BDSM play at all—but that isn't 100% accurate. Let me explain.

I like sex. So sexual activities are of interest to me. Specifically, playing with orgasms is super fun—either wringing every shudder possible out of Katie, or using her for my fun and denying her the right to orgasm at all. Super hot.

My main "kink", though, is playing with power with Katie. When we scene it rarely involves applying much discomfort to her. I'll tweak a nipple harder than normal, bite an earlobe harder than normal, or pinch the really ouchy bit on the underside of her arm. Nothing I do is ever enough to bruise—heck, even seeing a blemish on her skin is pretty unusual when we are done. Almost all of my touches and attention are sensuous. Kisses, caresses, brushing the hair from her face, gently lifting and cupping the weight of one breast, pulling her tight against me and grinding a thigh into her mound.

Our scenes involve me manipulating her body—touching her like I own her and am inspecting her, walking around her in a judgmental and appraising way, moving her head or arms to different positions like she is a poseable doll for my entertainment. Sometimes I move her body to create disorientation and trance by spinning her and tossing her head. Often moving her body involves wheeling her chaotically around a mat, like a drunken dance partner, so she is unbalanced and scampering to keep up, reliant on me to keep her from falling. I will also move her from standing to kneeling to laying in a wild flurry of position changes. Sometimes I push her to the ground and stand over her, or drape myself over her curled body, and communicate ownership from my position above her.

> Power-highlighting scenes where I fuck her up and rip orgasms from her for an hour are really valuable to us.

All these things are about communicating ownership. All of them are about making demands of her position or attention and having her comply with that expectation.

Combining these things, our scenes become a dervish dance of movement, with Katie feeling more and more powerless. She struggles to constantly move or behave to my demands and becomes singularly focused on quickly moving to please me. Then I start forcing orgasms from her. Over and over. Movement, compliance, sensual touch, orgasm.

For a tiny bit of unexpected difference, in very small doses, I will give a little pinch or swat. Not because she is a masochist, and not because I am a sadist, but because it is something I can ask of her and she can show compliance. I'll even kneel her down facing me, and I'll have her look me deep in the eyes, and I'll say "I'm going to swat your thighs now, and I want you to remain still and passive, without a sound. Just accept the hurt and look at me lovingly."

That isn't to say that a 5-minute spanking before I dive in for some hot doggy-style never happens. Her little squeaks are pretty hot. But that might be a handful of times in a year.

So … BDSM scenes aren't really important to us. My "tool bag" of implements I take to use on Katie is tiny, and I often forget to open it. On the other hand, power-highlighting scenes where I fuck her up and rip orgasms from her for an hour are really valuable to us. Huh— we actually rarely have those scenes at home though, and certainly could, especially since we haven't gotten a "fix" from attending a conference in the pandemic years. We usually just incorporate power into a nice fuck, but don't actually have a power scene when we are home. Worth considering there, Kevin.

How important is BDSM play and scenes in your dynamic?
Katie:

Bondage

Hardly at all. We have never gotten into the rope skills beyond the enjoyment of being spectators. In sex, Kevin's hands are my bondage. In a dungeon, he will restrain me with a command. "Don't move." "You better fucking hold still!" Once he tied me with thread to a St Andrew's Cross and ordered me not to break the bonds. Then he proceeded to fuck me up with a bunch of orgasms. Mental bondage perhaps? Ya, we like that shit.

Domination & Submission

When you apply this to being a Top or bottom in a scene we absolutely love this play. Sometimes primal, always highlighting Kevin's control and training of me. I will elaborate in a moment.

Sadomasochism

We are SM light. We mess around with some intense sensation to heighten sexual experiences and our roles in erotic play. I think in all our years I have had five bruises from Kevin and a few neck bite marks when the duration got too long. Mostly he chooses to do some amount of impact play just because he can. He does it precisely because I do not enjoy it. The act says, "You are mine. You don't much like this, but you will fucking comply and allow it." The yielding and obeying gets us ravenous much more than the sadomasochism aspect.

> Our kink is eroticism, some level of exhibitionism, and orgasms—especially mine because that is Kevin's ultimate goal in any scene.

Our kink is eroticism, some level of exhibitionism, and orgasms—especially mine because that is Kevin's ultimate goal in any scene.

When we play in a dungeon, we are on the wrestling mats, but not fighting—more like dancing. The dance has no choreography. It has a leader and a follower. Both intensely in their places. Kevin, becoming broad in the shoulders, straight in the spine, his stance coiled and balanced, laser-focused in his gaze. Demanding, commanding, manipulating me in full dominant roar. I quickly slide into an altered mind state where it is all about him and his demands. Anything other than him fades away. His actions are intensely sexual. Without any penetration he rips a cascade of orgasms from me.

At home our sexual interactions are very similar and most would say that that is sex, not BDSM play. But that is how we do BDSM.

Sensual domination is very important to us. It is intimacy. It is vulnerability. We need to have that saturated into our days.

Sometimes as a brief interaction, like Kevin taking the paring knife from my hand while I work in the kitchen, holding it to my throat and growling, "Mine!" Sometimes as a full out, bone liquifying primal domination fuck.

Doing "scenes" such as in a dungeon space are not essential to us. Mostly because we have ways to meet that need in our daily life. It's like having gourmet ice cream at home, but occasionally going out to a place where they scrape your dessert around on a rock, chop up some goodies, put it in a fancy cup with sprinkles on top and it costs you more. Delicious, treasured experiences. Not essential to us in our life, but hell yeah we're grabbing some if available.

Section 3: Mental and Emotional Gymnastics

The questions in this section explore the internal work we do and the way we reason through topics that are sometimes emotionally complex or challenging.

14) Transparency, vulnerability and openness—what do these mean in your relationship?
15) How do you manage the sacrifices necessary to make this relationship work?
16) Are manipulation, coercion, or underlying motives part of your interactions sometimes? Why?
17) How do you reconcile empowerment and independence with transferring authority?
18) Is anything off-limits in your relationship? Why?

Chapter 14: Transparency and Vulnerability

Transparency, vulnerability and openness—what do these mean in your relationship?
Dan:

As we sat here this morning, the topic was decided on and someone said "Go" and I started writing. I thought that this would be an easy one to answer and go on about my day. After all, I've said more times than I can count that vulnerability is my kink. And then, as I started to write I found myself stopping and restarting, over and over. Let's see if I can explain why in a slightly cohesive way.

I know that vulnerability is something that "turns me on". By that, I mean turned on emotionally, sexually, and mentally. Further, I know that as a Leader, I need to cultivate that vulnerability in my followers. What is the best way to have a follower allow themselves to be vulnerable (no, you just can't whip out the Dom voice and demand "Show me your soul!")? To have a follower of mine wholeheartedly trust me enough to share their inner heart is by sharing mine. I've heard this referred to as "baring your soul", and what a great way to say it. My follower dawn knows all my inner demons by name; my fears and where they live in me; and exactly how to attack my ego if she so chooses. By offering her this, in time, I get the same from her.

That process - having that follower being transparent with you - is not quick and should not be rushed. It is simply offered with an open mind and listening heart and as each part of that proverbial onion is peeled, acknowledged.

> Your follower does not need to see you impacted by whatever they shared and feel like they have just done you harm.

And here is where you as a Leader—if you decide to cultivate this—have to be skillful and able to accept what you hear. In other words, this is the scary part! When a follower for example *(and I am making this up just as an illustration, sorry if I step on someone's toes)* reveals that they were once mocked by Tom Hanks, you have to be able to hear that, emphasize, show compassion for them (and not feel pity). Granted, you might also be angry, or disgusted at the cruelty of humans, or have a wide range of responses. But, oh Leader, that shit gets put aside as you simply stand and accept what that follower shares. I'll note that now that you have taken on this information, you do want to process it. Scream or rage or cry, but do it elsewhere, not at that moment. Your follower does not need to see you being impacted by whatever they shared and feel like they have just done you harm.

And each time that follower shares a Deep Dark bit, hear them, then have them kneel at your side or get you a cup of coffee or whatever normal follower thing they do. An action that says "I heard you, that is fucked up, and we are still us and good, so serve me."

The above illustration was for a Big Thing, but should be practiced for the little things as well.

Transparency is that idea that nothing is off the table and no secrets are kept. This means at any time, if my follower thinks I am being a dumb ass or doing something unskillfully or just doesn't understand a choice, they can (in a proper way), ask me why and I will often tell them. Well, most of the time. Sometimes we Leaders flex and decide not to reply, and that also generates trust. "You don't understand, but do the thing anyway, because I want it."

Are there limits on what I expect a follower to share? On one hand I know all of dawn's passwords—email, bank account, OKCupid, and can go in there at any time. If I need something from the internet and my phone isn't handy, I grab hers and enter the passcode. Neither of us gives it a second thought. On the other hand …well, in our life, that is it, there is no other hand. This isn't to say she does not have privacy when she asks for it … but I can't recall the last time she did.

This vulnerability is a keystone of any power exchange I do. And that extends to my non-power exchange relationships as well (the polyam partners and my closest friends). Not that I know my pals' bank account info … but if they asked for mine and had a reason, I would not hesitate.

And finally—vulnerability literally makes my dick hard. When a person I am romantically interested in shares that in eighth grade they stole a chocolate bar and has never told anyone else before … that gives me a woody. I'm not sure what that says about me, but it doesn't do anyone harm and leads to some really … different fantasies when I self-pleasure.

Transparency, vulnerability and openness—what do these mean in your relationship?
dawn:

One of the things that drew me to this style of relationship was the whole idea of transparency and … wait. Let's start at the beginning.

Our relationship literally started because of these three core concepts. Two things were happening around the time that our friendship shifted from friendship to something much deeper. For one, I was tired of my vanilla relationship and was spending a lot of time discovering the world of naughtiness on this new thing called the internet. I was collecting pictures and stories and found that I was drawn to domination and submission, kinky play, sharing sexual partners, and more. I mean, that shit was really turning me on, but I had no one to share this shift with. My partner at the time had no interest and was actually offended that I was embracing this interest even if it was just me reading stories and looking at pictures.

At the same time, I was also spending time researching things for my healing and spiritual path .... I mean a whole new world had opened up to me and I didn't have to go to the library anymore looking for books that may or may not be there. So I spent hours and hours falling down rabbit holes on the computer.

Like I said, so much happened in these few months. I'm reading about power dynamics. Domination. Submissives being forced to share everything about themselves so their dominants would know everything about them. Submissives admitting to deep dark secrets and fantasies that they couldn't tell anyone else. Dominants that embraced all of this. It became a deep desire to find this type of interaction one day.

Over time I really needed someone to share this all with, and Dan and I were spending more time together since we worked at the same place. I slowly shared what I was researching. We shared our porn pic collection and realized we were drawn to the same thing—this thing called D/s. We both were drawn to that style of relationship.

Then, one day I was invited to a BDSM demo by some people I'd met on an IRC channel. I went, tried it out and found that I loved it! I even asked one of the demo leaders to give me a spanking. Well, it turned into a paddling and I walked away with some happy bruising. My husband was mortified. So I learned quickly not to share this desire with him anymore. Now I was hiding a core piece of myself. I'd already had to do that with another secret of mine since the beginning of our relationship. When we got together and I decided to become vulnerable with him and share something I've never shared with anyone before, he cut me off and told me he couldn't handle it. Now, here I am discovering something new about myself, and can't talk about it with him either. Because of this....and other reasons ... I decided I couldn't go on with that relationship.

> Over time I realized that this was how I wanted to live my life: open, transparent, and vulnerable. But only with those who could handle it. Not only handle it, but cultivate it.

But I still had a friend in Dan, and decided to slowly start sharing little pieces of my discoveries with him. Come to find out, he had the same interests and hadn't been able to share with anyone. I had showed him my bruise and that had turned him on. What I didn't realize till later was that it wasn't the bruise that had turned him on, but the fact that I had shown it to him. Nervous as hell, never having done something like that before, and I was showing him. I was trusting him with my vulnerability after having been told by my ex that what I was interested in was wrong.

Now fast forward just a little bit. Remember that I'm also digging into resources that can help me with my past baggage at the same time. I go to a workshop, Dan goes with me. We were both workshop junkies at the time … always looking for something new to learn, yet rarely went together. The fact that he was there this evening was a fluke. Or was it? His workshop had been canceled. He had the evening off, so he decided to join me at mine. Well, I could go into a lot more detail and I do during our presentations, but let's shorten this to say that the facilitator of the workshop was able to discover everything that has happened to me in the past and vocalize it to me. I had never spoken those words out loud. This totally destroyed all the walls I had built around myself. Add that to the judgment I had faced with the ex and I was running out the door like the hounds of hell were on my feet. I had to get out of there.

Dan followed me. He let me cry. He let me sob. And then he listened to my story. And just listened. All of it. When I looked up, there was no judgment. No resistance to me sharing. I had shared my deepest, darkest secrets with this person I had called "friend" for years and he didn't reject me. He sat there and let me know that he was still my friend and I was a courageous person for sharing.

That was my first time at really being vulnerable and open. Since then, it's become a theme of my life.

Over time I realized that this was how I wanted to live my life: open, transparent, and vulnerable. But only with those who could handle it. Not only handle it, but cultivate it. And what better way than in a power dynamic built around these concepts.

I tell my story when others new to this relationship style ask how much they should share with their new owner. I say, "Everything." Share it all. If you should be able to share with anyone, it should be the person that wants to own you, master you. For how can they master you if they don't know everything about you?

I'm at the point now, and have been for a while, where secrets feel icky to me. We have built our communication tools in our relationship to have ways to bring up those topics that are hard because we need that transparency, openness and vulnerability in all that we do. We speak the things that are hard to speak about. We lay ourselves open.

It's hard. But, shine a light on it all. Secrets, fantasies, all of it. If you don't, it will live in the shadows and rule your life without your permission. As a follower, that's your Leader's responsibility. As a Leader, if you don't shine a light on all your "stuff", you'll never know why you make the decisions that you do. You won't truly be in charge.

For me, all of this leads to trust. Trust in me. Trust in him. Trust in us.

Transparency, vulnerability and openness—what do these mean in your relationship?
Kevin:

The crux of this question is related to how available you, and your partner, are to each other on the important-yet-invisible topics, like emotional content. As a Leader, it is important for me to have as much information about my Follower as possible to be able to guide and support effectively. If I am making huge life affecting decisions and I am blind to Katie's internal state, the risk of me doing harm, or simply neglecting her, increases.

I need to know how she is doing. I need to know her emotional state: Is she worried about the upcoming visit to her relatives? Is she enjoying the current lifestyle we are experiencing? I need to know her thoughts: Does she think I'm spending too much time reading the news? Does she think walking might be more valuable to my health than jump-rope skipping?

What I don't need is her unfiltered thoughts. If every time she is annoyed by having to walk the dog, she vomits out a stream of "transparent" sharing regarding her annoyance—that's going to be no fun in a big hurry. So she has the additional expectation that she do most of the heavy lifting regarding her own internal state. She must process and evaluate her internal landscape and try to manage much of the monkey-mind nonsense that rides there in all of us. Each of us has a head full of old baggage, mistaken beliefs, sloppy mental habits, unrealistic viewpoints, and other flotsam and contaminants. I expect her to try to quiet all the excess noise, primarily so that she can reduce its impact on her and secondly so that she doesn't transparently share gunk with me. Not necessary, thanks.

> The Follower must be brave and trusting and share all their inner tender bits. They have to shine a light into their dark corners and then bring those ugly bits to the Leader on a platter.

I read a book recently where the entire reason the aliens attacked was because they picked up our TV broadcasts and spent a great deal of effort to translate them, only to find our TV broadcasts constituted a million hours of mind-melting nonsense. They considered transmitting that volume of useless information, that required effort to process, an attack. Similarly, I don't need Katie to share every bit of gibberish in her head for me to decipher. Just send the cleaned-up signal, please.

So, I do expect Transparency, Vulnerability, and Openness from Katie. I want to have the closeness and trust that openness and vulnerability bring. I also want to have the knowledge of her internal state so that I can lead in a way that is respectful of her.

Interestingly, one of the places that the Authority Transfer subculture draws a line is with the Leader having a reciprocal obligation to offer Transparency, Vulnerability and Openness. The Follower must be brave and trusting, and share all their inner tender bits. They have to shine a light into their dark corners and then bring those ugly bits to the Leader on a platter. The Leader usually has no such obligation. They are often allowed to keep secrets. They are allowed to feel sad but "bravely" soldier on and keep it to themselves.

They are allowed to have doubts and fears and resentments that they do not express.

What happens in a relationship with an imbalance in openness and vulnerability? Since those are elements that tend to build trust, is there half as much trust as there could be, since only the Follower is offering those things into the relationship?

Further, how pragmatically effective is it for there to be unilateral vulnerability and openness? If the Leader is veiled, is the Follower able to offer the support or understanding that they could otherwise?

In our relationship, I try to offer Katie the same vulnerability and openness that she offers me. I trust her to be generous in spirit and respectful of the things I share with her. I try to keep from leaving hidden emotions or secret thoughts as an ugly background noise in my head, rather than getting them out and letting us resolve them.

I'm not sure how I feel about Leader transparency. In some ways the hierarchical nature of AT is highlighted by the fact that I don't have to tell Katie everything. I don't have to explain myself. Sometimes I get to have some stuff I don't share - but that feels like it might go really poorly. I can decide to spend a bunch of money, and why and where and for what could be kept to myself. It is within my right as the Leader. But that could, especially if what is hidden is impactful, lead to loss of trust, and a negative outcome for the relationship. Non-Transparency is theoretically my right in this relationship, but just because I can doesn't mean I should. I'm not sure doing so would be wise.

Transparency, vulnerability and openness—what do these mean in your relationship?
Katie:

Transparency, vulnerability, and openness—this is both scary and reassuring. Getting beyond the scary part and growing into the security and reassuring aspects has been a very deep journey of growth for me.

Being transparent with Kevin is something I learned to do—even forced myself to do for an extended time before it had any ease. Even today I sometimes put on the steel-toed boots and kick my own ass into the conversations I need to have. Not only do I need to have those conversations, but as my Leader, Kevin needs that information to do an effective job, make good decisions and help me with my struggles.

I believe the first time I had to face this was when his parents moved in with us temporarily. Suddenly I was serving a much larger household. I was overwhelmed. Being very new to my role in our dynamic I was trying to be the ultimate accomplisher of all the things. I just kept on taking on more tasks, cleaning and cooking more than ever before, interacting respectfully with additional adults because they were *his* adults. I did this for much too long without transparency—to the point where it was shattering my resilience and joy. When I finally broke down and shared my suffering with Kevin it was intense and messy. It would have been much more effective and less painful if I had let him know as things unfolded.

> I do not need to vomit them out onto his lap in a mess of accusations, recriminations, and hurtful words. Who wants to sort through a lapful of vomit?

Once he had the information that I felt overwhelmed with the work, the mess, the confusion of hierarchy—once I had done my job— he could do his. And he did. The way he heard me, recognized the truth of it, didn't think less of me for "failing", the way he resolved the issue all deepened my trust and willingness to be transparent in the future.

91.3% of the time transparency for me is a crafted moment. Yes, I need to share my struggles and concerns. No, I do not need to vomit them out into his lap in a mess of accusations, recrimination and hurtful words. Who wants to sort through a lapful of vomit? I can say everything honestly and fully without putting words into our relationship that will echo on and haunt us. Without disrespect or unkindness. My sharing is about problem solving and information supplying, not an attack.

Every once in a while I will be in quite an emotional tumble. I will let Kevin know we need to have a conversation. I will then say something like, "I am really struggling to sort through this issue and I think it needs to be messy and disorganized and I need your help to discover the reason why I am upset." It's a heads up that where I start might not be where we actually land. That I am not convinced that I have the bottom line on the issue, but I know that there is an issue. Once again, even this delivery is not ugly in name calling and accusations. It is just disorganized.

Vulnerability goes hand in hand with transparency. With a slightly different flavour. To be vulnerable for me is to take that leap into sharing my struggles, my opinions, and my desires, and believing I will still be lovable and valued.

We keep secret what we are ashamed of, what we believe is unappealing, but in a long-term relationship secrets don't keep well. It might be the vulnerability of sharing a kink, a desire, a weakness, a failing. Letting him into my innermost thoughts and history is vulnerable in a way that I have never allowed before. It also allows for me to have exciting fantasies play out, and have long withheld desires explored.

This vulnerability exposes to Kevin the "ugly" parts of my past that I am ashamed of. History that sometimes bubbles up into my emotional reactions. Again, allowing for that window into katie gives him the information he needs to do his role and lets me feel seen, heard and loved.

I love that Kevin is also vulnerable and open in sharing his struggles, thoughts and desires with me. He is my leader, but he does not walk a lonely road of holding all his bad days, insecurities and struggles inside. Being met at this deep level of vulnerability is essential for me to travel there as well.

These aspects of our relationship create a depth of knowledge and trust that has seen us through very tough times. It also gives us the surety to face changes and challenges.

Chapter 15: Sacrifice

How do you manage the sacrifices to make this relationship work?

Dan:

I have a few core philosophies that have served me for over thirty years. One of them is "You can do anything you want, as long as you are willing to pay the price." Power exchange is like that. But that isn't a negative thing.

As a Leader, I do have to sacrifice some things for the health of the relationship. You'd think it is the follower who does all the giving up of stuff—the very name of it suggests that the follower is sacrificing their power. In truth, we as Leaders may make sacrifices as well. But let's get more specific—what have I sacrificed for this relationship?

I had to give up the easy path tools I had in previous relationships. I was pretty good at bullshitting my previous partners and could avoid issues by either skillfully lying about them or just giving up on what I wanted. I've heard actual relationship advice that suggested you have to choose your battles. I find that view pretty goofy nowadays as it assumes battles are the standard. I had to give up the idea that I can be lazy, that things would just work out, and that ... blah blah blah, you know the fucked-up stuff that goes on in fucked-up relationships.

> I've heard actual relationship advice that suggested you have to choose your battles. I find that view pretty goofy nowadays as it assumes battles are the standard.

In my current power exchange relationship with dawn, what do I sacrifice? Once more, laziness. Meaning if things are not going well for us, I need to step up and drive. I give up anger. Not to say I don't get angry, but I don't get to do that comfortably sitting in anger for a day or week waiting until someone notices and asks me about it. When I get angry, I huff, then I address the thing or lack of thing or fear that caused the anger to arise. OK, all this is kinda positive sounding, but let's step deeper.

Did I have to sacrifice that girlfriend or potential additional follower because dawn felt unsafe? I thought I needed to, and I did.

That was probably the part where I was closest to tossing in the towel. I was stuck with the conflict of the authentic *Dan is polyamorous and is a multiple relationship/multiple loving kind of guy* and my misguided thought that dawn was asking me to sacrifice that. What I figured out—eventually, after much gnashing of teeth and tears—was that what I needed to sacrifice was time and energy so I could lead dawn to address her fears around this. She didn't want me to not be me—but it was hard for her to navigate and I needed to provide guidance.

This is the real sacrifice—or cost—of being a Leader. Time and energy that you would devote to yourself is devoted to the follower and to the relationship. I want to follow that up with a caveat that it all balances out, what you surrender your follower gives back in another way, and I know it is true, but sometimes, when you are in the midst of it, it doesn't feel like it.

I want to sit and play a PC game. Dawn, on easy mode, asks me what I want at the grocery store or what I want to do tonight. On hard mode, she is having a bad day or needs help with a challenge. Either way, I have a responsibility to turn from that game and make a decision. Address an issue. Extend my energy toward something that isn't satisfying a selfish desire.

I am not going to sugar coat this for you, oh reader, or for dawn, or even for me. This is the lot I have cast, to put my relationship health first. But don't confuse this with it being a bad thing. When we talk about overall value, my relationship versus getting to level 14 on Star Battle Warrior has no comparison. I know this. But the feeling, at that moment, at that split second, is "Can't someone else drive for a bit?"

This leads to the development of tools to deal with that. Time management, Dan days, commands that say "Fuck off, I'm playing, I'll catch up later." And creating a follower that doesn't need to be micromanaged. Ninety percent of the time when dawn asks me what she should get at the grocery store, I say "whatever". She is skilled to not only bring back the things we need, but more likely than not has a little treat for me that had I thought about it I would have said "Oh, I want that!"

The point being—does Leadership require me to make sacrifices? Yep, for me, I say it does. Are those sacrifices worth it? Undoubtedly.

Good health required me to sacrifice daily ice cream; good work ethics means I am sacrificing late nights.

You can do anything you want as long as you are willing to pay the price. The price of power exchange Leadership is exceedingly worth the cost.

How do you manage the sacrifices to make this relationship work?

dawn:

Sacrifices?

Sacrifices?

I'm thinking hard on this one. Sacrifices, what stinking sacrifices? Come on dawn, think. What sacrifices have you made for this relationship? Everyone says there are sacrifices in any relationship. And I'm sure from the outside it seems like I've given up a lot. But life is so good right now, it doesn't feel like anything is a sacrifice. I'm going to start typing and see if anything comes up, otherwise I'm going to spend my next half hour staring off into space, thinking.

Let's get started.

Well, I just wrote this long paragraph about how the only sacrifice I could think of that I've made is to give Dan complete authority over me and us. But that it's really not a sacrifice because it's the foundation of our style of relationship, and therefore feeds me. Which is true.

But this is a dichotomy.

It also means I don't get to do things my way. Don't get me wrong, I don't want to be in charge, but there are many times I'd like him to be in charge, doing things my way. But that feels so wrong. It's like someone joining a group saying, "I want to join your group, but I don't like how it's being led. So change what the group does and how it does it, based on what I want, but I don't want the responsibility of being in charge." (Ask me how I know to use that as an example.)

It is the sacrifice I've made though. When I think my way is the best way, for whatever reason, that's the way I like to do it. It's usually based on a past experience or something I've read or with the idea that it will keep me safe or seems like the proactively safe thing to do. Dan has other ideas. Sometimes it's hard for me to say, "Yes, Sir" and do as ordered. Sometimes I still want to offer more information to make sure he's making a decision based on the same knowledge I have. I really have to look close when I do that to make sure I'm not trying to manipulate his decision and I'm just giving information.

We do life differently and this can be a struggle. No place can this be seen better than with how we play the video game Minecraft. Or any video game for that matter. In Minecraft, I'm building things like stairs and fences and marking holes we could fall into with torches. All about ease and safety. Hyper awareness of anything that could go wrong and making plans for it. Gathering resources so we can do all the things we want to do and build what we want to build without much

> I'd prefer not to have to go rescue Dan because he made the decision to go on an adventure. But here's the thing … if I live my reality in that manner all the time, I would not be on this adventure that is full-time RV living.

struggle. I stay indoors at night so the monsters can't get me. Dan, on the other hand, is running around in the dark, falling in the holes I haven't had a chance to mark and having a great time while I'm indoors making food for the next day's adventure. I clearly remember one evening, playing a game with Kevin and katie. All of us are indoors and it's nighttime (in the game of Minecraft). We are all preparing for the adventure we are going on the next day in the game. Then, in our headsets we hear one of the doors of our house open and close. Monsters don't open doors. We all knew it was Dan sneaking out.

"Dan, where are you going?" one of us asks. We all hear Dan's reply at getting caught, "Nowhere, what do you mean?' and then a "Whee, I've fallen down a hole, ah shit, can't get out." I go running for him with a torch and a coil of rope. Katie is speaking up that she wants to go play. Kevin is telling her to stay inside because there are monsters out. It was a perfect moment of seeing all our personalities in the form of a video game. Dan running off into the dark because that's where the fun is. Me off to the rescue with the items he forgot to bring. Katie wanting to join in even though she might get lost and Kevin telling her to stay put while he is filling a survival backpack. Once he's set, he and katie come to rescue Dan ... I'm still trying to find him and have gotten lost myself.

I'd prefer not to have to go rescue Dan because he made the decision to go on an adventure. I want to stay indoors and safe. But, here's the thing ... if I live my reality in that manner all the time, I would not be on this adventure that is full-time RV living. I would not embrace our power exchange relationship because I'd be handing authority over to someone and having to trust that they had my best interest at heart. I would not be living my best life. I'd be my hermit self, with a lot of fantasies that I'd be too scared to act on.

So, is this really a sacrifice? I don't think so. And most of the time, even if I think Dan has a crazy idea, or when he's doing something that is so different from how I would do it, "Yes, Sir" is the one and only response I need to give, and let the adventure begin.

[After reading my piece out loud, Dan reminded me that the main sacrifice I made was to let go of my anger. Acting on anger is not allowed in our relationship. As a survivor, when I'm in victim mode, that anger gets the best of me. I've had to do the work to release it. It's a goodness though.]

How do you manage the sacrifices to make this relationship work?
Kevin:

I sort of inwardly chuckle at this question because the myth of the BDSM subculture is that being the Leader is such a magical lucky thing. The "good to be King" myth. I get 24/7 blowjobs and coffee ... that's the myth, right?

My version of Leadership involves a lot of sacrifice and service. I want to be super super clear, however: *Sacrifice is not the same as cost.* I give up many things (sacrifice) in order to have this relationship with this particular person, but very few of the things I give up do I consider (or feel) are costly.

I don't get to live my life as an undisciplined bachelor, for instance. I must have a reasonable sleep schedule that aligns with the sleep schedule of my Follower. In order to have the life I want, I give up the ability to stay awake until 4am and sleep until noon. (Sure, I have the right, as the Leader, to do so, but that wouldn't be in keeping with my agreements and the needs of the relationship.) I don't get to eat candy bars and ramen noodles all the time. Sure I can, but I sacrifice those choices in the name of a healthier less hedonistic lifestyle. I don't get to freely engage in high-risk activities, because I have a Follower who depends on me to take care of myself, be alive, and not cave my head in doing some crazy stunt off the second-floor balcony.

I sacrifice the right to be unethical and inappropriate—which is zero cost since those are not goals I would ordinarily pursue anyhow. Still, if I contemplate a particular choice, part of the decision making is whether it honors my relationship and maintains Katie's awe and respect. So, no more random dick pics. *[Sorry?]*

I think that is the long way around to say that as the Leader I believe I must hold myself to a high standard and that I sacrifice the right to be lazy, incompetent, selfish, rude, etc. As our friend Raven Kaldera says (roughly)—I make sacrifices all the time in order to be worthy of the extreme sacrifice of having my Follower put their life in my hands.

The sacrifice *can* sometimes be costly for me. I've had to do some things that were pretty excruciating in order to be a good Leader, and to make the relationship work. I'll reiterate though: the majority of sacrifices I make are simply changes from what I otherwise would selfishly do, but not a change that causes me pain, or resentment. The way much of the *cost* of the sacrifice is mitigated is the point of the question, I think.

> I see the sacrifices in my relationship as part of my role duties, or as the price of getting the relationship I want.

My sacrifices are not costly because I see them as the price of admission. You must be this tall to ride this ride. The things I sacrifice in order to own Katie are reasonable and acceptable to me. So I don't get to sit on my ass and play video games every day, and as a single dude I might. Giving that up was (and is) a significant impact on who I might otherwise be, and what my life might otherwise look like. In return for that sacrifice I get to hang out with the bestest girl I know. I get her loving service and devotion. The sacrifice is big, the cost is minimal—and I am mindful of that.

I think people can easily get wrapped up in the sacrifice, and see it as a costly loss. This is related to the concept of "construal" to me. I see the sacrifices in the relationship as part of my role duties, or as the price of getting the relationship I want. I construe those sacrifices as proof of my strength, as evidence of my determination. I construe those sacrifices as outward expression of my self-discipline—my ability to give up those things that are necessary in order for the relationship to be healthy. Those sacrifices are not heavy costs imposed on me by Katie, or shitty shackles that chain up my ability to live hedonistically free! Those sacrifices are my legitimate payment into getting the treasure I value the most.

It is a rare time that I must do something hard, suffer a loss of some sort, and then suffer a sense of unfairness or unreasonable cost. I simply can't think of the last time a sacrifice felt costly.

How do you manage the sacrifices to make this relationship work?
Katie:

Give the sacrifices happy drugs and throw them in the volcano. Hope the relationship gods are appeased and you don't have to scrub the toilet again.

There's a saying about choosing your hard ... Hang on, I will take some of my 30 minutes and find it.

* *Marriage is hard. Divorce is hard. Choose your hard.*
* *Obesity is hard. Being fit is hard. Choose your hard.*
* *Being in debt is hard. Being financially disciplined is hard. Choose your hard.*
* *Communication is hard. Not communicating is hard. Choose your hard.*
* *Life will never be easy. It will always be hard. But we can choose our hard. Pick wisely.*

Being in a negotiated, intentional relationship is hard. Being in the chaotic, undefined relationship I had before Kevin was insanely hard.

It takes a great deal of internal conversation to navigate sacrifices and effort made. I am constantly rewriting my perspective on what I must say and do. Changing negative thoughts to more realistic viewpoints. After all the years this has become a habit that enhances my satisfaction, my joyful life and ease of following Kevin.

Ahhh, examples will help.

Kevin and I are similar in many ways, but almost always our methods are different. Neither one is wrong. Just different.

The sacrifice: katie has a schedule and a plan for a task. Kevin steps into her day and decides the task is big enough that he should be involved. Kevin has a manner of accomplishing tasks that is different from katie.

Every.

Single.

Time.

The sacrifice is not getting to do it my way. Not being allowed to work in the manner that makes the most sense to me. I have to do the mental gymnastics to become unattached to my plan. I do this by sometimes sharing what I had in mind and why I thought it was important to do it that way. But many times I just have the rapid-fire internal conversation, "He is leading. He is making the best decisions he can. His intentions are for success. My method isn't as important as our relationship and what we can accomplish in harmony."

> Things would be different if Kevin was a selfish asshat, making poor decisions that followed his cock and cravings.

Daily schedules have a flow and order in my head. I love the autonomy of working in service to him, but without oversight and supervision. I can accomplish so much and attend to details that he might dismiss as unimportant. I can shine and bounce through an incredible workload in this structure. Not much sacrifice beyond labor, time and effort. Meh. That's an inconsequential sacrifice to me.

When we work together—which is almost always at the time of this writing—I need to slow my brain and body down to hear his wishes. Not jump ahead or off on my own endeavors. Again, the mental discipline. I love working alongside him. I enjoy the structure of him giving orders and expectations and working within that framework. This is quite contrary to the previous paragraph of me having my own flow and order. But sacrificing that means I am attending and highlighting our relationship style and our roles.

My most difficult sacrifice is about management and scheduling. Secondarily in the method of task accomplishment. And somewhere below that is the sacrifice of the final decisions.

Things would be different if Kevin was a selfish asshat, making poor decisions that followed his cock and cravings. I have handed over authority to a person who is wise, compassionate and very intentional in his decision making. This means I have not sacrificed my safety or mental health.

When he makes a decision that I disagree with, I "sacrifice" my inclination. This is usually after I have offered my ideas and perspective upon the Decision-Making Altar. And down comes the Hammer of Obidin or some Greek god. Kevin decides where we are headed and not only do I follow, I also support, jump aboard and do my utmost to make that decision a success. His success is our success. His failure is … human and not caused by me undermining and sabotaging the endeavor.

Sacrifice is a weird word, it sounds negative in that I am killing off or giving up something. But is also a very positive word in that it means I am offering a gift, I am pledging allegiance, I am giving evidence of my devotion to him and therefore to us.

It can be hard. I choose this hard.

Intermission

A fictional account of how four authors make important decisions.
(By Dan.)

"So", Kevin said, "when we arrange the chapters, let's just do the names alphabetically—so it will be Dan, dawn, Kevin, Katie".

"But," Katie spoke up, "alphabetically, Katie comes before Kevin."

"Well," Kevin replied, standing up and flexing, "you come when I tell you to."

"Ohh," dawn said. "I have a lady boner."

"Can we be serious?" said Katie. After a stunned pause, everyone started laughing.

"I don't know if I am comfortable being listed first," said Dan. "After all, how will people know how humble I am if they don't realize it wasn't my idea—not that it is a bad idea, mind you, I am after all … well, The Dan™." Dawn reached over and punched him in the upper thigh, eliciting a yelp.

Katie, who when no one was looking took her shirt off and tied it into a bow on Kevin's head, said "I respect my Dominante too much to argue, so I'm fine with Dan, dawn, Kevin, katie as the order".

"Great!" exclaimed Kevin. "It is decided!" They then broke from writing for the day, went on a hike, grilled chimichangas, and played a game of Terraforming Mars, which, just like always, Dan won by so huge a margin they had to break out a calculator and an abacus.

Later, after Dan and dawn left, Kevin, snuggled into Katie's bosom, said "Halfway through, I'll switch it to you and me being first. Dawn won't notice because she'll be writing three new books by then and Dan won't notice because he can't pay attention to one thing for more than 30 minutes."

[For those who don't speak Dan-ish: The author order from here forward is: Kevin, Katie, Dan, dawn.]

Chapter 16: Manipulation

[Note: This was supposed to allow us an opportunity to answer a question with comic bluntness and humorous derision, but dawn missed the memo and took this seriously while the rest of us were ridiculous. Also, the time limit was set to 3 minutes since we thought the question didn't deserve additional attention.]

Are manipulation, coercion, or ulterior motives part of your interactions sometimes?

Kevin:

No. That would be a terrible idea. Like … I dunno … is this question asking whether I want to have my relationship ruined by the same awful habits other people use on a regular basis? Am I missing something? No, I don't choose to do, or allow, relationship-destructive idiocy as a way to manage my relationship.

Katie:

Absolutely not. Why? Because it is only good if you want to shit the bed, squirm around in it, stand up, and see if anyone still wants to kiss you.

Dan:

No, because my MASSIVE PANTS DRAGON brings all people to their KNEES with its mighty PENIS POWER. Also no, because that isn't who I am. Also no, because I don't suck at being a human.

dawn:

Our relationship has no room for these underhanded techniques. As a matter of fact, we work very hard to make sure that this doesn't become part of our dynamic. Been there, done that, in past relationships, and I believe it undermines our dynamic. I'd rather have honesty and transparency to build the trust I need in a relationship.

Chapter 17: Empowerment

How do you reconcile empowerment and independence with transferring authority?
Kevin:

Ah yes, another chance for me to talk about the language people use chaotically and haphazardly! Woot! First though, I should actually talk about myself and the answer.

I want Katie to be powerful. I want to respect her as an individual with full agency. I want to recognize and nurture her authentic self. That seems, on the surface, to fly in the face of the idea that she must follow my direction in all things, and is often considered an extension of my will. She is also a tool at my disposal or a doll for me to manipulate. Those two aspects don't seem to be possible to integrate.

This exact dilemma is part of the reason we swapped from Master/slave and Power Exchange as our preferred terminology. Those two terms felt like they were dis-empowering to Katie. Those terms felt like they made her "less". Master/slave certainly highlights the idea that Katie is my property, but it felt like it did a terrible job doing the secondary task of honoring her power and independence. Similarly, "Power Exchange" gave us the feeling that she was handing over power to me, and thus becoming less powerful. The beauty of Authority Transfer as a term meant to us that she is a powerful, functional, person with full autonomy and agency, who has consensually allowed me to manage our lives.

> The beauty of Authority Transfer as a term meant to us that she is a powerful, functional person with full autonomy and agency, who has consensually allowed me to manage our lives.

So part of the way I reconcile those seemingly different aspects is in my Leadership beliefs and techniques. I believe Katie is a valuable asset—and so I work to empower her. The benefit to me of having a powerful Follower is immeasurable.

I also make the choice as a Leader to delegate a great deal of responsibility to Katie. I set a task before her, and I let her function independently on that task. I don't believe she needs

LEAD, FOLLOW, LOVE | 167

micromanagement. I don't need to stand over her shoulder and make sure she does it the same way I would do it—I can simply check at the end of the task and verify that the outcome I wanted was attained. I recognize that demanding that she become a mini-me and execute tasks in exactly the same way I would is a ridiculous use of a valuable asset, is stifling to her ability to provide optimum service and is a gigantic investment of time to somehow get her to do things my way. And I'm not so arrogant as to think my way is the best or right way. Frick—let her do it her way and we are likely to come out ahead.

As a Leader I don't infantilize my Follower. I don't see that I am the supreme and omnipotent authority on all things, and she must serve with perfection or suffer my lordly wrath. Fuck that noise. So when Katie does something wrong I treat her the way I would a powerful and independent human who I like and who provides me great service. I teach her how I would prefer that service be performed. When something goes sideways, I say "Go fix that, and hey, next time I'd rather you try this instead." She's not in third grade— she's a fucking genius. Having her write sentences or pull down her panties for a spanking because she booked our hotel for May instead of March isn't a way to get better service. I'll have her stand in the corner or give her a spanking because I want to make her wet, not to teach her how to wash the floor better. Again—she is powerful, wise, independent and can do a good job serving without treating her like a naughty child.

The language of the BDSM subculture perpetuates this confusion and myth. I own Katie. She is mine and she does as I will. Yeah, but really? She could grab a bus this afternoon, change her number and I might never see her again. I "own her" in that she has, as a fully independent and consenting adult, agreed to join me in the sexiness of that illusion. She is mine because she says she is mine as a powerful woman with full agency.

Finally, I want to point out that this clarity regarding her power, independence and agency is supportive of her mental health and overall well-being. I'm not sure that the BDSM myths support the long-term growth of Followers. Katie is constantly aware that she is a powerful person choosing to follow, and not an automaton who is trapped in this role by virtue of society or her genitals. She is free and strong, and only from that place can transfer authority in a healthy way.

How do you reconcile empowerment and independence with transferring authority?
Katie:

Feeling empowered and independent is part of being healthy and competent. Being healthy and competent offers valuable service to Kevin. But having someone with authority over me, able to change my course or life if they wish, can completely destroy my agency. There can be a precarious balance. "Choose wisely, grasshopper." And I did.

I can reconcile the handing over of authority in my daily life and relationship because it is a powerful move. This is one of the reasons Kevin and I shifted from the label "Power Exchange" as a relationship style. I am powerful, He is powerful. I do not give up power, I give him authority.

> I am not the crushed pioneer woman slaving from dawn to dusk while shooting offspring out my baby cannon every year until I am 35.

Following and serving can be done with incredible strength and competence. My manner of following Kevin is not by being managed in the minutia. I do not pursue feeling fragile and unable to function.

Insert disclaimer—which we are intentionally avoiding as much as possible in this book.

Disclaimer: Not bashing the doormat-identified or heavily dominated follower. This can be a very healthy place for a person to serve and grow into being more competent. Stop bashing doormats! They have other labels for their manner of serving and choose it for a reason.

Kevin's manner of leading and taking charge is one of compassion and deliberateness. He encourages my success and self-esteem. He finds it an asset to delegate tasks to me and have me function independently within that realm. All of this supports my sense of agency, and even autonomy.

I am not the crushed pioneer woman slaving from dawn to dusk while shooting offspring out my baby cannon every year until I die at 35 and get replaced. I am not a person who had this misfortune of being born without the penis accessory that gives me a "Lordship" label just because I dangle. I am not part of a faith that says my husband must be in charge no matter his inclination or skills.

I am in this relationship style because I choose it. Together we designed what it would look like and agreed to what we needed from it. Part of that design is ongoing growth and improvement. How empowering is that, muddafookers?

The business model of CEO and COO brings this point home. I apply to work for a company. I research what that company is likely to achieve, what the values are of the company. When the CEO of the company is interviewing me, I am also interviewing them. Is this someone I can work underneath with respect and regard? Do they have vision? Are we aligned with our work ethics and goals?

If I do all of that and then excitedly share with someone, "I just got hired by an incredible CEO and this company is going somewhere!" that person wouldn't say, "What? You have a boss? How does that empower you and allow for independence?" Absurd.

Of course you can have a leader and still have the ability to be confident, empowered and flourish.

How do you reconcile empowerment and independence with transferring authority?
Dan:

Isn't this a one-sided conversation?

Let's start there. Do I give up any empowerment (no) or independence ... now, I can't say a flat "no" to independence as I am picking up responsibilities. But for the sake and intent of this question, the answer is no, as I only surrender that independence that I want to. I know, we could argue that (I am doing that in my head right now) but since I made that decision, not dawn, again, not in the intention of this question.

So I will flip the question to how am I OK with taking away dawn's empowerment and independence. Well, let's do the easy one first.

I did not take dawn's independence. She surrendered it. She consensually and knowingly gave me her right to make decisions. And if she tries to get her own way and I disagree, I can respond with anything from "no", to a mild rebuke, to removing additional rights like using the internet or attending an event. The biggest challenge to me in this was many years ago when during my spiritual exploration it was suggested that no one person should ever, for any reason, control another. But I ... well, I got over that. Because another aspect of that same spiritual exploration advised that no matter who tells you something is a great idea—be it a teacher or a guru or a respected elder—you should try it on, but if it doesn't work, dump it. Instead, the agreement is that dawn surrenders her independence and in turn, I actively manage the decisions she would have made and accept responsibility for that when they are not the right ones.

How much independence does dawn really give up? Although we are in a full time "everything under the sun"-style relationship, I ... OK, I just had to change direction. I thought I was going to say "not much", but in truth, all of it. Because even though I don't manage her day-to-day decisions, I don't tell her when she can pee or that she cannot eat until I have finished the meal or that she can't go visit a certain friend ... I can. At any point. You think it, I own it. Just because I don't micromanage doesn't mean I can't at any time. Why, just a week ago I told her to call me something new (Belum instead of Sir, as in Yes Belum). She hardly ever asks permission to do a thing—but that doesn't mean I can't speak up and say no.

> You think it, I own it. Just because I don't micromanage doesn't mean I can't at any time.

For clarity's sake, in the past 24 hours or so, I've probably made 1% of the decisions in regards to dawn and maybe changed what she decided another 1%. For 98% of the decisions she does what she does and I feel no need or desire to interject.

This is balanced by the fact that if at any point she can say "I'm done," then the power exchange is over and she can do what the hell she likes. And in twenty years, that has not happened ... yet. (Suspenseful music.)

Now, part two, empowerment. Has dawn transferred or exchanged her empowerment for this relationship? No. I'm tempted to stop writing there. But I did go and peek at the definition of the word and came back with "authority or power given to someone to do something" which is what we've been talking about. But the second definition listed is "the process of becoming stronger and more confident, especially in controlling one's life" and that is a more interesting one. Dawn has become stronger and more confident despite not controlling her own life. Directly. But if we really look at it, she is in control of her life. Not the little things like who has to get my coffee or walk the dog, but moving her total life toward her dream of who she wants to be—a sexy vibrant supported human who can explore nearly anything life has to offer with the guy she is quite fond of. Hells, this book is very reflective and in reading what dawn has written, you have in a sense met her. That isn't the "right words to sell the book" dawn you are seeing, it is the real deal, the actual person I live with. You, oh reader, tell me—do you see an empowered person? Someone who is living the life they want, bordering on it being a fantasy come true? And do you doubt that if she wasn't where she wanted to be, she would not make things different? That she is so feeble she could not tell me to fuck off and she was outta here, probably taking the dog and the best BDSM toys?

Maybe once more I am off the rails and this isn't the true definition of empowerment. To that I say, fuck Websters. If Homer Simpson can get "D'oh" added to the Oxford Dictionary (yes, really, look it up) then I am not feeling bound to defend someone else's definition.

How do you reconcile empowerment and independence with transferring authority?
dawn:

Well, this is a heavy question for me at the moment and I will probably need to look at it again later when I'm not on the edge of a spiral. Let's play with the question though and see what I can come up with.

I am an independent person to a degree, and I'm definitely a strong person, most days. I have stories from the beginning of our relationship where I certainly didn't feel powerful or empowered, but I would not have made it as long as I did or as far as I did without having a massive amount of strength to begin with. Also, it may not look from the outside like I'm independent at times, but look closer at how much I do on my own.

At the beginning of our relationship, I can remember driving around and talking with Dan about co-dependence and making sure that I was not falling from independent to co-dependent during the transfer of authority. This was very important to both of us. I was becoming dependent on him, and I needed to make sure that I didn't fall completely in as I submitted and surrendered to him.

> I was strong to begin with, but I'm so much stronger now, because I have him at my back.

I'm sure that was part of my resistance at first. I felt like I was giving up my independence. Even though I was married before, I felt I pretty much raised my kids on my own. I created and ran Cub Scout packs, I put myself through college with no support from my husband. He actually didn't want me to go because it would make me less dependent on him. I home-schooled one of my sons while going to college full-time, and running the Scouts. Then I started therapy on top of all of this and really didn't have his support. I think he felt that if I "got better", I'd leave. Well … guess what happened?

And hell, this started back in high school. I led two different community service groups there, one of them international, along with being the youngest leader in the women's group of my parents' lodge. I had no support with the high school groups. I did that on my own. And only had support from my parents with the lodge because it made them look good.

Wait, let's go back further. Elementary school. I was in the gifted program. Not because my parents thought it was a good idea; they didn't. They thought I was trying to be better than them when I brought it up, which was a big no-no. So my math teacher put in the paperwork for me, so that I could join the program. I learned early on that if I wanted to make something of myself, I had to do the work, I had to have the drive and I had to make it happen. No one else was going to support me.

OK. Enough of that. I didn't even realize I was going to share that much. I just wanted to point out how important my independence was when I came into this dynamic. The thing is … my independence was important because I didn't feel that I'd ever be supported. I needed to do for me if I was ever going to accomplish anything. Then, along comes Dan and the idea of an authority transfer relationship.

You mean, I could hand things over to someone that wanted to Lead, AND be supported in the things I wanted to do and be and create and accomplish? Sweet! Except it was so very hard! Just handing things over should be easy, right? Not. I want to do things one way and Dan wants to do it another. Guess who wins, usually?

Hah. Trick question. This relationship isn't about winning and losing. And once I figured that out, my resistance smoothed out a little bit. Once I realized that Dan wasn't out to "win", but to empower us both, the resistance smoothed out a little more.

We had something totally new to us here. What started out as something hot, sexy, kinky and naughty, was turning into a deep relationship where we supported each other and empowered each other. He was helping me not only become the best follower I could be, but the best person I could be. And in turn I was helping him by the best Leader and person he could be.

Remember those conversations I mentioned just a little bit ago about our worry of becoming codependent? We were definitely becoming enmeshed. And honestly, I'm OK with a little bit of enmeshment .... OK, a lot of enmeshment if I'm honest ... as long as everyone is self-aware enough to know what's going on. But what Dan and I have is more about being interdependent. We are dependent on each other. We are opposite sides of the see-saw with our own strengths that we give to the relationship.

So, oddly enough, my fear of losing my independence, my voice ... seemed to work itself out. There are things I don't get final say on. Sometimes I do, but it's only because Dan has said, "Make a decision."

The structure we agreed on and built has actually empowered me. The lack of power struggles has empowered me. Dan supports me in most if not all of my endeavors, which empowers me. And he actually likes me to have some independence, so that he can tell me to get something done and he knows it will get done.

I wish I had time to write more about how this relationship has given me confidence in myself not only as a submissive, a follower, a woman, but as a person. I was strong to begin with, but I'm so much stronger now, because I have him at my back. I sit in my seat of power, which helps him sit in his seat of power.

Chapter 18: Off-Limits

Is anything off-limits in your relationship? Why?
Kevin:

The inside of Katie's wedding ring says "Bound—No Limits." Holy crap, is that a sexy fantasy. There are a handful of ways that wedding vow is entirely inaccurate, and maybe one way that it is true.

Katie has obviously got some limits. She's not up for murdering her family and burying them in grain sacks in a shallow grave beside the railroad tracks by the pale moonlight outside of Mundare, Alberta. (That's in our contract.) She's also not up for me sneaking into the bedroom and shitting on her face while she sleeps. We've negotiated these things and I respect those limits. Most of them are pretty reasonable.

She also has some limits that are less clear why she would call red, but she still has a strong aversion—like cruises, monkeys, skydiving, and polyamory. I've accepted those limits and have agreed that unless the plane is on fire, the island is being consumed by a volcano, the monkey can piss gold coins ... you get the point.

> I could order her to move to some deep South American jungle but I am unlikely to do so because, although it is within my power, it would be a huge thing to require of her. Also, I would miss her.

Katie is also squicked out by a whole range of foods. They are not "off limits" exactly, but if I forced them on her, she would beg, then cry, then vomit ... so my lack of sadistic inclination pretty well keeps food-related acts of power off the table also. Ha! Food is off the table.

Other things are off limits simply because they are not healthy and my job is to protect and enhance our well-being. I can't order her to suck my cock for the next 24 hours because it would likely cause her injury. Sure, she's talented, but can't unhinge her jaw like an anaconda.

So our relationship is theoretically no limits, but what that actually means is "No limits within the boundaries of the ethics and responsibilities you have demonstrated, and the trust in your Leadership I have offered." Katie is protected in her "no limits" vow by the fact I don't want to cause her injury, or to behave in ways that are contrary to our priorities and ethics.

And she gets to inherit my limits, since she is mine. My limits about scrapbooking, drinking alcohol, and making babies are all limits she is stuck with. She has some limits because I have those limits.

So we can fuck other people, but not love them. We can go on kayaks but not cruises. We can ... nah, monkeys are all bad. She can do any creative endeavor the world over as long as it isn't scrapbooking. There are limits, but they are all reasonable, right?

On the other hand, I can compel Katie to do a great deal of things that are far outside her comfort zone. I could order her to go up on stage at a kink event and sing a song—she would be aghast but would comply. I could compel her to flash a stranger. Uncomfortable, she would still do it. I could force her to eat foods she finds gross but would pay the price in responsibility for the therapy sessions necessary afterwards. Much of what would be "off limits" in terms of her preferences are not literally off limits, but I would have to have a really compelling reason to demand them of her.

Also, her happiness is important to me. So I could order her to move to some deep South American jungle but I am unlikely to do so because although it is in my power, it would be a huge thing to require of her. Also, I would miss her.

In summary, as a good friend pointed out recently "Within an extremely confined and tiny range of choices I have absolute unlimited power."

Is anything off-limits in your relationship? Why?
Katie:

Off limits is such a strange concept once you have actually finished the exploratory getting to know each other. I don't think of things as *"Off Limits,"* because it suggests that without those magical words I would race out and do it. It's like a kid yelling "Time Out" in a game of tag and suddenly he doesn't get touched like he has a force shield.

But I will stop fucking around with the concept and answer the spirit of the question. Are there things Kevin isn't allowed to ask of me? Are there things he refuses to do? Gosh, I still cannot answer straight.

There are acts, interactions, sexual activities and relationship styles that Kevin cannot ask of me because of the profound distress it would cause me. The list is short—especially after you take out the ones that he would not be inclined to do.

We have more common things that are off-limits to both of us. We decided early on that Polyamory is not for us. I could tell you why, but that would open the door to debate and defense. We have talked about Polyamory. It does not fit who we are and what we are focused on. So, look! I'm not answering the "Why" part of this question.

Off limits is having sexy fun times with people that are very close friends. It is too complicated for us. It has the risk of ruining or changing beautiful friendships. We can find sexual adventure in many places, we don't have to make puddles in our close social circle. Again, this is not one of us setting something as Off Limits. It is both. So then it just becomes something we don't do.

Off Limits—Kids, Kaka and Killing?

When it comes to BDSM play the list is huge. The fact that we are sadomasochism-light is enough information for a person to know many of the play styles we don't use. The BDSM world is full of extreme play that Kevin and I do not even have to discuss to know that it wouldn't be part of our eroticism and fun.

We never fuck other people without both of us present. If we flirt with someone, our partner is immediately updated or involved. All sexy fun is a together adventure.

We do not play separately in the dungeon with others. We've talked about this quite a bit—though also nobody in all our years has ever asked either of us to play. Because our scenes are so full of our dynamic, our relationship, so erotic and full of lust and orgasms, it would be too … intimate? … as well as difficult to play the way we do with others.

We have talked about how it would feel to be doing a power exchange scene with someone else. How it would feel to watch each other in that situation. Kevin is inclined to think he could pretty easily have those experiences and stay disentangled, and that it likely shouldn't have an effect on me. I'm pretty sure it would feel like I was sharing the very best of my universe. And the reverse of me being in the hands of another Dominant or Top in a scene would have his protective instincts in full roar. The dungeon players are better off without us giving this a whirl.

We have done Body Drumming scenes together on other people. It was fun, profound and everyone had a great time. Not as intimate as what we usually do. But also not so compelling that it is a must-have in our life.

If I had my choice, leashes would be off limits. I pretty fiercely dislike being on a leash. But they don't harm me; I just get fired up. So Kevin puts a leash on me sometimes when we are sceneing together. Because he can. And to exercise my ability to take reaction, get it under control and turn it into compliance. That makes his lordly sword shwing!

> Off limits is having sexy fun times with people that are very close friends. We can find sexual adventure in many places, we don't have to make puddles in our close social circles.

The inside of my wedding ring says "Bound—No Limits." This is a statement of trust. I know he knows me. I know he wishes me to be healthy and thriving. I can make that vow with the level of trust I have in him and be assured that it will be wonderful.

Once a person asked, "No Limits! What if he asked you to chop off your sister's head and put it in a burlap sack?" I replied, "I would take him to the doctor."

Is anything off-limits in your relationship? Why?
Dan:

Off limits? An interesting question and I thought I had a straightforward answer but now I'm not sure. Let me start with the much more fun things that are *not* off limits. Things such as having sex with dawn, having sex with other people named dawn, having sex with people regardless of their name, watching porn, masturbating to porn, not having sex with dawn, practicing celibacy, having non-sexual power exchange relationships. Other things that are *not* off limits include staying out late, getting up early, having ice cream for lunch, having pineapple on pizza, having pineapple on peanut butter sandwiches. Not serious enough? Other things that are not off limits include making dawn do what I want, doing what I want, doing what I feel like doing even when it annoys everyone, going on hikes, bike rides, car trips with no clear destination.

OK, now I am just making a list for the hell of it, but hopefully you get the idea I'm trying to get across— if there are two or three things off limits, then compare them to the fantasy and freedom that is my life, I'm happy with that arrangement.

> If I need the satisfaction of stomping out and slamming a door, I use a closet.

There are a few things off limits. These are things we came up with when we first decided to try this power exchange thing and none of it has changed.

If dawn and I have an argument, it is off limits for me to leave the house and slam the door. Not sure I recall why this was important to dawn but it was in our initial agreement and is still a thing. If I need the satisfaction of stomping out and slamming a door, I use a closet.

Me using drugs and/or alcohol is also off limits. I have already had enough and would become very self-destructive if I returned to that part.

Cheating is off limits. And dumb. We are open, poly, and sexual adventurers. And dawn doesn't get a vote in who I fuck (and I have a kink about her getting fucked) so just no reason to do it. Speaking of sex, if there is one area where dawn has 100% equal voice, it is our safer sex practices.

And we have some hard limits we agreed to in our early days. Consent is essential, so no children, animals, or dead.

Now, we have other stuff we don't do because we don't dig it, but not because it is off limits.

Maybe there are other things that don't come to my mind right now. But overall, we have a relationship built on trusting each other and that we want each other to be fully comfortable seeking out whoever they are.

Is anything off-limits in your relationship? Why?
dawn:

I'm not exactly sure how to answer this question. Dan and I are in a total power exchange relationship. That means total. Nothing off limits. And relationship-wise, this is true. Though, I'm catching myself thinking hard about this. Is there anything off limits?

I know for some people, their family or finances or job or children might be off limits. This isn't the case for us. Dan absolutely has my and our best interest at heart. When he has told me that I can't have a relationship with a certain member of my family, it felt odd. How could I let someone keep me from my family? Isn't that a sign I should be looking out for? But, he was absolutely correct. This person is toxic for me and therefore for us and has no business in my life. Dan saw me suffering way more than was needed in this situation. I was trying to be a good person to someone that didn't deserve it. Dan has every right to limit who I spend time with.

> I have told Dan "no limits". If he ever decides to abuse that, I have the power to walk away.

In classes, I usually give the example of me finishing my degree when I was going to college. Dan had the power to keep me from graduating if he wanted to. I could be on my last credit hour and he could tell me no. Again, he has my best interest at heart. I have no clue what his reasoning would be, but he would have a good one, and I would say, "Yes, Sir." Maybe with some confusion or a request for a reason, but I would comply. Some people would argue his right to do so. I need him to have this right.

I can't think of anything that is off limits, including my spiritual path. When we are in front of a class talking about our needs and wants, I list my spiritual path as one of my Needs and it is. I Need to be able to follow whatever path is calling to me at the moment. That does not mean that it is off limits to Dan. If I got involved in something that became harmful to me or us, he'd have something to say about it.

Dan has the right to veto any of my poly relationships. He hasn't and wouldn't do so lightly, but he has that right. In the poly world, this is a huge red flag. In my world, I need him to have this power as he would only use it to protect me.

I think the thing that has me stumbling at the moment is that I definitely have a list of hard limits when it comes to play. But they are not for Dan. I trust him completely. There are a couple of things that I have a visceral reaction to. Not to yuck anyone's yum, but there are a few kinks that I never intend to participate in, unless Dan tells me to. Again, he would have a good reason and would never have the intent to have me do something just because he can, especially if it might break me.

Dan leads. I follow. And this is how I need it to be. I don't want to have limits. How can I fully surrender if I have limits? Surrender is not everyone's goal, it is mine. If I can no longer surrender, that means I've lost my trust in us. And if I've lost my trust, I can no longer follow. If I can no longer follow, my only option is to follow the steps in our contract for dissolution and walk away.

I resisted writing that sentence. But that is the truth of it. I have told Dan "no limits". If he ever decides to abuse that, I have the power to walk away.

Section 4: Struggles and Challenges

Any relationship between people has the potential to have some rough spots. Make the relationship long-term and intimate and you can pretty well guarantee that it won't always be silky smooth. The sea might get choppy now and again. There might be unexpected cave-ins or avalanches. Authority Transfer relationships are not immune to struggles, but they are perhaps more resilient, or at least have tools and processes in place to help quickly get back on track.

19) Share a time you fucked up and how it was resolved.
20) How do you deal with being disappointed or causing disappointment?
21) You want to fuck but they don't—what do you do? Now reverse it.
22) What does a shitty day look like in your relationship?
23) Tell us about a significant disagreement and how it was resolved.
24) Describe a time your partner was compromised in their ability to fulfill their role. How do you manage when it happens?
25) Have you ever been in a slump with your partner? How did you resolve it?

Chapter 19: Fuckups

Share a time you fucked up and how it was resolved.
Kevin:

Tricky!

I'll try to answer this a couple of ways in the time I have. First, as a broad overview, when I fuck up, I take responsibility, I make amends to the best of my ability, and I work to never repeat that fuck-up. That's the underlying formula. Each step could probably be a chapter (if it was me writing) or at least a paragraph (if it was Katie).

Fuck-ups happen all the time. I'm, unfortunately, not cut from the same infallible cloth as some of the Dominants I've met. I seem to make mistakes on the regular, and often open my mouth only to change which foot I have jammed into it. So I'm not the cat vainly scratching at the linoleum trying desperately to cover a wayward shit that everyone has already seen. I'm pretty open (to Katie) about fuckups and once they are processed and in the past, I'm even comfortable sharing them with a class when we present.

Most of my fuck-ups are relatively minor. A few have been large. And just a couple have been relationship straining. I'm not fond of letting those last ones replay in my head, let alone shining a light on them.

I'm also going to assume this means a fuck-up with regard to my relationship with Katie, and not just some other random bone-headed moment.

I'll just pick a current fuck-up: I have a habitual phrase that I regularly use that Katie interprets in a negative way. When Katie does something that isn't as I expected, I'll say "I'm surprised that...." For instance, if I look over at the RV and the door and screen are both hanging wide open, I might say "I thought we were worried about bugs. I'm surprised you left that open." To Katie, that sounds (putting words in her mouth here) like criticism, or passive aggressive, or like I see her as incompetent. My actual intent when I say those words isn't super important—what is important is that my incautious phrasing has created a problem and has communicated something I did not intend. So we have talked about it. We've each calmly explained our viewpoint and feelings. We've each said we will try to remember how the other feels—I will break the habit of using that phrase, and Katie will know I don't mean it as offensively as she hears it. Since that discussion we have jokingly been using that phrase intentionally, and in silly ways, so that we both know it is being attended to and some of the weight of that heavy discussion can be lifted. We have been playing with the phrase to rob it of some of the history and discomfort.

> Rather than bring it up and point out our shared failure, I let that unfortunate order lie dead in a shallow grave.

I think that most of my medium-size fuck-ups are omissions rather than actions. I think I get lazy and don't do enough leading or fail to be decisive. Those fuck-ups are harder to notice, and hard for me to correct. If I'm being lazy then notice it, it is far too easy to simply continue being lazy. These are the mistakes that I have the hardest time fixing. Not only are they harder for me to recognize, but if I've been neglecting a job or responsibility, it is harder to lever myself into action to correct it. I think this is because the harm is slow and subtle rather than being an obvious impact on Katie.

I have occasionally put a protocol or expectation in front of Katie, then failed to enforce the expectation, but also failed to revoke the expectation. It is just a haphazard demand that I failed to manage. Then I realize Katie hasn't done as asked, but I also realize I've not done any leading. I feel upset she hasn't done her job, but I feel worse that I haven't done mine. Rather than bring it up and point out our shared failure, I let that unfortunate order lay dead in a shallow grave. I should do the work of digging it up and putting it to rest or resurrect it if it really should have had life.

So my failures of Leadership are the ones that plague me the most. My formula for noticing and correcting them is less clear. And the long-term impact of those failures is potentially more profound than the mistakes that slap us in the face and are immediately addressed.

Share a time you fucked up and how it was resolved.
Katie:

Woowee this will take some balls. But I'm not a cup of baby carrots, so let's go.

We are not obligated to share our biggest fuckups, but my baby carrot balls are pushing me in that direction. My biggest fuckup with Kevin and our relationship was when we first met.

We met online in a chat room—the old MSN chat rooms that showed up in a list of topics you could scan and click into. Masters and slaves. In retrospect that chat room was crap. It took all the online and fantasy M/s ideology, put it in a pot and boiled it down to a syrup. But that is where Kevin and I met.

Somewhere in this book I wrote "Don't do what we did to start out. We did all the wrong things." That includes the way we met and the following fuckup.

When I entered that room I had to create a profile. The profile was bullshit. My age, my singleness, my childlessness was all a lie. The only word I have in my defense is that I was not chatting in that room to find somebody. I was only there for a little group chat and curiosity. I purposefully removed anything real beyond "female."

In a freakish level of fate/luck/random lottery win, Kevin was chatting there too. My fuckup was that as we chatted in the "room" and then later in private chat windows I didn't fix my misrepresentation. I was a total lie. I slid down the slope of being someone I had never been before—a person who had no integrity or ethics. I was deep in limerence, deep in lies and deep into hurting us both. What a fucking disaster. If there was any chance that we could be together, I had to lay all my failings out before Kevin—or ghost away like so many did online.

> One of Kevin's first statements after my confession was, "Let's see if we can salvage this relationship."

Whether I confessed or disappeared, we both lost and we both were heartbroken. So I did the right thing. Confessed it all. He was amazing and I was a bullshit creation. I don't know how Kevin was able to hear that and still give me a chance. I wouldn't have.

How did we fix that? Kevin.

One of Kevin's first statements after my confession was, "Let's see if we can salvage this relationship." I have no idea how he saw any glimmer of the real me—of my value as a partner. But I am so grateful he did.

Part of resolving the issue was to meet in person as quickly as possible. We were 4000 kilometers and two countries apart. We needed to see each other and know if it was worth the effort. I booked the tickets and made the arrangements to travel within the week.

During that week before getting on the plane I was completely focused on exposing and being the real me. Anything he needed from me, I provided. I was precisely on time for each scheduled chat online. I spent as much time talking as he wished. Answering previous questions over again from a place of honesty and vulnerability.

When we first chatted as "fake katie" he would call me his perfect girl. It was a knife every single time. I wanted to be his perfect girl so bad. He deserved one. He was so wonderful, funny, kind and brilliant. It was up to me to show him who I was and for him to decide if I was his perfect girl in this new light.

Beginning our journey into Authority Transfer right from the start supported us in this rocky launch. It gave us a structure that allowed us to resolve this huge fuckup. He was my Leader. He set out expectations of me that I stepped up to time and again. He asked questions and made demands that I answered and complied with. Kevin was in charge of our journey to trust and love each other. I supported and cooperated in any way I could.

This fuckup was resolved because we were able to rebuild the trust and he was able to forgive me. Forgiving myself took a prolonged time. It was resolved because we both put tremendous energy into healing and bonding at a deep level. We moved beyond it because we could see the prospect of something amazing together.

Is it forgive and forget? Hell no. Forgive, heal and rebuild trust. But we do not forget. It was a brutally hard lesson learned. That doesn't disappear. It was also an incredible situation that showed our true character and devotion to our relationship.

Share a time you fucked up and how it was resolved.
Dan:

Let's start off by determining what a fuck up is. Then I can pick one of my many options.

You know, the first thing that comes to mind as we approach this is "Give yourself a break." Sure, I screwed up on occasion over the past twenty years. Probably the central theme around those screw ups is "I didn't remember." Didn't remember what time the thing was, or what date, or that we were doing it, or that someone told me a thing. On one hand, no big deal. On the other hand, I am responsible for a relationship, so maybe it is. Let's dig in.

Is forgetting to do something a fuckup or just something humans do? As with many things, it isn't that simple. You need to account for more than just the *thing* (in this case, I forgot) and extend it to "why".

The reason this was becoming a big deal was twofold—first, dawn and I building a trust based relationship. So when I committed to something and then had to toss out an "oops, I forgot", it impacted her innate ability to believe in me. Sure, she could be forgiving and understand I was human, except for the second part. Not only that I was forgetting things, but it was happening a lot.

When you say "I told you we were going to have dinner tonight but I have a date with Karen and I forgot to tell you," even when it is 100% valid that you forgot, is still disappointing. And when it happens a lot, and the person hearing it has been lied to a lot in the past, this little mistake moves to being a little fuck up.

> What I do with any mistake, whoopsie, or fuckup is the same. Acknowledge it, own it, address it, resolve it.

What I do with any mistake, whoopsie, or fuckup is the same. Acknowledge it, own it, address it, resolve it.

❖ Acknowledge—yep, I said A and instead, we have B. Never an excuse or dodge or "Well, if it wasn't for the whatever." It really isn't that hard to be humble enough to speak up when you screw something up.

❖ Own it—I did or did not do something that brought up this situation. Me. The trick here is to know what you are owning. When we address it, we talk about this situation. But owning it is about the root cause. Why did I forget? More on this below.

❖ Address it. Here is the fuckup and here is the impact of the fuckup. I told you I'd be home for dinner at 6pm and it is 7pm. The impact is that you are going to lose trust in me when I say I'll be home at a certain time. Now, you might think this is drastic—"I was home late once and you'll lose trust?" Not for one time, no. But if it is a pattern, you betcha.

❖ Resolve it. Since it is fucked, I'll unfuck it. Or preventing the fuck up from happening again.

Back to "own it", and specifically, in regards to my forgetting things. On one hand, you might say that my poor memory is due to circumstances beyond my control—my brain is what my brain is. Even if we assume that is right (which I don't, but back to that in a moment), that does not mean I don't have options. In this case, I started to develop habits of note-taking, task management, and calendar competency to mitigate the deficiency caused by a poor memory. This was how I "owned it".

I also tried a variety of things to improve my memory and still do. I can't advise you on anything that worked empirically but getting the right amount of sleep, eating smart, and exercise seem to help. But there was another aspect that I realized that it wasn't about memory after all but about attention. Good listening skills and a meditation practice led me to realize that sometimes when the conversation was dawn saying "I told you about the thing" and I said "I forgot", what I really meant was "I wasn't really paying attention because I was thinking about something else".

To switch gears for just a moment, one other aspect regarding not just this fuckup but all fuckups is the intent. Making a mistake is not good, but sometimes it is important to look at the intent as well as the impact. Address the impact, but realize the intent wasn't to ignore you, leave you less important than someone else, lie to you, or to pay you back for something you did to me. By keeping myself at a high standard of ethics, my intention around the fuckup are less questioned and the fuckup is just that—"I done did fuck up."

Finally, I am picturing my writing partners and what fuckups they describe and wondering if they are writing about Huge Momentous Fuck Ups. I picked a series of little fuckups. But it is worth noting that little fuckups unaddressed can mutate into a big, big fuckup.

Share a time you fucked up and how it was resolved.
dawn:

Do we really have to talk about the fuckups? Sometimes it's hard to remember these things and write about them in such a way that they don't bring all those memories back. But I guess if they didn't have strong feelings, we wouldn't still consider them fuckups.

I'm trying to come up with an example that we don't use in class but nothing else comes to mind and I only have a half hour to come up with something. So, here I go dredging up the thing that happened at a small private Leather event.

We had been invited to someone's "Gifting of Boots" ceremony. They were just starting their Leather journey and someone in the group decided that this Master needed to be gifted boots to signify the beginning of his journey. Honestly, this is one of the things I like about Leather, rituals and recognition.

Dan knew he was going to be wearing his Leather garb like his boots, vest and cover (a cap/hat that had been given to him as a Master by other Masters). But he also knew that the cover made him sweat, so he didn't want to wear it all evening. There would be a point that he'd want to put it down somewhere instead of wearing it or having me hold it. So he wanted a square piece of cloth about the size of a bandana put in his hat box to use. He already had a bandana, but wanted something a little more special. I was tasked with finding this cloth.

> Dan's tone of voice left no doubt in my head or heart that he was disappointed in me.

The story of how I found this piece of cloth … irrelevant.

I put the square of red satin in the box under his cover and we dressed and headed out to the house event.

How does satin fray on its own? It's not like it was moved around in the box. I laid it in there gently and placed his cover on it gently. So, it had to be the friction of the cover as we traveled. That's my only guess, but it doesn't really matter.

We get to the event, place the box down near the ritual space, socialize for a little bit. Then, it's time for the ceremony. Dan pulls out his cover and wears it long enough to get through the special occasion. Ritual done, he goes to the box to pull out the cloth, which he's going to lay on a small table and place his cover on it. He reaches in and pulls out that sad-looking scrap of cloth. It's frayed and wrinkled. It doesn't even look like the same piece of cloth I put in there. I mean, of course it is, but it certainly doesn't look like it. I would never have put it in there looking like that. I would have ironed his bandana and put it back in there if I'd known the satin was going to look like that. But there it is and I know I'm in trouble.

Of course, Dan doesn't know this. Instead, he pulls out this sad-looking thing in front of other Leather folx. He asks me what it is as he holds it by a corner. I start to make excuses, trying to explain, knowing there is nothing that is going to fix this.

He knows everyone at the ritual and asks the host Master if he minds if he punishes me right there. Crap. Dan is not one for putting on a show of punishing me. This has really hit him in the gut. I can't fix this. The host says of course he doesn't mind, and the Masters call their slaves over to kneel at their feet as I'm to do the same at Dan's feet.

Once I'm on my knees, he proceeds to show me the cloth and let me know how disappointed he is not only in the cloth, but in me. That he'd made a simple request, and I didn't care about him enough or how he looked in front of other Masters during an important ritual to even follow through with a simple order.

I could feel his disappointment. I could feel the other submissives and how witnessing this punishment affected them. Dan's tone of voice left no doubt in my head or heart that he was disappointed in me. And to chastise/punish me in front of others, there is no worse punishment for me.

At the end he made sure to let me know that was the end of the punishment and I was to take the lesson and move on. Punishment over.

Punishment is what was needed. Without it we would not have been able to lay that moment to rest. Otherwise I would have beat myself up way longer than necessary. This was a fuckup that shouldn't have happened. But it did. I was punished because of his disappointment, but ultimately it helped me atone for what I'd done so that I could let it go.

Chapter 20: Disappointment

How do you deal with being disappointed or causing disappointment?
Kevin:

This one strikes a little close to home and might be a vulnerable writing for us. Recently Katie has found herself struggling to hear my corrections in a positive or loving way. We are still trying to figure out the cause and the repair, so that's not going to show up in this writing.

As a compassionate and loving partner, I never want to be the source of discomfort for my partner. This statement reminds me of the story of a young guy who got a bulldog as a puppy that hadn't had his tail cropped yet. Upon taking the dog to the vet he learned that cropping the tail isn't really optional, it is done for health reasons. But being a kind and compassionate guy, he can't bring himself to cut off the entire tail, so he has the first inch of the tail removed, then lovingly takes care of his sweet puppy during its recovery. On the next vet visit the vet says that the tail really needs to come off, so the man, who is very caring and compassionate, and can't bring himself to harshly remove the puppy's whole tail, has them cut off an inch... *[My co-authors thought this was a confusing story to have included. Mostly the point is that it is possible to do shitty things, describe it as "kindness" and feel like you are being a "nice guy." I think this was a reminder to myself to do my fucking job as a Leader, even when uncomfortable for each of us, instead of taking the "nice" way that could be unhealthy.]*

> I ache when I think that I have lost even a smidgen of her respect for me, as a person, or as her Leader.

As we've said in other places in this book, Katie and I work to have openness and honesty. We work to be vulnerable and to listen with generosity. This means that even if I was not her Leader, I would still need to speak any concerns I have. As the Leader of the relationship, I have the further obligation to not just speak my personal viewpoint, but to speak from my position of authority and responsibility to shape the relationship and my girl, into the design I envision. My obligation, then, is to say things that are going to be upsetting sometimes. Sure, I can be cautious in my phrasing. Sure, I can use the shit sandwich technique ("I love you. This thing was a terrible choice. I am grateful for your service.") but it doesn't really hide the fact she's eating shit.

Am I answering the question? Focus, Kevin. Fucking free-writing monkey.

I handle being disappointed by first checking the situation and my perception of it. Was the disappointing thing intentional? Were there factors at work of which I am unaware? Usually at that point a disappointment becomes a simple logistical issue. Something is/was not to my liking. If there is a way to correct the issue, then I will typically order Katie to go make it right. Beyond fixing the immediate concern (if possible) I will usually express a preference as to future management of similar situations. "When I ask you to come pick me up, I expect you to be on your way in under 10 minutes. If you will not be, I need to know that."

I suppose technically, I am rarely actually "disappointed" in Katie. Sometimes things don't go as I wish. Sometimes she makes decisions that I would not. Sometimes she dumps the entire filter full of coffee grounds onto the floor, instead of the trash can three inches thataway. I guess one might say I'm "disappointed" that the floor now needs cleaning, but that seems like a frivolous use of the word. I don't think I can recall any mistakes or errors or failures by Katie that made me think any less of her. She is sometimes haphazard, but usually that happens when I've run her ragged in service to me, then kept her awake as a sex toy all night. Am I actually disappointed that the coffee grounds missed the can—or is that just the consequence of having the girl I do, serving me the way she does?

Being truly disappointed is so rare that I don't recall it happening. Wanting her service to be improved or different or corrected happens occasionally and requires me to bravely express that I need that change, even though she might hear it as disappointment in her.

And that circles me back to where I started. It is really hard for me to look at the extraordinary service, devotion, and love I receive and then feel like it is needful to say "Hey Katie, you dried my wool socks in the dryer and you know that is not the way they should be cared for. You are naughty and a failure and now must be smote." Fuck that. So I correct the spots that I believe are important and let minor mistakes or hiccups go unremarked. They are so insignificant that I see it as the price of doing business.

When I have actually disappointed Katie is a much bigger and different topic. I have made choices that, I believe, have made her think less of me. Where I failed to do my job, or was selfish, or I didn't protect her well-being. I think those things disappointed her in me. Those things just kill me. I ache when I think that I have lost even a smidgen of her respect for me, as a person, or as her Leader. I know that being a human means fuckups. So I strive to correct those disappointments I have caused. I strive to learn from those disappointments and never repeat them. I strive to validate and respect her experience and not become defensive when she brings to my attention the place where I have disappointed her.

How do you deal with being disappointed or causing disappointment?
Katie:

What a powerful word in our relationship. Disappointment. Not achieving goals. Not getting what you wish for. Not having your partner do as they agreed to.

I think I will focus on personal disappointment with each other instead of the world in general which has no agreement with me or Kevin beyond spinning about and gravity. If I am disappointed with Kevin or our relationship this better be about issues that are important or I need to snap a knot in my thinking. Usually this would surface more as confusion and floundering about. I get lost when we aren't on track. Is it his doing that initiates this?

I do get disappointed sometimes because I have plans and ideas that are all about my inclinations. Then they get modified by Kevin to be about us or—more rarely—about what Kevin wishes. Sometimes I am very attached to my stuff. There can be a letdown in the moment. But it is uncommon for that to have a prolonged effect on us.

Example: I had an idea that I thought would be fun and exciting for me and likely for Kevin as well. I struggle with being sexy and flirty with other people. I would love to, but there's a lot of sandbags still attached to my air balloon.

We were headed to a kink event. (Now this was in the olden days before Covid.) I shared with Kevin that I would like to go to the event with little coupons and mints. I would selectively hand those coupons and mints to folks that I felt comfortable with or attracted to. The coupons would say something like, "You are welcome to one kissing/groping interaction at any time during the event that I am not otherwise busy," or something like that. I hadn't totally formed the wording. (Don't you love the mint addition?) My thought was even if very few used the coupons, it would be hot to be aware that I was available for sexy interactions. In my imagination the flirting had an open door without too much bravery necessary.

Kevin replied that he did not wish for this to happen. He is a cautious soul. He had concerns. What if I got sick, because everyone goes to kink events even though they are sick? What if some folks were insulted when they realized they didn't have a coupon? What if some folks felt awkwardly put in a situation? What if random people saw and assumed for a free-for-all? There was a whole list of risks that hadn't entered my mind. I was disappointed.

> I have used the Double Ended Dildo of Disappointment on us and forgot the lube.

I'm pretty reticent about sexual fantasies with others and this was a bold suggestion for me. But I totally saw his reasoning and that he was making a decision from care. I handled it by letting that shit go and focusing on how intentional he is in making good decisions even when it taps into his kink of sharing me with others.

Being disappointing to Kevin is huge. For me, it is the ultimate way to be disciplined. I do not need caning, or physical correction. All I need is for him to say I have not met his expectations. The punishment of that is profound. I deal with it by seeking improvement and forgiveness.

When he corrects my behavior or interactions it is usually with instructions on how to do better. Who doesn't want to give the ultimate service? As programmers become aware of bugs and glitches, don't they correct those so that the program works as smoothly as possible? Kevin's corrections are working out the bugs and glitches.

If my CEO says, "That was not what I expected of you. Here's the results I was hoping for. If you did it this way instead it would be better. Now go fix it," I am aware that I have failed him or not met expectations. I am sad. I have used the double ended Dildo of Disappointment™ on both of us and forgot the lube.

Most of the time this is resolved in my head and heart by fixing the error. Correcting my manner of speaking. Putting effort into righting the wrong. It is actually further punishment if he steps in and fixes what I have done. There is healing in giving me the space to make things right.

Feeling like I have disappointed Kevin is a monkey on my back, though. It is perhaps my most emotionally weak characteristic. I have a natural inclination to beat myself up to the point of despair. There's a dark vortex that has a constant pull on me saying I'm not enough. I'm aware of that bad place. I know it is about me, not about him. Kevin is also aware of my struggle because … communication.

Dealing with the above issue has been an ongoing mental reprogramming. It is a checklist I run through when I feel like I am not pleasing. A mantra he says when he sees me headed for that dark spot.

I deal with him disappointing me with generosity and I deal with being or feeling disappointing with brutality.

How do you deal with being disappointed or causing disappointment?
Dan:

I deal with being a disappointment by doing better next time. I don't cling to it. I recognize I am a human who will make mistakes and do what I need to do to avoid that mistake again. I apologize when called for and acknowledge any harm I have done.

Sorry if the above seems simplistic or even immodest but, for me, today, it really is that simple. Even if it feels unjust (you say you are disappointed but in truth I didn't do/not do the thing) then I might get annoyed. But even that is nothing I hold onto.

The reality for me today is I just don't hold onto stuff. I don't cling to the mistakes I made and I don't worry about the mistakes I will make. My expectations for myself are high, but they are also aligned with my understanding of my limitations.

If I sound like I have my shit together, well, in this one area, perhaps I do.

Dealing with being disappointed is actually no different. If it is external (not getting tickets to a show I want to see) then I say "Ah, man," and move on with life, maybe grousing about it the next time or two we tell stories of missed opportunities. If it is within the power exchange, I address what it is ("From now on do x instead of y" or "When I tell you to do the thing, do it then"). That addressing it—in our relationship—is everything from a simple comment to correction to punishment. If I say the words "I am disappointed" regarding her actions, dawn knows it is significant because it isn't a term I use much. Some people, I know, don't have a discipline dynamic in their power exchange, but when I say "I am disappointed in you," then that is indeed a harsh discipline in dawn's eyes.

> Some people, I know, don't have a discipline dynamic in their power exchange, but when I say, "I am disappointed in you," then that is indeed a harsh punishment in dawn's eyes.

I suppose just in case you are of a mind to wonder how I got here, my answer would be by cultivating the mind that is rooted in the present (you can only be disappointed now, not two weeks later when you happen to think about it). And by realizing the world, contrary to what I'd like to think, is going to be what the world is, not what I want it to be. My sphere of influence is tiny and even within that, "Man plans, god laughs."

How do you deal with being disappointed or causing disappointment?
dawn:

Do you know what is the easiest and most effective way for Dan to punish me? Telling me I've disappointed him in some way. I'd much rather take a caning or have to write sentences for days on end instead of being told that I've disappointed him.

Most days I'm a perfectionist and take pride in the things I accomplish. Most days I put him first and everything I do has Dan and my service to him in mind. One of my ultimate goals is for him to be proud of me. So, to find out I've disappointed him, that's crushing.

How I deal with it now is much different than how I dealt with it then. It still hurts to find out I've disappointed him ... huh ... almost wrote "I'm a disappointment" ... there is a difference in the wording there and that is probably the difference between now and then. Then, at the beginning of our relationship, I took that personally. Not only did I disappoint him, but I *was* a disappointment. That can be soul crushing if you take it that way. Not only did I have to deal with not living up to my end of the bargain, but I saw my whole being as a disappointment and therefore why would he want to put the time into the relationship.

If you haven't noticed by now, there was a lot of stinkin' thinkin' that was going on at the beginning of our relationship. I was internalizing the disappointment and making it about me, not my action.

I'm looking back in this writing and questioning the use of "soul crushing". Is that too strong and dark? Well ... No. Remembering how I felt as I knelt and listened to him tell me how I had fucked up. Soul crushing. I'd much rather have had a cane taken to the back of my legs. The atonement I felt would have been much easier to accomplish.

I'm sure there's baggage involved with that physical, soulful response of mine, and Dan recognized that. So, this is sparingly used for punishment or just in conversation. Though even in conversation it was super hard to deal with, until I learned to separate the action from the person.

This skill has come in handy with dealing with being disappointed as well. Because I attached the action to myself, I also attached it to others when they disappointed me. The person became a disappointment instead of their action.

OK, let's flip this whole thing. I did not learn to deal with disappointment in others because of learning how to do it with myself first. It was the other way around. Because disappointments happened with Dan, I had started thinking of him as a disappointment, the same way I thought of me as a disappointment. Not the action. But that's not how I wanted to feel about my Master.

How could I submit to him? Surrender to him? If I felt like he was a disappointment? A lot of head talk happened here as I tried to figure this out. He wasn't, the action was.

Case in point … We go to Kinky Kollege in Chicago. We had talked the whole way there about how we were going to scene, what we were going to do, how exciting it was going to be. Then, we get there, and it doesn't happen. We walk through the dungeon and Dan just isn't feeling it. We'd driven all day, had taught a class once we got there and run a 12-step group and he just wasn't feeling it. I wanted to push and say, "But you promised," and I may have made a noise or two as such. But it wasn't going to and didn't happen. This is where things started to make that final shift in my head.

> Do you know what is the easiest and most effective way for Dan to punish me? Telling me I've disappointed him in some way.

Dan wasn't a disappointment. I was disappointed that we weren't going to be able to play. There is a separation in the result and the person tied to it. There is also a shift in what the disappointment or any emotion is about.

So, if Dan wasn't the emotion, but I was feeling an emotion over an action … that's my responsibility to work with.

This also means that when Dan is disappointed in me it's in response to my actions or state of mind at the time, like forgetting something or not realizing that a command he's given me and I've forgotten was super important to him, not just an exercise in domination. It's not the big ME that is disappointing. I'm not sure I have the exact words for this. But it was a huge revelation for me. One of those super growth moments.

And now when Dan says he's disappointed, I can look at it, and I still feel that little pang, but I can look at it and hear him and fix what needs to be corrected, not taking it as a sign that I'm a broken person, but that an upgrade to my service is needed and anything less won't be tolerated.

Another fucking opportunity for growth.

Chapter 21: Mismatched Libido

You want to fuck but they don't—what do you do? Now reverse it.
Kevin:

As with many of these topics, the non-lordly answer is, "It depends." Generally speaking, Katie is my free-use little slut. She is a fucktoy for my pleasure. That means that I have the authority to interrupt any task and use her in sexual ways, whether that is a 30-second boob nuzzle, a 3-minute make-out session, a "pull down your pants and bend over" visit or drag her to bed for the rest of the afternoon. But I also live in reality and conform my behavior to that reality in most ways. When she is halfway through making chicken salad, I only interrupt her for a minute or two so that the fixins aren't out on the counter for a long time. If we have guests over, I pull her into the pantry (when we had one) for some smooches. When we are out on the town, I will subtly brush my hand across a nipple or send her a text message that she's in for a ride when we get home.

I also pay attention to input from my toy regarding her fitness for use. If she says "Wow, I have a crushing headache," I say "Awww, sorry baby. Would you let me know when you are feeling better, please?" Until she feels up to it, I confine my touches to sweet caresses, gentle hugs, and pets on the head. I like those also—it doesn't have to be sex organs to be fun.

(As an interesting aside: sometimes when Katie is actually having a migraine, I will lay next to her in the dark and try to rub her neck or offer some comfort. Sometimes she suddenly gets really needy, wanting sex. She says she feels like the migraine is somehow part of some scene, and she gets weirdly turned on. The migraine gets pushed aside by sex and she suddenly feels great. Unfortunately, the migraine usually crashes back once the sex is over. Booo.)

> I am rarely so far from sex that I can't see it from where I'm standing.

I suppose if I answer the question specifically, if Katie said to me "I'd rather not right now..." I would absolutely honor that. Whether she has an upset tummy, is worried about her daughter, or just accidentally ate a frog—I know that she is willing and available for my touch, even at inconvenient times, so when she does request to not be used, I totally respect and honor that. It would be a very strange use of my authority to say "You willingly, happily, enthusiastically serve my sexual appetites 98% of the time, and I insist on you serving them the last 2% even if you really don't want it." So I'll wake her up at 2a.m. and use her, but if she ever said "Not now, please..." that'd be a "no."

Usually if she wants sex and I'm not in a sexy headspace, all she has to do is be sexy at me for a minute and that changes. I am rarely so far from sex that I can't see it from where I'm standing. It only rarely happens, since she is free-use and I use her pretty thoroughly. But sometimes I've had my fun and she is still hungry. So I bravely press forward and have even more great sex.

I think we've both learned that sexuality is a beautiful and loving thing that can and should be woven into our daily lives on a continuing basis. We've learned that touch and pleasure is an important part of giving and feeling loved to us. We've learned that "not having time" to caress one another, or "not being in the mood" makes for less connection and joy in our lives. We've learned that refusing touch is a minor rejection and that unless we have a strong reason to do so, time and love and touch should be shared and accepted as often as possible.

So I sometimes "Not tonight, dear" when I've had a rumbling stomach and don't want to fart my way through sex. She sometimes says "Now isn't good" when her headache is severe. We each respect those times because sex is almost always present in our lives.

Generally when we aren't "in the mood" (or feeling up to) for sex, we are still touching and stroking and groping ... and sure enough, happily having sex.

You want to fuck but they don't—what do you do? Now reverse it.
Katie:

Weeeheee sex question!

96.3% of the couples in the universe don't have matching sexual drives and activations. I believe that Kevin and I are closer to a match than most partners.

Fucking is a multi-faceted activity for Kevin and I. Sometimes it doesn't even involve orgasms … I know, right?

If I feel a desire for sexy fun times and Kevin is not inclined, I give him some medicine or tuck him in bed. Something is almost always awry with his health or sleep if he isn't down for it. Me initiating a sexual interaction often looks like snuggling up to him in an intimate way or getting on my knees for a crotch nuzzle. If he does not desire sex at that time, I rarely experience a blatant rejection or refusal of intimacy. That is an extremely important detail.

Every once in a while he would be like, "Off, you fuck, you little slut, I am busy right now." Which is the hottest rejection I can imagine. It holds onto our dynamic, highlights his authority to have sex entirely at his wish and whim, supports my kink of being a sextoy that is sometimes left in the drawer. All of this being healthy, sexually charged in its own way, and leaving me comfortable and willing to make the next approach when I feel inclined.

He is aware that a message of non-desire can have lasting effects. Rejection sucks. It stays as a whisper in my mind. It takes courage for me to put myself out there with desire. This has him being supportive and encouraging of me acting in that way. Even if I don't get sex, I get appreciation, a groping, a smile of delight—actions and words that say, "You are being hot, katie. I love it when you are on a burn. Do this more. Do this often. No, we are not having sex right now."

> Kevin's not an asshole. I don't get fucked when I am crying because the cat died or when I am sick.

If I told him I craved an orgasm and he wasn't inclined, I know he would be happy to offer me the opportunity to satisfy that need on my own—likely with pictures, watching, or a later accounting of the incident.

The flip side.

Some Authority Transfer folks would say this is simple. Kevin wants sex. He has sex. Which is mostly true.

Ahh … fucking is not just insertion and orgasm though for us. It is all the sexual interactions. Kevin freely does as he pleases with my body, through the day and in the bed. It is an intrinsic part of who we are and our joy in life. Yes, sometimes I am mid-task and he is dropping my pants and bending me over the counter and it would not be my inclination—and yet, it is. Because that is who we are together. I am his to use and enjoy,

Kevin's not an asshole. I don't get fucked when I am crying because the cat died or when I am sick. He is considerate if I am stressed and crushed for a task.

Most often his sexual inclinations not being matched with mine happens when I am exhausted. I can certainly be his human Fleshlight in that situation and that becomes hot to me and exhaustion will fade. Or he will use me without expectation of much interaction. This does not make me cranky or think him selfish. This is part of who we are.

I am the luckiest girl in the world. I have a sexy guy who desires me. He has an incredible energy level and inclination to eroticism. I love that about him. I don't want him to feel undesired just as I do not wish that for myself. He is kind to me in his refusing my advances. I am gracious to him in accommodating or I have a good reason for not being available.

Part of us trusting and respecting each other is recognizing that we are sexual beings and that is a vital part of us being intimate, vulnerable and adoring of each other even on the days we don't match desire levels.

You want to fuck but they don't—what do you do? Now reverse it.
Dan:

In my fantasy world, we both wanted to fuck all the time, so no problem. And when we first got together, that was the case. But as time moved on, things shifted—and in twenty years, more than once. For most of our time together, dawn and I have had mismatched libidos, mine being lower than hers. So the Part One of this question— "you want it, they don't"—didn't actually come up. When I was ready, so was dawn. And there is another aspect. Sometimes I would be ready to fuck and just not ask dawn, we'd just be fucking because I wanted to. And that was hot for both of us—it was about my sexual pleasure and her service pleasure. So coming home for lunch, bending her over and fucking her and then back to work with no thoughts for her having an orgasm, no problem, mutually exciting. Or at least I am told—perhaps when we read dawn's response to this question I'll find out something else...

Yet, I'll admit that there are times, few and far between (although one was just a week prior to this writing) where dawn has conveyed "No." And I respect those. I don't have to—authority transfer includes her sexuality—but in that situation, I don't need to fuck her. I either jerk off, or just pass.

(An odd side note about me: I don't mind not orgasming or not having sex. I wonder sometimes if I enjoy the desire for sex more than sex.)

Add the fact that we are sexually open (extra partners are part of our life), there really isn't a reason I can't fuck ... well, someone. But I need to remember that part of our bond, part of who we are, is when we connect sexually. And after twenty years, it is still important that we make the effort to create time. Doesn't sound sexy, to have to make time. We often tell people we are not good at relaxing—this means we often work on projects and such until we are both falling down tired and then flop into bed. So creating "date nights" where we put intent into that part of our relationship is important.

On the reverse, if dawn wants to fuck and I don't, then we don't fuck. She fucks herself (sometimes after I am asleep—apparently I am a sound sleeper!) or I'll play with her (oral and fingers) until she comes. I enjoy that ... and sometimes that moves my needle from not wanting to fuck to hell yeah!

> Sometimes I would be ready to fuck and just not ask dawn, we'd just be fucking because I wanted to. And that was hot for both of us—it was about my sexual pleasure and her service pleasure.

An area we are just starting to work on is that I want dawn to convey her desire to me more. This is new for us and an adjustment for her, as she is used to me being the lower libido person and often goes without my dick. So her learning—at twenty years in—to be more forthcoming when she is in the mood is a new thing we are teaching her. (No jokes about old dog, new tricks ... OK, maybe one.)

Finally, here is the fun part. As I mentioned, we have had different levels of libido during our time together, primarily dawn being higher and mine lower—sometimes being very low (low enough that when I considered celibacy as part of my spiritual path it didn't scare me at all). But as time passes, the body we are in may throw us the occasional curve ball. In the past twenty years, I personally went from horny a lot, to horny sometimes, to not so horny. Recently, I've been treating some physical issues around low energy, and a side effect is that at fifty-six years old I now have morning wood every day again. (I forgot how that makes it annoying to get out that first morning pee.) So looks like my libido is climbing. Is dawn's? Will it drop when she hits some of the biological aspects of being in a woman's body? Very likely.

So here is the most important part—and the part dawn and I remind ourselves of often. The first is because we've had more than one friend suffer from physical issues that made the desire for sex disappear. This leads us to acknowledge that if sex is the only thing in your relationship holding you together, then you are taking a risk based on your biology that—like it or not—you can only partially control.

Secondly, sex is fun. So if dawn wants sex, I may say no, but I never say "...so you can't have it either." Instead, she is free to find other partners, surf porn, masturbate, or create an OK Cupid profile and roll the dice on a hook up. I have the freedom—and do—for the same. Why not allow pleasure for yourself and for those that you love?

You want to fuck but they don't—what do you do? Now reverse it.
dawn:

It's actually more common than you might think that partners have different sex drives. Everything from hormones, stress, where you are in the curve of a normal sex drive ... so many things affect one's interest in sex at any time. The trick is not to take it personally when your sex interest doesn't match up with your partner's. The great thing about our relationship is that we have tools to talk about this and we've discovered things we can do about it.

As a follower, if I want sex, but he doesn't ... I can bring it up and he will help me solve the problem. It doesn't mean that I'm getting it, though. He's not a vanilla husband that needs to please me to keep me happy. He will let me know what he wants me to do about it. Should I not ask for sex each time I want to? Should I keep asking, even if he might turn me down? Do we have a code word? There are many tools that can be put into place here.

Dan and I have been through mis-matched moments more than a few times over the last 20 years. His rule for me is to keep asking and be OK with a "no" from him.

Now our situation may be a little different than others in authority transfer relationships, because we are also polyamorous and sexplorers. What this means is that I have permission to have sex with others. Not only do I have permission, Dan finds the idea super hot. So, if our sex drive or whatever is out of balance, we have options.

Luckily, with the way we've built our dynamic, we also have a lot of communication tools in place for talking about this, but the main one is to "not take things personally". For me, I have had a harder time with being told "no" because I've taken it as a sign of him not wanting me, rather than what it is, which could be anything from him not being in the mood to the fact that he's flexing because he can. So most of our communication would be around the "how I'm feeling" more than the sex not happening, itself.

> I get turned on by being with someone in control. If I wasn't in the mood, and Dan said, "Tuff," well, that would turn me on.

Honestly though, our dynamic allows him to say 'no' regardless of reason. If it's because of me … and I don't think that's ever been the reason … he'll let me know and we'll fix whatever is going on.

So, let's flip that. Dan wants sex and I don't. Dan's in charge. I've agreed to follow.

According to our contract that means that if he wants sex, he can have it anytime he wants from me regardless if I'm in the mood … but here I was going to say "Dan's not a dick and wouldn't do that to me." But he could. And would that make him a dick of a Master? Not necessarily. And just writing about it is more than a little hot.

I get turned on by being with someone in control. If I wasn't in the mood, and Dan said "Tuff," well, that would turn me on. I've given him the authority, the power to say "Tuff" and we are having sex regardless.

If our sex drives flip-flop and he wants it more than me, which very well may happen ... sure, we are poly and he can get more sex elsewhere, but I like sex with Dan. That is part of our connection. That is part of my drive to be in a hierarchical relationship. Not all of it, but part of it. I find power exchange sexy.

Now, if I'm sick, that's something different. Just recently, I think I turned Dan down for the first time. I was just getting over being sick. I felt awful and was exhausted. He could have said "Tuff, bend over." Instead, he took care of me so that I'd be in better shape the next day. And then, I was told that's what he wanted. Turned me on. Not only that he cared enough to not take it personally when I said I wasn't in the mood (I mean, that was a new experience for him), but that he followed through the next day and said that's what he wanted and that's what was going to happen. Totally hot and totally within his rights as a Leader and our expectations of me as a follower.

Chapter 22: The Bad Days

What does a shitty day look like in your relationship?
Kevin:

There are so many ways a day can seem shitty if you let it. Is it a shitty day related to terrible things happening around us or to us? Or is it a shitty day related to how we feel or how the relationship is going?

Sometimes the world around us just kicks the shit out of us. A total-loss house fire. Children being wayward and difficult. Having a business do poorly, or even a business do so well we hate it. There are also the heat-of-the-moment terrible times—like discovering a couple days ago that the recent rains had driven a nest of ants into the RV.

An example of a shitty day is when we landed at an airport following a trip to warmer weather. The temperature was well below what we were dressed for and there was snow falling—about 4 inches by then. I did a bunch of prep at the luggage carousel so that our transition to shuttle then car would be really smooth. We got to the car— cold and snow in our shoes—but still doing pretty well. Then I could not find the keys. Four inches of snow could hide dropped keys

> That represents our general approach to shitty outside experiences: Circle the wagons, take care of our precious partner, and assume everything else is solvable and temporary.

pretty well. Or maybe I lost them on the shuttle. Or maybe while rearranging at the luggage carousel? It was well over an hour, literally, out in the cold trying to solve the problem. When it did resolve, it was my incaution and failure that had caused the entire thing.

We were kind to each other during that experience. Katie never said an unkind word or offered recriminations. She was patient and understanding as we got colder and more miserable. I kept my temper despite the huge frustration and the burden of knowing that getting Katie safely into the vehicle and home was my primary, even solitary, responsibility and I was failing at it. Instead, we continued to work at supporting each other and solving the problem. That represents our general approach to shitty outside experiences: Circle the wagons, take care of our precious partner, and assume everything else is solvable and temporary.

What about when our shitty day is internal? We both have rough days sometimes. Katie has migraines occasionally. We sometimes are exhausted and lack the resilience to be upbeat and charming for our partner. Our patience is frayed and our emotions are thin, or too near the surface. On those shitty days, the mental process is very similar: First, we almost always make the effort to check in and confirm where the issue is located. If I am cranky (not often) it would be really easy to take that out on Katie, or to let my monkey mind tell me that it is probably some bullshit from her that has prompted my crankiness. When I take a moment, either because I recognize I'm cranky or because Katie calls it out, I am almost always able to say "You know what, baby … this is a me thing. I have zero reason to be cranky, I just am. I'm going to go fire up a game (or do X job) and I'm sure I'll sort out soon." Sometimes a 20-minute nap is a sufficient reset.

Recognizing that the "shitty" part of a shitty day is unrelated to how much I treasure and adore Katie makes a difference—it is helpful in correctly positioning where the "shitty" is located. We gain the ability to say "That thing out there (not Katie or the relationship) is a problem right now. It is external to us and we are still great. What do we do about that external thing?" We can, by externalizing the problem, be a Team addressing a shared concern, rather than an individual floundering around unsure if our partner is part of the problem, the solution, or just an innocent bystander.

When Katie is having a shitty day, I have to decide the intervention I believe is wisest. Sometimes I take more direct control of her day. I tell her she must stop working and go chill with some art or a game. Or I tell her to shut up and come for a walk with me. Or I tell her to take some headache medication and come have a cuddle, instead of being so fucking tough and brave. Usually I trust Katie to prescribe her own solution to a shitty day, but occasionally I intervene. And, in a great Follower move—Katie will sometimes say "You seem frazzled and that job you are about to start is probably going to be a huge frustration. I recommend you hold it until tomorrow and come have lunch. After lunch you can see if you feel like tackling it." She helps me tune into my own experience of having a shitty day, and she makes some suggestions for altering that experience—but without blame or personalization. Something is out of sorts, and we both have trust that it isn't between us.

Worst is when we double-dip our shitty. I'm frustrated and feeling a bit low or down, she's wrestling with a headache and frustration with accomplishing so little—and we still are committed to being kind and appropriate to each other. No excuses for harsh words, bad attitude, or in any other way taking it out on our partner. No excuse for letting our shitty moment turn into a negative impact on us. So we share that we are out of sorts. We acknowledge that we are both in a shitty spot together, and we circle the wagons, make the world small and bearable, maybe eat a comfort oatmeal or cup of tea, and be patient and understanding that this shitty moment will pass.

What does a shitty day look like in your relationship?
Katie:

Ahh—this book was too full of ultimate service, perfect solutions and conscious interactions. Time to balance that Dessert Buffet with a Poo Parade.

A shitty day—general overview first, example to follow. It's a day where I am feeling low as regards personal worth and competence, combined with some high-demand tasks and deadlines. Stir in Kevin's burden of making many decisions, doing his jobs and taking care of me. That's a rough day.

There was this time we were renovating a house. An old house. They are full of Easter eggs. You think you are starting to fix one thing and four more issues show up. That was this house.

This particular day everything was going wrong. All aspects of horrible had shown up for the occasion. The renovations were labor intensive, the floor we were laying wasn't going down properly. I was days away from emergency surgery—I knew I was unwell, I did not know how urgent the situation was. Our Autistic child had just had a full meltdown and we had had to cancel Thanksgiving plans. They could not cope with the upheaval and change of schedule.

Kevin and I were sitting on the floor of that old, nasty house, surrounded by the tiles which were not working. If you have already read a story slightly like this in the book, yes, we had two renovations reach this level of despair. I was feeling so ill. My heart was aching for Kevin and all the burdens that were upon him. We were stressed out and sad for our child and the broken Thanksgiving. Not only was this a shitty day, we both knew it was going to last a while. We had quite the gauntlet ahead.

Each step forward seemed insignificant. We trudged. We kept solving the next issue. Aware of the impression that we were making so little progress, but suddenly looking around and thinking "Wow, we are almost through!" Gradually resolution was achieved.

> We are extremely kind to each other when things are horrible around us.

A more "minor" scale of shitty day would look like Kevin being stressed out and suffering from decision fatigue. With me in an emotional low, tears not far below the surface. Usually with a topping of a deadline and time-consuming tasks on the list.

It would look like us both openly acknowledging the struggle and not taking it out on each other or lashing out in frustration. We talk about how to get through that tough spot. Seeking out ways to work together and as best friends.

Days like that need affection, loving words and solutions. We are extremely kind to each other when things are horrible around us. We cling to each other as support and strength. We are a strong team. We know we can survive and thrive.

Each shitty day has a couple of Post-It Notes stuck to the front. They say:

Not shitty forever
Not a shitty relationship

If a day is particularly hard due to emotions, tiredness and low resilience, we often are extremely generous with each other. Kevin declares it to be "Fuck-off Day."™ This is a day where we fuck off from all responsibilities except what is absolutely essential. There are gentle walks, napping, comforting meals (oatmeal, toast with cinnamon sugar or other such soothing foods.) We play games, watch a movie, cuddle and chat together.

A shitty day is sometimes a flashing red light that we desperately need to recharge.

What does a shitty day look like in your relationship?
Dan:

Selfishness is the first thing that comes to mind. Me being selfish, self-centered, and/or self-absorbed. Actually, self-absorbedness isn't always the indicator of a shitty day unless it is an escape tactic.

A shitty day starts via some input that is improperly processed. Meaning, stuff happens that is not aligned with how I want things to be. Boss gives me crap, dog barks all night, dawn laughs when I am trying to be serious (I joke a lot so this happens on occasion). Or sometimes just random unexpected emotional responses that we call land mines. You didn't know it was there, but once triggered, boom.

Example: Me and the family were out at dinner, having a nice meal, on my birthday. Everything seemed fine. I yawned, and dawn said something like "Now that you are this old, maybe you need a nap." I had no indicator that my age was something that, somewhere in the way back of my head, was bothering me. But that simple comment caused a pail of anger to drop upon me.

As I said above, it starts with some input, but the input alone is not enough to make it a shitty day. The rain causing the awning to collapse does not change my day from great to shitty. How I interpret that can. If I responded by assuming dawn blamed me for the oversight, or blaming myself, or blaming Kevin (for no good reason other than his awning isn't broken), or with the ever-popular FML, which many people think stands for "fuck my life" but what I think really stands for "The universe does not guarantee you happiness or sadness. Chaos and change are the standard. Your life is what you make it." But I digress.

> A shitty day is never caused by a thing or a person, but by how I digest it.

So, to restate, a shitty day is never caused by a thing or a person, but by how I digest it. Now, yes, dropping my brand-new phone and having the screen break, or getting laid off, or not getting my dick up when I had people to do, all are less than desirable. But they are not things that cause a shitty day unless I have a pity party about it and let it. I will point out that I will allow myself a "fuck me" or such to slip out. I am not above being annoyed or upset when a bird flying by decides to take a dump on my head. But allowing that to spiral into a day-destroying event is what I am talking about.

Let's expand this same view into what makes a shitty day in the relationship. Dawn and I are very intertwined. When I let my day start to be shitty, it impacts her. She wants to help or fix or resolve and have me be happy. Well, on those shitty days (note that previously I only explained how they happen, not suggesting I am immune) the more she tries to help, the more grumpy I get. So a shitty day in our relationship when I am being the shitty one is me being mopey or self-absorbed or whatnot, and dawn giving up on helping me and enjoying her non-shitty day. Don't assume this is bad. I've trained this exact response. Just because I am stuck in shit doesn't mean she should drown as well. Let me realize that I am the problem to my own happiness and I'll work it out. Dawn is patient and present (and might change the calendar to have my favorite meal for dinner instead of what she planned) but needs to give me space. Because the worst case is, she takes it personally and then her day goes to shit as well. Now we are both in the crappy zone. More about that in a moment.

If things are reversed, I'm digging life and dawn is in the crap, then it pretty much works the same. I check in, see if she needs anything, and let her deal with it. If she asks for advice or acknowledges she is having a challenge, I may remind her of some tools that might be of value.

At times, it is a shitty day because we have argued or not seen eye to eye or something where we are misaligned. The last time this happened, we went from quietly gathering our wits (which sounds much more pleasant than mutual silent treatment) to me taking the lead by explaining how I am feeling. Not defending or blaming, just how I feel. Dawn explains how she feels. I make a decision about action. We act. This simple sentence is the difference between a shitty day and a shitty hour or a shitty week. At this point in our relationship, we have shitty hours but very rarely more than that.

Just to push back on myself a bit, when kame bat died, was that a shitty day? It was gut wrenching and terrible and fucked—but as a Leader I had no time to be in my cups about it. Things had to be accounted for. Later, when it was time to grieve, I grieved. Not fun or enjoyable, but not to be avoided either. It was both shitty and very ... real.

For me, shitty days are often a result of avoidance—avoiding what is going on, avoiding how things really are, avoiding owning my failures and limitations. My ego demands a shitty day when I am not the center of the universe. My sense of humor reminds me it hasn't happened in the past 50 years, but maybe tomorrow is Universal Dan Day.

What does a shitty day look like in your relationship?
dawn:

We are currently sitting at a coffee/ice-cream shop with a view of the river bank ... and huge, loud trucks driving by. It's too loud to talk to each other, but focusing on this question isn't as hard as I thought it would be.

I'm trying to think back on a crappy day and a specific one isn't coming to mind, but I know a crappy day when it happens. It usually happens when something has either angered one of us, like work or politics, or we are feeling emotionally thin, which is usually because of something physical. When these things happen, tiny annoyances tend to escalate into larger annoyances if we aren't careful.

Or somehow we've fallen into old relationship habits. We know something is wrong. We can feel the energy is off but neither of us wants to do the work of asking what's wrong or to admitting something is wrong. It could be that we've fallen into the cold shoulder habit, or that we are internally processing. Or the anger starts to leak out of one and the other doesn't want to touch it with a ten-foot pole.

Or depression ... fuck depression. But it still happens some days and it's hard to pull through sometimes. And it's hard not to suck your partner down with you. We do our best.

So crappy days still happen, but they are rare and neither one of us looks forward to it happening again. Our days are so good for so long that a crappy day is a real crappy day.

To be proactive about days like this, we've built some tools along the way. We mention these in other books, but I'll go over a couple of them quickly here.

The 48-hour rule: If we have something that is bothering us, we have 48 hours to bring it up or it gets dropped. Even if it's to say, "Something is bothering me that I'm chewing on right now. I'll bring it up later if I need to." This is a great tool for us because we are so aware of each other's emotions that we can tell if something is wrong and though we do our best not to think it's our fault, sometimes that doubt leaks through the cracks of our good intentions of not taking things personally or thinking everything is about our relationship.

> Sometimes we misstep and land on the other person's foot like a two-stepping elephant that's lost the beat of the music.

"I'm going to take you at your word." The other trick we've learned is that if we ask "Is anything wrong?" when we feel that shift and the answer is any version of "No, nothing is wrong," we take that person at their word. This is their chance to speak up. The person asking may ask a second time just to give room for the answer to change if needed, but if it's still "Nothing is wrong," our response is "OK. I'm going to take you at your word." This puts the work in the lap of the person feeling crappy. They are always able to ask for help or to speak up about the 48-hour rule, but they can't punish the other person for not asking enough, or not reading body language or whatever. We've both agreed to this tool. Just the other day Dan asked me twice if I needed something. I said no. He replied with, "OK, I'm going to take you at your word and go work on the satellite dish." I thanked him and said I needed him to take me at my word. That's how we've built trust in those types of situations.

We've also built language in these situations to be used as needed. Maybe it's a crappy day, we are not talking to each other for whatever reasons, we feel such a disconnect that even wanting or giving service isn't happening, which makes it worse of course. We are letting it drag out ... not using our other tools. If one of us takes the courage to ask the other if anything is wrong, we can also use the language that sort of happened out of the blue. It's great when one of us realizes we need to admit to these moments. We call them WAMs, blips, or hiccups.

I share something with Dan. I can feel an emotional reaction. I ask if anything is wrong. He says, "I just had a blip." That tells me he's had an emotional reaction but may not be sure what actually caused it. My story, yes. But, why? I ask if he needs help, he says he'll work on it. I back off.

It's a dance that we've learned over time. But sometimes we misstep and land on the other person's foot like a two-stepping elephant that's lost the beat of the music. We've hurt each other's feelings. We've let politics affect us and leak out. Sometimes other relationships affect ours. Sometimes we are dealing with memories that have nothing to do with either of us.

So, the best thing we've figured out is talking ... communicate, communicate, communicate. But there are other things we do as well. A car ride to talk about things. A walk in the woods where we can just breathe in the fresh air and ground. We've even used play or sex to reconnect. There are so many options and it depends on the day as to what we try.

With all these tools there isn't a reason for a crappy day, but they will happen regardless of how proactive we are. We are just more aware of them now, and also aware that if they continue for too long, it's our own fault. We know what to do about it. We just have to remember that it's important enough to do something about it.

Chapter 23: Disagreements.

Tell us about a significant disagreement and how it was resolved.
Kevin:

[*An interesting pre-writing note: We all cheated just a little on this one. Apparently we all have significant disagreements so rarely that we all asked for a minute or two to dredge one up before starting the timer. That in itself is noteworthy.*]

When Katie and I first got together it was via Katie moving from Canada down to Lexington KY, where I lived at the time. Prior to leaving Canada she had supported herself and five children through teaching painting, and also by doing a number of profitable art shows each year—selling painted goods.

My employment was supposed to be with my family's business (some VA health contract), but it was going so poorly they couldn't afford to give me any work. I decided that the best idea ever was to capitalize on Katie's amazing success with painting in Canada and open a studio in Lexington. That included buying supplies and renting a fairly expensive office space where we could have displays and hold classes.

> I was sad that I had made a bad decision. I was embarrassed my plan had failed. I was chagrined that I had ignored Katie's concerns.

Katie said it was a terrible idea—one should start a business small, then expand the business as it has success. Apparently, her silly preference isn't to start a business with zero cashflow and a huge lease payment. I essentially told Katie, who you might recall had years of experience and success, that I knew better than she did. She was going to be much loved by Lexingtonians and very successful in this new city!

Katie literally got on her knees and cried, beseeching me to reconsider and not sign the lease. Of course, seeing her pain and recognizing her wisdom, I immediately relented. HA! As if. No, that is what should have happened. Instead, I reminded her that I was in charge and that we were going to dive in and make it work.

For fuck's sake. What an unmitigated disaster. We worked so hard to make my bad decision turn out OK. We painted late into the night. We sent out fliers for classes and our grand opening. I don't recall that we actually successfully booked a single class. Maybe we did, but I doubt it. We ended up breaking lease on the building, nearly going bankrupt, and soon thereafter moving to Canada. I was sad that I had made a bad decision. I was embarrassed my plan had failed. I was chagrined that I had ignored Katie's concerns.

I'd love to be able to say we had a huge disagreement and we settled it successfully and with wisdom. Instead, we had a huge disagreement and I used my authority to make the choice I believed was best. Unfortunately, that is still likely to be the way a similar disagreement would play out again today, twenty years later. As the Leader, it would be my responsibility to hear my Follower and then to make the best choice I can in that circumstance. In the case of any serious disagreement, my job is to do the best I can for the relationship and for us, whether or not Katie agrees.

It isn't about winning or losing a disagreement. I don't care which one of us comes up with the best idea. I must make a choice that I believe is wise. I cannot let Katie's opinion be the factor that decides all disagreements, or her opinions get to be in charge, not me. That said, I sure as hell learned a valuable lesson about listening better to her input.

It is extremely rare that we disagree. When we do, I try to hear Katie's viewpoint and concerns. Then I get to make the final decision, meaning there is no longer a disagreement. Once the decision is made, Katie will drop her objections and throw herself 100% into making my decision successful. She will never drag her feet or undermine the success of the mission, just so that she can say "Told you so" when it fails. The failure of the Lexington business was because I was foolish, not because Katie let it fail. She worked so hard to make my choice be a good one. She put all her energy into making that studio fly. So I also learned that even in disagreement we are a team and we have each other's back.

Katie saw me take responsibility for that choice and that failure. She saw me learn that her input should be taken seriously. Our disagreements ... Gah. Time.

Tell us about a significant disagreement and how it was resolved.

Katie:

Shhh ... I'm going to cheat a little. So far all my companion writers are clicking away on their keyboards like a vagina with teeth after a fisting. *[Kevin-note: For fuck's sake, Katie!]*

I have wasted way too much time trying to remember a significant disagreement between Kevin and I and how we resolved it. We don't fight. It just makes no sense to us.

No.

We.

Are.

Not.

Robots.

We are too reasonable and have no inclination to be unkind to each other in frustration and anger. We do have disagreements though. Differences of opinion. They don't get ugly, and very rarely even get intense. I think this is the reason I cannot come up with a significant one. Well, I can remember one from the first year we were together, but for sure Kevin's going to hit that like a slippery cockpocket. So my little cheat will be talking about a disagreement with no measure of significance.

> I can remember one from the first year we were together, but for sure Kevin's going to hit that one like a slippery cockpocket.

If Kevin and I are in conflict, we sit down together. We hold hands. If I am upset he will sometimes have me kneel at his feet with my head in his lap. We discuss, we listen. For many people listening is so often not about listening but instead all up in their own coconut planning a reply. He is a great listener because that was his job. I have learned from him.

Because he is my Leader, Kevin has the power to say that the conversation is over at any point—or even that the conversation isn't going to occur, he has made a decision. That is an extremely rare occurrence. He might play the Authoritative Decision Card™ because time is critical, or I am not taking good care of myself.

Since we already know that a disagreement isn't about one of us winning, it takes so much of the stupid out of our interactions. Kevin will hear me out, Kevin will explain his viewpoint, Kevin will make the best decision he can. And forward we go.

Best decision for who? Best for us and the relationship. Time and again I see him take the responsibility of making a decision when we are in disagreement. I see that his decision is not guided by his cock, his ego or his inclinations. Rather, he is thoughtful and intentional.

Even if I disagree with him, I cannot fault his intentions.

At that point I fall into step alongside him. On his team, doing the best we both can to make his decision a success ... for the sake of us. If he is wrong, then likely I will be writing a book twenty years later, like this minute, and be unable to remember a significant disagreement we had to navigate.

What if we lose money, or waste time, or end up with a failed endeavor? Oh well. We can get through that and repair those kinds of damage. The harm caused by arguing, vying for power, yelling until we get our way, being unkind and hurtful—those damages are so difficult to heal and repair from.

We've had disagreements about me wearing clothes that reveal my scarred leg, about the people we have sexy fun times with, the businesses we have gotten involved in, what to do to help family members, whether to invest in this company or that, what kind of crown molding to put up in the bedroom, whether or not that huge dildo will fit inside me, whether it is OK for me to wear transparent tops in public, whether to clean the truck today, how many cans of refried beans fit in our pantry, whether the dog farted or the sewer line is leaking. Some of the disagreements I listed are bigger than others. But all of them are addressed in a calm, loving manner seeking resolution and best decisions.

Tell us about a significant disagreement and now it was resolved.

Dan:

I'm trying to come up with something that isn't related to polyamory. No luck yet.

Although we have stumbled through the early days of power exchange as we found tools and support and our own footing, significant disagreements were rare. Sure, they happened—during the housing crash over a decade ago when I decided that we needed to surrender our home; when we failed to communicate about a walking exercise we were doing (seems silly in retrospect but it was pretty contentious at that moment); these disagreements were resolved by me calming down and re-establishing dominance. I, as the Leader, had to lead, so step one was to get my own emotional turmoil under control and then lead us out of whatever dispute we were in.

Our mixed *polyamory + power exchange* moments were also challenging to navigate, but didn't often result in significant discord. One of dawn's fears was that I would find her unworthy and reject her; thus when someone else who was also a follower came into my life, it would bring up some challenging emotions for dawn. Again, we managed.

Egalitarian polyamory—in other words, when I fell in love with a vanilla girl—was a more significant predicament. Because I could control my temper to have even-handed conversations in the previous situations; but love is harder to navigate.

That is the oxymoron of power exchange leadership. "I am in charge, I get to do what I want," is always countered with "I am in charge and responsible for the well-being of my followers."

You see, both dawn and I got stuck in the same "What about me?" loop. Actually, that included the other person in this, who we will call Karen (since that is her name).

Dan: I love me a Karen, I want to go spend the weekend with her.
dawn: But what about me?
Dan: I love me some dawn, so I will not go away for the weekend with Karen.

Karen: But what about me?

Dan: ....

Also Dan: Hey, what about what I want? When do I get to put myself first?

And that is the oxymoron of power exchange leadership. "I am in charge, I get to do what I want," is always countered with "I am in charge and responsible for the wellbeing of my followers."

The way to resolve this was for me to make a decision. Now, that simple sentence sure sounds easy, but it was years in the making. This conflict between what dawn wanted/needed, what Karen wanted/needed, and what Dan wanted/needed. What I needed to do was parse the wants and the needs; then, determine the best path. I stumbled all over the place. From "Fuck it, I'm doing what I want," to coddling dawn, to full martyrdom mode. I had few tools and was stuck in my own suffering a lot.

How did we resolve it? The formula doesn't change. I made a decision and acted. This was far from easy and took patience from both dawn and Karen, but we got there. We developed tools, I helped dawn feel cared for, but stuck to my guns on what I wanted; I stopped treating dawn with kid gloves but instead with actual compassion; I stopped thinking so much and started acting. As the old saying goes, "Better to flounder about than be passive when your shoes are on fire."

I don't think I actually hit what this question really was so allow me to summarize. Leader, when there is a disagreement, it is up to you to lead out of it. Get your emotional shit together and come up with a plan. If an argument last days instead of hours or weeks instead of days, you are responsible for moving things forward. Balance compassion with decisiveness.

On an aside, Karen was my partner for twelve years, those last five living together with me and dawn. Although Karen and I went our own way, just the same, a very happy ending to the story indeed.

Tell us about a significant disagreement and how it was resolved.

dawn:

This question seemed to be hard for the four of us, and we actually put the question aside at least once before deciding just to tackle it.

So here we go.

Dan and I do things differently, so it only stands to reason that we would have some disagreements with how things can be done. Dan has the vision and is a broad-view thinker, whereas I concentrate on details and the moving parts of projects. This can get a little tricky when one seems to be in conflict with the other.

The conflict that pops into my head and was significant at the time was about 12 years ago when we ran for the Master/slave title for our region. We both really wanted to run for title … well, actually I was probably a little more attached to it than Dan. But because it was a new experience, he jumped right in. Once our application was accepted, I started coming up with all these ideas of how we could win; matching outfits, learn who the judges were and everything about them, read answers to questions from prior contestants that could come into play, do our two-minute speeches based on something important to a judge with clout. You know, all the stuff you do to win the thing.

Except this is not how Dan wanted to do things. It should not matter if we dress the same. We do not do that at home, so how would that reflect our real dynamic? And learn about the judges? That wasn't our responsibility to know who they are. They were judging us, so it was their responsibility to learn about who we are. I really had a hard time with that one. Shouldn't we know about them as if it's a job interview? How do we figure out how to answer so that a judge would vote for us? Well, when Dan heard me say that, he put his foot down. "Do not read the judges bios." Don't read the bios? Well, I had already read a few and really, really, REALLY wanted to read the rest. I wanted to be prepared. I was feeling a bit foot-stompy because I thought my way was the best way and I kept expressing this, thinking Dan wasn't listening. He was hearing me but not understanding what I was trying to say, or so I thought.

After finally having had enough with my pushback, Dan sits me down. "We will be ourselves. We will dress nice but do not need to match. We will have fun and be real. I do not want you reading about the judges, because it will affect how we answer questions. We will go on car rides and ask each other some hard questions so we aren't surprised on stage. We will learn some Leather history. We will be our best selves, nothing more, nothing less."

I had to take a deep breath and respond with "Yes, Sir." Actually, I'm betting he had me say, "Yes, Master," to show how important this was to him.

Sometimes his orders are stated and I can say "Yes, Sir," and then flip my thinking so that we are in alignment. This one was a slightly harder struggle. Oh, how I wanted to read more of the bios than I already had. But it was a no, so I didn't follow through with what I wanted.

When we have disagreements, the resolution is usually pretty simple. For the most part, Dan lets me have voice. Though, he certainly doesn't have to, and doesn't always, it helps us work together. Sometimes he'll explain his reasoning for doing it his way. Sometimes he doesn't. And sometimes he'll take my information and change his mind about doing something he wanted to do.

> And once I've said, "yes, Sir", the discussion is over. I don't "punish" him later for not doing things the way I wanted it done.

And once I've said, "Yes, Sir", the discussion is over. I don't "punish" him later for not doing things the way I wanted it done. This is not how our relationship works. I agreed a long time ago to follow his lead. And even though I may have resistance sometimes, I still want to follow his lead. He's a smart guy even if he does things differently than I would. He has our best interest at heart so why wouldn't I follow? This relationship and dynamic are where we are our best selves.

Keeping this in mind has helped us through moving out of a house where I didn't think that was the best idea, investing in stocks at a time that seemed risky, moving in with one of his poly partners when all I could think of is reasons not to, getting a puppy with a poly partner, putting our condo on the market with only 2 weeks notice and selling all our stuff … we did it his way and all of that has turned out ok.

By the way, we won our regional contest. We did not win the international contest, but it was not because we didn't wear matching outfits.

Chapter 24: Compromised Partners

Describe a time your partner was compromised in their ability to fulfill their role. How do you manage when it happens?
Kevin:

The interesting thing about this question is that it allows me to talk about times that Katie had reduced functioning in her role, or I can talk about a time that she was totally unable to engage in her role. Maybe I can hit both?

Katie has had a few times in our relationship where a medical issue has totally side-swiped us. She was in the hospital for days, or she was in recovery at home for days. (Hey, you don't get magnificent breasts like those without some down time, right?) In those instances where she is 100% unable to do the mental or physical duties of her chosen role, she is still my treasured Follower. Her prime directive at all times is to take care of my most valued possession. When she is impaired in some way her obligation as my Follower is to do everything in her power to be healthy and recover. Her absolute best service in that instance is to rest, or do the physical therapy, that leads to her rapid and full recovery. She may not feel guilty or like she is neglecting her role, as she should be focusing her attention on doing the most important task—her health.

In another instance, I think mentioned elsewhere in this book, we were facing a lot of challenges and Katie was extremely low in resilience. She was exhausted and irritable and sad. She explicitly said to me "I'm sorry, Sir, but I am unable to do many of the things you ordinarily expect of me. I can't problem-solve. I can't be creative. I can't add energy and enthusiasm. What I can do is follow your explicit directions, and plod forward on the tasks you assign me. Tell me what you want done, and how I should do it, and I will do that thing with the energy I have." For some period of time after that I micro-managed Katie and

> Our dog can tell I'm not the real Katie, but I do my best to maintain our world in exactly the way she would do if she were able.

did not count on her to be my powerful second-in-command. Instead, I used her as a robotic extension of my will—aimed at a job and left to grind away toward completion.

I think the general formula for full or partial disability (of the temporary sort, anyhow) has been to recognize that continuing to do the role, in its fullness, is not in Katie's best interest. I think in every instance we have either known it was going to happen (like surgery) or Katie has recognized a reduction in her capacity and announced it to me. I don't recall ever telling Katie that she was unable to perform her duties and needed a reduction in expectations.

The important internal part has to be present. I continue to see Katie as my treasure and my Follower, and I recognize and honor my responsibility to care for and maintain my property. She's my sweet toy, and if she's broken I want to do all the things that take care of her. I joyfully take on any tasks that are usually hers to do. I serve her, as her Leader, to the best of my ability to maximize her comfort and health.

I sometimes tease her after she has lost most of a day to a migraine that I was "being the real Katie" and had accomplished a whole list of Katie chores in her absence. Our dog can tell I'm not the real Katie, but I do my best to maintain our world in exactly the way she would do it if she were able. My stepping into her chores is critical, I believe. She needs to trust that the world will continue to run or she will not have peace with taking the necessary time for herself. She needs to know it will mostly run well, so she will not dread or fret about the laundry piling up or the dirty dishes attracting ants. She needs to know the dog will be fed and loved and that I know how to make a meal. My competence to do most of her tasks, although never as completely, competently, or gracefully as her, allows her to release them into my hands.

I'm also a bit of an asshole. Nothing like adoring your sweet Follower, offering to bring a cup of warm broth, then backing out of the room saying "As you wish, Mistress" just to fuck with her. Also, pro-tip: if you can arrange it so you clean the floor on your hands and knees in front of your Follower, it also is worth a chuckle to see their discomfort.

And, as a bit of objectification, yet adoration, I often continue to sexualize Katie even when she feels like shit. I'll say "I know you aren't much use to me right now, but at least you still have a nice ass for me to squeeze." When she has a migraine I say "Tell me when you feel better so I can fuck your face." Adoring, right? That's totally care-taking, I just know it.

Describe a time your partner was compromised in their ability to fulfill their role. How do you manage when it happens?
Katie:

Kevin and I attended a Power Exchange discussion group and a person of the Leadership flavor said, "People think being a Master is the best. You get all you want. I say being a Master sucks. I can't have a bad day. I can't make mistakes. I always have to be viewed as perfect."

> Like a teeter-totter, he wasn't as high in the air, but I carved out the ground beneath me so the dynamic was still in proper position.

I'll admit I was very candid in my response to him. I said, "Bullshit!" (… OK, not quite that candid.) I said, "What you are describing is the fantasy version of a Master or Leader. Living according to that expectation is unrealistic and cannot last."

This topic asks me to describe "a time" Kevin was compromised in his role. We've been together twenty years. There have been many times—of course!

He's been sick. He's been grieving. He's been overwhelmed with stress. He has been injured. Those occurrences compromised his ability to fully lead. That did not mean he was failing me or the relationship.

Kevin spent a couple of years in a doctorate program to further his ability to do research. We thought it would be like him having a full-time job. It wasn't. The workload was crushing. The demands of the program had me alone for 12-14 hours a day. His stress levels were way up. Exhaustion was pervasive. Kevin's role of leading us was compromised by a lack of time and energy, and constant fatigue.

Since Kevin could not lead as much as before, I served more than before. In an odd way, this keeps the balance. If you think of a teeter-totter, he wasn't as high in the air, but I carved out the ground beneath me so the dynamic was still in proper position.

I did everything I could to lessen Kevin's burdens. Continually, I was aware that he was doing his best and right then his best looked different. Of course I missed him. I missed sex and light-hearted laughter together. I missed working beside him. I mostly missed my Leader having a joyful life.

I would still come to him for decisions, but I would choose my timing wisely. Often it would be as he gulped down a meal that I would share updates and ask if he had any orders or final say. I would choose my need for oversight. Many, many decisions were made by me, in his service.

We would look for the spaces in his schedule to reconnect. Those breaks students get that aren't really breaks but chances to bend over gasping and try to catch their breath.

I didn't actually feel like I personally was suffering beyond my heart aching for his total exhaustion. I had time to accomplish household management and errands. I had time for art. I got a gym membership and spent a great deal of time working on my well-being, immersing myself in yoga classes. We were both seeking to improve ourselves.

I never thought less of Kevin's leadership or commitment to us. He was doing a hard thing. It was temporary. I adore his level of commitment and dedication to his pursuits.

Time and again I saw Kevin pull himself out of that crushing schedule to hug me, to sex me, to find a way to still contribute to my day. It fed my soul that he was so lovingly appreciative of my service and help.

My view of Kevin through this was that he was brilliant and amazing. He was doing the very best he could. His compromised ability was just a situation.

Perspective. That is how I managed it.

Describe a time your partner was compromised in their ability to fulfill their role. How do you manage when it happens?

Dan:

I kind of dig it when dawn is unable to fulfill her role. I am not opposed to change and chaos in small doses just to see what happens. Since dawn is so good at her role (compliments to her, and to brag a bit, the both of us) I don't have to ever do the things she is assigned to do. Her current role includes all the domestic tasks (quick note: not because she is a follower, it is logistical) so her being down and out means I get to do laundry and cook and clean. I am not being facetious—since I do it very rarely, currently it is kind of fun to see how I do.

Also, I get to take care of dawn. One might suggest I always take care of dawn, but not in a "Can I get you a pillow?" or "Would you like some more soup?" sense. Regardless of our Leader/follower status, I am in love with dawn, so taking care of her basic needs feeds a part of me that doesn't get out much.

The above is around the time that dawn had surgery. Another time she was ill, I let her sleep for twelve or so hours a day, asked nothing of her from our normal list, and made sure she had whatever meds she needed. All of the physical-based "compromised" days are pretty straightforward. Let meds and time do what they need to do, realize that our to-do list (I had 130 items on mine last time I checked) is nearly all an illusion, and relax. The biggest Leader-y thing I have to do is, at the beginning and toward the end, remind dawn to chill out, stay in bed, I'll walk the dog, and to take care of herself so she can go back to me taking care of her. And then I secretly revel in looking around the kitchen and wondering if I should call for delivery or maybe I'll try to make something ("This quick and easy peanut butter chicken recipe is sure to become a weeknight favorite!").

> It is always a weird balance between being emotionally supportive but intolerant of self-pity.

I've already talked about how we handle being emotionally compromised; for examples see the chapter on "What a Shitty Day

Looks Like". Beyond that, though, emotionally compromised is challenging to answer as each situation is unique.

A long time back, in the very early parts of our relationship, dawn had something happen that put her in an emotional tailspin. I don't recall what it was exactly. But she had had enough, sat down on the kitchen floor, and was done with everything. It is hard to describe the anguish she was in. My reaction was to simply be there. To be present. To let her know although she felt alone, she was not, and I was in reach. Even though she felt unlovable, I was proof she was not.

It is always a weird balance between being emotionally supportive but intolerant of self-pity. A more recent example was that dawn was mad as hell. Crying in rage levels. I told her I was open to listening and gave her my full attention. I did not respond with either sharing her rage or feeling bad for her. Instead, I just listened and agreed that what she was mad about was a real issue. Once she spoke it out, I told her to make me a cup of coffee, sweep the floor, recommended she use a tool (called draft email, a form of journaling) and that we needed to think about an action around this. (We are both ethically opposed to the thing she was mad about; so what could we do about it?) I was there for her emotionally, I let her bleed off some steam, and then I reminded her she was loved and cared for and had a place in the world, or more importantly, in my world.

Describe a time your partner was compromised in their ability to fulfill their role. How do you manage when it happens?
dawn:

Running through the Rolodex of time, trying to remember when Dan was compromised and unable to fulfill his role. I know things he could do but hasn't that could compromise it, but it hasn't happened, so no need to focus there.

I could talk about some moments of depression or anxiety, but he's such a "live in the moment" kind of guy that those are rare and don't last too long.

I'm sure there were some small moments or something I'm just not remembering from the last two decades; things happen, after all. But the only one that sticks out in my memory was a time of Dan needing surgery. And then a second surgery to fix a problem caused by the first surgery. He was in so much pain that that took all his energy. He had broken his wrist and surgery was needed right away. My role was to keep him comfortable and make sure he took his pain meds. And keeping an eye on his pain meds as this was his first major surgery since becoming clean.

I'm trying to come up with how this affected us. I remember him not being able to give orders. He needed to sleep and be taken care of and have me drive him to doctor appointments and hold his hand when Doogie Howser tried to pull a wire from his wrist, not realizing it had hooked around a bone they were pulling on, requiring a second surgery. My role didn't change.

He was not able to actively participate in our power exchange dynamic, but in moments like this, it doesn't really matter. We've designed what works for us. We've designed a complete system, which means when times like this happen, I step up and do what needs to be done. I take him to the hospital. I sit by his side when he comes out of recovery. I laugh with him over the pain of the catheter being taken out. (An inside joke there.) I make sure the kids are taken care of and the house is taken care of. I buy his prescriptions and make sure he is comfortable when he comes home. As his face turns white from the wire pulling, I hold his hand and back him up when he clearly states for the dude in the white coat to stop what the fuck he's doing.

> It doesn't serve him or us for me not to be able to jump in when needed.

I step in. I take care of things. This does not mean I'm out of my role. Everything I do is in service to Dan and us. I do it all as his follower. There's never a doubt in my mind who's in charge regardless of the circumstances. From the outside, it may look like I'm leading, but that's just not the case. I know how to get shit done that needs to get done. Dan depends on that and this is just one of those situations where that skill needed to be put into play. This is one way I have of taking care of him and us.

It doesn't serve him or us for me not to be able to jump in when needed. If I need direction from him all the time, or for him to "receive" my service in a domly-dom manner for things to be right with or dynamic, there will be moments of me floundering and us being unstable just because he is not able to fulfill his side. I don't even want to think what that would look like in a bigger situation. Let's not go there. I need to be able to step in and be confident in my ability to take care of him and us when needed. It doesn't make me any less of a follower or him any less of a Leader. I think it makes us more powerful as a Power Exchange couple, and makes it easier to ride the ripples in the pond or the tsunamis life brings.

236 | Dan, dawn, Kevin, Katie

Chapter 25: Slumps

Have you ever been in a slump with your partner? How
did you resolve it?
Kevin:

Authority Transfer is mindful and intentional. In order for me to
do it well, I have to consciously remember to make use of the tools in
the toolbox. In order for it to function as designed, I have to make the
effort to remain in my role and do the jobs that come with that role.

That clarification makes the answer very clear. _[Re-reading,_
Kevin says: "Clarifications making something clear? I'm stunned."] You
betcha we've been in slumps. And by that I mean there have been
times when the Authority Transfer slipped out of focus. We were still
in a loving relationship, but we were not consciously doing our roles
and making use of the tools.

This has happened for us for a few reasons. Most of the times we
have slumped have probably been due to complacence and laziness on
my part. Being the Leader, especially of a competent and powerful
Follower, means that it is easy to see the world as running pretty
smoothly and not needing constant attention and effort. As the Leader
of a super-successful organization (our relationship) it is easy to
imagine the profits are high, the shareholders are happy, the employees
love their jobs, the cafeteria serves all my favorite foods, and porn plays
on all the monitors in the lobby. I might as well sit behind my desk
with my feet up and let it coast, right? It doesn't take much laziness to
turn huge success into stagnation.

A few times in our 20 years, the Authority Transfer has suffered
because of my failure as a Leader and good partner. Times that I've
been hurtful, for instance, have led me to feel I shouldn't be leading, or
don't have the right to lead, or that Katie would be justified in not
following. Authority Transfer is founded on trust, and the handful of
times I have really failed to deserve that trust have been trials to
maintaining our roles.

LEAD, FOLLOW, LOVE | 237

Other times we have had slumps have usually been related to pressing outside matters causing the Authority Transfer to become a background hum, instead of a vibrant focus. It was still there, guiding much of how we interacted, but it wasn't being fed. I spent two years fruitlessly pursuing a Ph.D. During that time Katie was almost a widow. Our Authority Transfer was getting thin and pale from lack of sun and feeding. Another time, we had a total-loss house fire and we spent nearly a year trying to get our feet back under us. It wasn't a great time to make additional demands on Katie, so we defaulted to a less explicit, less vibrant Authority Transfer. It still guided us, quietly, from the background, but it certainly wasn't center stage.

> As the Leader of a super-successful organization (our relationship) it is easy to imagine the profits are high, the shareholders are happy, the employees love their jobs, the cafeteria serves all my favorite foods, and porn plays on all the monitors in the lobby.

How did we fix it? Often we fixed it by talking about the fact that it felt "off" and that we missed the vital Authority Transfer in our lives. We admitted the relationship was changed, and we checked whether we were both still wanting Authority Transfer as a priority. Each time we have had a slump, we have had a discussion where we said "That's enough of that. We want to put in the effort to revitalize the Authority Transfer and do better."

And I think that brings to focus a critical portion to me—almost every time this has happened Katie has been faced with the decision whether to trust me and fall to her knees, or whether I no longer deserved her devotion. Each time I have caused, or allowed, a slump has been a failure as a Leader and so far, each time I have seen that our path has strayed, Katie has agreed to follow me back to the path and trust me to keep trying. Not everyone gets that gift. Not everyone who fails at their job gets to try again. So part of the way we have fixed our slumps has everything to do with Katie being gracious, trusting, and willing to put herself back into my hands.

Have you ever been in a slump with your partner? How did you resolve it?

Katie:

Vague questions are awesome for getting random answers. Like asking "How's that thing going?"

Yes, I have been in a slump. We have been in a slump. We got out of it with effort, patience and attending to the importance. There. Katie's section done.

We have had low spots regarding how "intense" our dynamic was. Low sexual times. Low emotional times. And these are very contagious. If one of us is sliding, the other can easily fall down too.

Not too long ago Kevin and I were under an incredible physical workload. It had gone on for months. We were deeply exhausted. No matter how hard we tried to add energy to each other's empty tanks we had less and less to offer. I remember one particularly hard day when not only were the long hours of labor bashing us, but also everything seemed to be going wrong. We found ourselves sitting on the floor with each other, tears in our eyes, foreheads pressed together and just breathing. A complete emotional slump, physically beaten. Neither of us with anything left to give.

At that moment we weren't casting blame or hitting out at each other. Out loud we said the words, "This is now. This is not the rest of our lives. No matter how ugly our surrounding circumstances are, we adore each other." It might seem odd to quote what we said, but this is a mantra we say when things are going to shit. The awareness that together we have a deep love and together we were facing a bad time that wasn't going to be forever.

We connected to each other in comfort. We worked alongside each other for support, instead of at individual tasks. We literally trudged on with agonizing determination until days and months passed and the issue was resolved.

When we have had low times in our relationship—I am speaking of how intentional we are with our roles and dynamic—this has been attended to in much the same way. Together recognizing the source, the suffering and seeking solution.

Once early on, I got my feelings hurt hard and deep. I seriously doubt that the problem would be a big one if it arose today, but we now have a foundation built and methods in place to seek early solutions. But back then, while establishing vulnerability, respect and deepening love, it was intense for me and had a profound effect on being Kevin's follower.

We stumbled around, making everything worse with our inexperience, but we still found solutions. Kevin asked what I needed to heal. I opened up and told him where the pain was. He resolved everything within his power and ability. I did my work of changing my monkey brain thoughts whirling round and round. Replacing the statements in my head that hurt with the reassurances that he loved me so much he would take extreme measures to repair—even if they seemed not critical in his perspective. Internal statements that he was an amazing leader and humbly helped with the unpleasant task of cleanup.

> This is now. This is not the rest of our lives. No matter our surrounding circumstances are, we adore each other.

It took weeks to get my head straightened out, retrain my thoughts and perspective and fall back into place as his follower. But we diligently pursued pulling our relationship out of that slump. Again, trudging alongside each other with agonizing determination until the issue was resolved.

As the leader Kevin's skill set and attention to detail helps us recognize low spots and find the path to resolving the struggles. He is almost hyper-aware of changes in attitude, compromises to our interactions, straying from what we know is essential. This allows us to intercept many slides into a low spot early in the tumble and attend to "Onward and Upward!"

Have you ever been in a slump with your partner? How did you resolve it?
Dan:

For me, what I hear in this question is a sense of "blah". The relationship is blah, my feelings toward dawn are kinda blah, maybe life in general is blah. I am not too concerned with the Little Blah. The Little Blah is when I am just tired and lazy and I'm going to play PC games all night; any questions get answered with an "either way" or a shrug. It isn't to be dismissive; instead it is me doing some self-care by pretending my life isn't full of responsibilities or work or Leadership. This could be the slightly more dangerous "avoiding thinking about something", so I make sure these sessions don't last too long. But sometimes that is the process for me—let it sit for a bit before I take it out and examine it. Some emotional states are best examined after they have had a chance to sit on the counter and cool down for a bit. As long as this entire process is infrequent and doesn't extend beyond a night of self-indulgence, I have no problem with it for me. Nice to give yourself a break on occasion.

The Big Blah then, for me, is when that feeling of "Meh, this is OK, I guess," extends beyond a few days. Happens to people for different reasons, I imagine, but for me, it is when I have periods of lack of creativity. Although I am no painter or musician or poet, creativity is a big factor for me and my internal ballast. My "artistic muse" is fed by many forms—a new book dawn and I are writing; coming up with a membership model for a lifestyle club; or a spreadsheet that changes color when I enter a certain value. That idea of applying inspiration into action and having something created is a driver for me. So the Big Blah for me within my relationships happens when nothing is new, progressing, being ... well, created. Although there is value in long term stability, it isn't very interesting. And I do this with the relationship with myself—a lot. Shake things up and see the world in a new way.

How I get out of it is self-evident from the above I imagine. And it happens organically. I continue to do the day-to-day things that I do, but I do so with an openness to things—both new and existing—that creeps into my awareness. Different ideas, alternative views, or the same thing I've heard a hundred times but today hear it in a different perspective. And then one day I'll realize I should do something and bam, a new project is started. Or, within my relationship, a new 'add on' is included. From a Dan & dawn perspective, one example of this is when we heard a term that meant "serve me in silence" which led us to a great conversation, a deepening of our relationship, and had a tumble-down effect to remind us what a great power exchange relationship we had. Another example is when we visited friends who were more full time/naked-slave-girl focused than we were. We loved being around that and even though we didn't adopt it, we felt refreshed with what we had. Other examples for us are teaching classes about power exchange or the rare title run. Both are great ways to not only create something but to dig into ourselves and make sure we have something authentic to share.

Sometimes it happens *to me* instead of *because of me*. They say "When the student is ready, the teacher appears," and I've found myself cast in both roles, regardless of if I think I needed to add anything. Just a few days ago someone asked me to mentor them. Suddenly I find myself in a position of suggesting they read a certain book … and realizing I haven't read it in a decade and can't recall much of it, so I'd better pick it up myself.

I'll be honest—I don't really tolerate that blah in myself much. As I said, I'm fine for a night of gaming or sitting around moping around. But more than a night annoys me.

There is a third blah I'll address very briefly. The legitimate depression blah. That is a different animal which I am not qualified to advise you about, oh reader. Except to say this—do something about it. I've had depression and I know that the last thing you

> The Big Blah, then, for me, is when that feeling of "Meh, this is OK, I guess," extends beyond a few days.

want to do when you are depressed is "do something". But I reflect on the time I've wasted knowing what I should do (eat right, exercise, meditate, talk to a professional) and then, after I do it, realize how good I feel that I did.

Have you ever been in a slump with your partner? How did you resolve it?
dawn:

Dan and I have never been in a slump, either emotionally or sexually or … and "More Lies" for $200, please.

Over 20 years, how would it be possible to not go through times of being in a slump? I would assume this is pretty normal as we grow and change in a relationship or even individually. The difference is, we've become self-aware individuals creating a conscious relationship;

we have cultivated a life of mindfulness and being in the moment; we've created communication tools; and we know how long slumps can last if someone doesn't take care of it. We've also learned that it's not a particular person's responsibility to drive the resolution of the slump.

When we first started this power exchange dynamic, and came across others trying to do the same, it was actually a big question ... whose responsibility was it to fix the slump? Was it the Dominant's because he was in charge of the relationship? Was it the submissive's as a form of service? I've never been able to figure out the answer, because I think the question is faulty. It's both of our responsibilities.

There have been times that I've crashed hard. I was suffering and therefore our relationship was suffering. The same has happened with Dan. We've been through many life shifts, many stressors over the years. Though, it's not just this that causes slumps. Surprisingly, sometimes life is so good that we get complacent, and that can cause a different kind of slump.

Regardless of what kind of slump, the answer to the first part of the question is yes, we've been in slumps.

How did we resolve it?

Well, the most important thing we did was to get out of the power struggle of whose responsibility it is to "fix" it. This is a co-designed relationship. Both of us do the work. Both of us recognize when there is a slump. Sometimes it will be a little bit before one of us has had enough and figures something out to shake up the energy.

I'm sitting here trying to think of a specific story I can share ... are we in a slump now? No. Our life has just changed and we are still making adjustments. We've sold everything and have become full-time RVers. We don't have rituals like we used to. We don't play like we used to. It's the time of the Covid pandemic, so we haven't been able to attend events. We lost the Columbus Space, so we aren't busy there every weekend anymore. But I truly wouldn't consider our current situation a slump.

When was the last slump? I feel like something should be popping up in my head, but all that is there are moments from the beginning of our relationship. And were they slumps? Or just shifts as we changed and grew? (…thinking…) Yes, some of them can be defined as slumps. But why aren't they making an impression on me right now?

I think it's because we don't let them last for too long.

Huh, I'm betting they don't last for too long because we've moved beyond the blame game. In my last relationship, if there was a slump, I would think it was because of something my husband was or wasn't doing. Even if it was my depression, if he cared enough, he'd do something to fix it. And I never talked to him about it, so I have no clue what he was thinking. Probably something like, "There she goes moping again."

Whereas in this relationship, we are proactive as much as possible: meditation, journaling, speaking the unspeakables, transparency, confidence in ourselves and "us". Hell, just doing these writings is one way of making sure a slump doesn't happen.

And because of our mindfulness practice, we are able to catch a slump much faster and are able to do something about it, which usually involves talking … or just getting away for a little while to recharge. I might go for a trike ride. Dan might go hiking. When we had the motorcycles, we'd go out for a couple hours or a weekend trip. Sometimes, we'd recharge at an event or with other authority transfer friends. Or an intense kinky scene is a big help for us.

> Surprisingly, sometimes life is so good that we get complacent and that can cause a different kind of slump.

Why didn't I think of that before? Sometimes I've actually asked for an intense scene just to bring some of my emotions to the surface that I can cry over and release. Or if Dan is in a slump, I'll ask for a scene when I'm not sure what else to do. What a tool that is.

So yes, we've had slumps. Yes, we make a point to get over them, I still can't think of our last one and am curious as to what Dan wrote.

Section 5: Myths and Reality

People believe a lot of things about Authority Transfer relationships, and some of those things might not be entirely aligned with reality, as we (the authors) see it. Some of those beliefs are driven by uninformed popular press, some are driven by myths perpetuated by the BDSM subculture, some are simply the result of misunderstanding or confusion. In this section we give our blunt and unfiltered viewpoints about a few of the common myths we've encountered.

26) Does it matter who's stronger, smarter, makes more money or any of the other regular power issues?
27) How do you view a "Do as I say, not as I do" style of leadership?
28) How do you handle it when someone questions or challenges your dynamic?

Chapter 26: Strong, Smart, Rich, Sexy

Does it matter who is stronger, smarter, makes more money, or any of the other regular power issues?
Kevin:

Nope. Next question please?

One of the benefits of creating an Authority Transfer relationship is that the normal struggles over power don't happen. But that also means that the normal techniques by which one might gain power no longer apply.

I don't want this to be just a cerebral class on power, but the highlights might help. In most relationships power is seated in the person with the loudest voice, the most muscles, the biggest income, the larger social clout, or the most options for alternative partners (to name a handful). The people who have those things tend to be the same people who have the power in interpersonal interactions—with romantic partners (and often otherwise). If one has a look at politics, you might begin to suspect that the people with a lot of those determinants of

> I am the CEO who was smart enough to hire the absolute best. Just because Katie is amazing doesn't mean she gets to run the company.

power don't actually have the skill to Lead. Being the richest, or the one with most social clout, or the loudest obnoxious voice in the room doesn't necessarily mean they can be Leaders, but it does mean they have a lot of power.

As a momentary aside, being a great Leader also has nothing to do with the genitals you carry around. So walking around as a dick-swinging muscle-basket doesn't mean they'll be a good Leader or should automatically have the right to lead. Similarly, being famous, well-liked, or having celebrity probably also has little to do with Leadership but can certainly bring significant power.

The great thing about Authority Transfer is that the person with the inclination, skill, and consent to lead gets to be the Leader.

I'm stronger than Katie in my upper body. She's probably got stronger legs. I'm pretty fucking tough, but she's given birth to four kids. She's been through trials and hardship that I can't even imagine from my cushy, privileged position. She is smarter than I am, but I have more formal education. She is wiser than I am, but I've had a career providing therapy as a clinical psychologist. Most of the years we've been together she has made more money than I have—and at this point we live entirely on her income. She is probably actually more skilled and suited to the role of Leader.

Our agreement is that Katie follows. The fact that her income supports us does not change that. The fact that she often suggests better solutions to our dilemmas than I generate does not change that. Metaphorically, I am the CEO who was smart enough to hire the absolute best. Just because Katie is amazing doesn't suddenly mean she gets to run the company.

The other unspoken vector of power is the person willing to push the hardest, play dirtiest, manipulate the most, or cut off access to valuables (like sex). Those covert methods of gaining and maintaining power also get short-circuited in an Authority Transfer relationship. Being in the subordinate position but being the true power-holder through use of covert (for lack of a better word when I'm hurrying) techniques usually doesn't happen in AT, and is fairly common in egalitarian relationships. "When momma ain't happy, ain't nobody happy" is a phrase that exists for a reason. But those vectors of power simply don't fly if you are doing AT well. Not only are they unlikely to be attempted if the Follower is following in good faith, but they are unlikely to be successful, if attempted, if the Leader is attentive to how power functions within their relationship.

That isn't to say that those power issues are not present! We've heard of a Follower inheriting a fortune, and everyone in the family suddenly deferring to their preferences—despite their "slave heart" and their total lack of interest in having the money impact their chosen role.

The emotional reaction of one's Follower can impact what orders, what leading, a Leader is willing to give. If I know Katie will struggle with an order, or will be made sad by a new direction, I might shy away from asking it of her. That allows the emotions of the Follower to be in charge of the relationship. I'm a nice guy. I don't want her sad or hurt … so my attempting to avoid those things prevents me from acting in the way I might choose otherwise. That is a source of accidental power for Katie that we must both be mindful to consider. I must be willing to take "right action" regardless of how her emotions might buffet me.

Damn it…. Time's up. I think I had more to say…

Does it matter who is stronger, smarter, makes more money, or any of the other regular power issues?
Katie:

Ahh, the power issues that bubble up in an egalitarian style relationship and try to poke their little dragon heads into Authority Transfer.

It takes mental discipline to clear out old measures—common ways of viewing power, of "winning your way," of gaining the upper hand..

Break it down, break it down, break it down, bitch.

Let's start with smarter. This relationship is not about me being inferior or superior to Kevin. We are both decently intelligent people and individually we have specific skill sets. I'm good with finances. He is exceptional at being prepared for problems that need fixing. I am good at time management. He is good at planning and keeping us on track. I am good at cleaning and organizing. He is amazing at administration tasks and writing. That's reality. Not ego or vanity. This offers incredible diversity to what we as a couple can accomplish in life.

> Life is a bitch who has puppies and they are all female puppies and the neighbor won't tie up or fix his randy dog. Life is full of struggle.

Who's smarter? Damned if I know. And what is more critical is who is wiser. We are aware of who is the source of the best knowledge in each aspect of our life. We tap into that asset without attachment to our roles.

Who is stronger and does that have an effect on our dynamic? Physically stronger is Kevin of course. By a heap and a honker. Physically he is extremely agile and strong. This is important to me as his follower for a couple of reasons—neither of which makes him my Leader, but certainly enhances our life. It is super hot and sexy to me to be aware of his power and strength. I love feeling his ability to crush me, have the endurance of a machine, tap into a more primal fuck. That's the erotic side of the relationship. Not the role.

His physical strength matters in that it is a sign that he is attending to his health and wellness. So when I see him do strong things, that heightens to me his attention to exercise and fitness. Following a partner that is unhealthy and weak due to laziness and neglect would not work for me at all. Way too much undermining of my respect for their dedication to themselves and our life together. If there comes a time that he is unhealthy due to issues beyond his control, that is an entirely different matter. Of course I would still be devoted to him and make incredible effort for us to wring out all the delicious parts of life still available.

Emotional strength, fortitude and resilience. Well, these are quite different. Does it matter which of us is stronger in these aspects? I have to say an umbrella No. This is because life is a bitch who has puppies and they are all female puppies and the neighbor won't tie up or fix his randy dog. Life is full of struggle. Kevin and I have individually gone through tough emotional times. Grief, stress, hormones, brain chemicals, family issues all take their toll on us. Sometimes I am the calm, determined, and resilient one. Sometimes he is. We have had this happen often enough to smoothly step into the need for each other without it affecting our dynamic or high regard for each other.

I don't need or want a leader that is an unfaltering rock of strength and stoicism, never showing a struggle or an emotional low. I want Kevin to be real and honest, even if it is not a powerful moment for him.

I don't feel a need to be weak—to be less so that I stay in my place as his follower. I love bringing my strength and determination to our relationship. It is fulfilling for me to use my brain and abilities to help us accomplish goals.

Money. Shit, we have five minutes. I hope Kevin started here.

Money is such a power tool—a weapon in relationships. How sucky is that? Money is supposed to make things better and for so many it causes fighting and activates a feeling of superiority.

For us, money has been a very conscious aspect that we decided means nothing as regards to who holds the authority in our relationship. I make a significant amount of money. Kevin sometimes has made more than me, many times I have a higher income. It is a number in a bank account that we use to reach goals, fund life and plan for the future. That doesn't belong in our dynamic. Off, you fuck, financial dominance!

We are very conscious of what power and authority means to us and the things that influence it. Money, strength and intelligence are ... And the timer buzzes, haha.

Does it matter who is stronger, smarter, makes more money, or any of the other regular power issues?
Dan:

Before I answer, let's take stock of where things stand with dawn.

Stronger—me. Well, are we talking about physical strength? Then me. Stronger from a courage perspective (me) or strength of character (probably a tie). I'm sure there are some other ways to view strength but start with these.

I am stronger physically and it doesn't matter. It means I get the first shot at opening stuck lids or such. But we are close enough matched that when our naughty play involves dawn struggling back, I have to be on my "A game". In general, it has nothing to do with our power exchange.

Smarter. The ability to learn and retain information? Dawn, no contest. I am smarter in some areas—Excel, video games, navigating my workplace. But overall, dawn is smarter. She has a college degree (I do not), understands how to study, and more.

Makes more money. Me. But that is a design choice. I work in an environment that pays me a fair wage. After dawn was no longer with her last employer, she started taking care of not just the home-fires but also the business of Dan & dawn (we have a podcast, do presenting, etc.). It is a full-time job that doesn't pay very well but the value to me and us is not in the monetary value.

There are many other areas where we can play this game—who is better at finances, better agility, more skilled in writing for a corporate environment, etc. But who cares? Earlier I mentioned "strength of courage" and that I had the advantage there. That works great for us, because I can lend that courage to dawn, which helps her grow it. Strength of character is an area we can keep each other in balance— are you the ethical being that reflects who you want to be?

I get the point of this question—does one person being more powerful in an area make things unbalanced? Alternatively, unless the Leader is stronger/smarter/more, will the follower follow? Or (and I've seen this) they will revolt and take over.

But the actual answer to the question, in our home, of who is stronger or smarter, is "it doesn't matter". It only matters that we know the answer. Because if we know who has what skills, I as a Leader can make use of them. To quote my old friend Master Hank, dawn is an extension of me. Therefore, if she is the smartest person in the room, then I am the smartest person in the room—if I use her as my proxy. When someone asks me "What is the main difference between Jung and Freud?" or "How do you cook a turkey?" I can say "dawn, answer that for me," and she will.

You might suggest that I am disempowering dawn or that I am stealing her thunder, but that would only happen if you don't know us. Because when it comes to power exchange, this is about us as a single working unit. Is Dan stronger? Then we are stronger. Dawn is a better cook? Then we have good cooking.

> Sometimes dawn is so smart that I have to tell her "Da'quill" (serve me in silence) so I can try to figure things out and make my own mess.

So it does not matter as long as the Leader can lead. As long as the Leader is humble. And as long as the Leader gives credit (generously) where credit is deserved. The Leader gets this huge benefit of doubling their capacity and often gets acknowledged doubly. Not only do they get the benefit of having an extra set of hands and eyes and a follower's intellect, they are likely to be the one getting the compliment (dawn is such a good follower, you have trained her so well, she has grown under your collar) which may or may not be said to dawn at all. When I am a good Leader, I make sure to not only convey that to dawn, but to convey my own praise upon her for the great value she adds.

Sometimes dawn is so smart that I have to tell her "Da'quill" (or serve me in silence), so I can figure things out and make my own mess. I like that I can have dawn figure out things for me—and sometimes I like wandering around in the dark and figuring it out on my own (which is likely to cost more, cause swearing, and need Band-Aids).

Does it matter who is stronger, smarter, makes more money, or any of the other regular power issues?
dawn:

Timer (for answering question) set …Go.

"No!"

Done. (Hands in the air.) I win.

It's really that simple.

Seriously, we have found that these perceived "power issues" don't really matter in the long run. It just doesn't. It can make it challenging if it's out of balance … but out of balance with what? And which part? And is everything really ever in balance? Life shifts and changes, we've had to learn to go with the flow and roll with the punches life has given us over the years.

"No!"
Done.
(Hands in
the air.)
I win.
It's really that
simple.

I'm actually sitting here a little confused with the question. Let's break it down ... which is going to lead to more questions. Does it matter who is stronger? Well, what does that mean? Stronger physically? Stronger mentally? How do you measure strength? And on which day? And does it matter? Do you want the Leader to be the stronger one, or the follower? Depending on how you define strength, you could have arguments for either side. A stronger leader because he's leading and (at least for me) I like to follow a strong leader. But don't you want a strong follower as well? One with resilience for the changes in life and one that can follow through with orders? Hell, maybe it's someone that you just want to be physically strong so they can do the heavy lifting. I mean, it really depends on what you are wanting out of the relationship and from each person and role. Though don't get too attached to that, because there are going to be days that the person in the role can't fulfill the role. Life fluctuates.

Same for 'smarter' or 'makes more money' or any of the other power issues. I find in a power exchange dynamic, it matters even less. You'd think a Leader would take an ego hit if their follower was smarter or made more money. Well, in a vanilla relationship that is probably the case more often than not because those relationships can be built around power struggles. The roles are supposed to be 50/50 according to those that say what relationships are supposed to be (though I really don't know who *they* are ... probably marketing companies). Anyway, with power struggles someone is going to be butthurt if someone else is making more money and it's not the person they think it should be. In a power exchange relationship, where we have our roles to try to keep the struggle over power to a minimum, it's easier to adjust your thinking. At least after a few hiccups, it was for us.

I'm sure Dan, as the Leader, thought it was his responsibility to make more money in our relationship. If he'd clung to that idea in 2004 when he was laid off from his corporate job, we would have had some major relationship issues. (That was fun to watch ... my Dominant being led out of the building at work during the layoff, yet I still had my job there ... not.) Instead, after some concentrated effort to shift his thinking, he realized it didn't matter who made the money. It didn't matter that I was still working a corporate job and now the breadwinner.

Though, I had to take a moment and shift my thinking as well. So what? Though I was making more money, I was doing it in service to him and our relationship. Problem solved.

The questions we ended up navigating were more about "Who takes out the trash now that Dan is home all day with the kids?" The person that took out the trash was who he wanted to take out the trash. He was still in charge and got to make those decisions.

How about who is smarter? Dan is a pretty smart guy. But I'm high on the smart meter myself with some things. Luckily for me, Dan uses that to his advantage. He doesn't try to squash me down so that he looks taller. He recognizes where I have knowledge and experience and when he wants to use it, he does. That's not all the time. Simply because I want to do or not do something based on my knowledge or experience, doesn't mean we do it that way. He may have different ideas. Or he wants to figure something out on his own. But he doesn't squash me down and make me feel dumb just so I will follow him. I've seen that happen in relationships. The leader is so scared of looking dumb that they don't allow their follower to be the smart one. I don't see that as a healthy relationship.

Who is smarter, stronger, makes more money or anything else ... take a close look. Does it really matter? Whose ego is making those decisions on whether it matters? Everyone has strengths and weaknesses. That's part of what makes these relationships so exciting to design. If we can separate reality from fantasy and ego ... and use these strengths and differences to our advantage of building a strong relationship ... none of this outside stuff really matters.

Chapter 27: Congruence

How do you view a "Do as I say, not as I do" style of leadership?
Kevin:

Many folks say "I wouldn't ask my Follower to do something I wouldn't do myself." I'm not sure how true that is. Would that person actually be willing to kneel down and kiss the feet of another person and look up with adoring eyes and say "You are my world, and serving you brings me completion?" I'm guessing that we ask our Followers to do many things we don't do. And for fuck's sake—please don't load the dishwasher the way I do or make meals the way I do. Why should I suffer my Follower lowering her skillset to match my personal incompetence?

The critical piece of this question to me is: why do I have a Follower? What do I believe about Leadership? For me, owning a Follower is about having a strong and competent second-in-command with a diverse skillset, high intelligence, profound wisdom, and exceptional organizational skills. I want to make maximum use of her in all of those aspects. If I wanted her to only be able and willing to accomplish the same tasks and challenges as I can manage, we would be much the worse for that decision.

However—to the other portion of the question—those leaders who have bad habits and make terrible choices, but then hold their Follower to a higher standard. Is that OK? I'm torn. I don't want my Follower to speak to me in a disrespectful tone. I occasionally speak to Katie in a disrespectful tone, sometimes for fun, sometimes as a flex on my role (because I can) and sometimes as an embarrassing failure of my self-control. The first two are excusable and are great examples of places that Katie should not do as I do, but only as I say. She may not be disrespectful, and I can, by virtue of our roles and agreements. But if I am going to hold her to that expectation, I should also foster the self-control that I am asking of her. I should only speak to her with disrespect as a tool within the bounds

> It means, "I am a failure as a Leader, but I still want a success for a Follower.

of our agreement, not as a failure of my self-control. She should not do as I do, she should do as I say. And I should have the ability to do as I am expecting of her.

If I am going to eat unhealthy food choices, and fail to exercise or maintain my health, I have little room to expect her to eat carefully and be at the gym every day. This is a matter of congruence. I personally need to be congruent to my beliefs and expectations. If X thing is important, I need to congruently treat it as important. My actions and my statements should align. If I say that fitness and health are a priority and I fail to be congruent in my actions, then she sees a spot where my word and my deed don't match. This undermines trust, which undermines devotion, which undermines both the Authority Transfer and the loving relationship. My word and deed must be aligned to the best of my ability. I must be congruent—my priorities should align with my choices and my actions.

The challenge here is that I know the Leaders this question is actually aimed at. I know the Lords, the Tyrants, the Omnipotent Alphas that believe that they can be whoever and however they want to be, and also believe that they can make decisions about how their Follower will be—and those two things need not align. LadyBananaclit can have sex with whoever she wishes, but their Follower must be monogamous. MasterMooMoo (with apologies if there really is someone named that) will demand great service but will be a slovenly hulk of a disaster in their personal life. MasterMooMoo can leave dirty socks and underwear in the living room, can pile up soda cans beside the bed, can piss on the toilet seat—but still expect their Follower to keep a clean house.

Sure, if they both love that arrangement and have agreed to the Follower having the shittiest job ever because that calls to them, I don't want to yuck their yum, right? But otherwise? Fuck that "Leader." That isn't how Leadership works. You don't use up your Followers and force them to fix and cover up your own incompetence. As a Leader you strive to inspire. As a Leader you show the way. As a Leader you blaze a path that others wish to Follow. Leading from a place of incompetence is where "Do as I say, not as I do" becomes an ugly and poisonous policy. It means: "I am a failure as a Leader, but I still want a success for a Follower." It means: "I can't make myself be great, so I'll compel you to cover for me."

In summary—be congruent. Have reasonable expectations. Use your Follower wisely, even if it is to do things you do not. And don't be that fucking incompetent who uses power to hide their failings.

How do you view a "Do as I say, not as I do" style of leadership?
Katie:

This question highlights the label of Leadership to me. Leading by tyranny? Leading by self-serving indulgence? Leading by example?

For me to align myself to Kevin I have to hold him in high regard. What he does shows me his dedication to high standards, ethics and the well-being of us.

An example would be health. Kevin has an expectation of me that I'll eat well, take supplements, take good care of my body as regards hygiene and exercise. If I do as he orders me, but he is eating HoHos, watching hos and fapping with Cheeto-stained fingers while I munch celery and jog three miles, there is a problem. Not only in the fact that he expects more of me than he does of himself, but also he is working hard to make sure I am well, healthy and long-lived, but not doing the same for his body. I am likely to lose him early to avoidable illness, disease or accelerated aging.

I must hold him in high regard—awe, even. Yes, I know he is not perfect, and will have bad days. But the balance must be tipped towards him being a Leader I can follow with respect and trust. If the majority of his actions show that he is aligned with what he expects of me, then I can see his commands and expectations as important and worthwhile.

> I'll take the rotting-boot leader, farting from MREs and fighting alongside me any day.

I think of the military and leadership. The respect the troops have as their leader eats the same food, does the exercise drills, stands in wet trenches with rotting boots alongside them vs. the leaders that sit on their fine stallion drinking from a flask and waving about for their underlings to do all the shitty stuff that wins a battle. I'll take the rotting-boot leader, farting from MREs and fighting alongside me any day.

Sexy dominance is a totally different interaction. Having Kevin order me to do things he would not do—kiss his feet, serve him refreshment with a gentle voice of devotion, flip my legs over my head and cry while being torrentially devastated by fuck—well, in that regard it is a great deal of doing as he says, not as he does. We've been together for two decades and I am yet to say, "Hey bend over like a slut, shut up and take this, and cum over and over until I decide you're done." Total coin flip for fun times.

Leadership is about daily life, goals, and priorities. Setting a vision for us as a couple and us individually. The entitlement of "Do as I say, not as I do" would deplete my energy and investment.

There is incredible joy in having Kevin translate what he wishes of me and values me attending to, into some version personalized to himself. He masters himself even more than he Masters me. The trust and respect that generates in my soul is intrinsic to the strength of our dynamic.

How do you view a "Do as I say, not as I do" style of leadership?

Dan:

My initial reaction is not really ... useful. After all, how can someone be comfortable following me unless I am willing to lead? But then you realize there are many nuances to this that make it less cut and dried. Let's dig into it.

Some areas for me are indeed straightforward. I need to hold myself accountable for my behavior, my ethical standing, the way I treat people and the way I compose myself in all situations. And I expect my followers to do the same. Lead by example.

I am not willing to tell my follower to do something I would not do. And here is where I run into an annoying self-realization (and realize that this book in particular has been a journaling exercise). I want my follower to be healthy and eat well. It would be of benefit to her to have a better diet. But ... I like to eat. I like to explore food, try new things, have cake I've never had, eat international foods, try all the things. So I won't tell my follower to change her diet/eat better because I am not doing it myself.

This is an area of reflection for me. And an opportunity to be more self-disciplined so that I can command discipline for followers. As I sit here and write, I realize that being a Leader is being responsible for the entire relationship, and that includes the physical aspects of both of us. As I realize that my weight is not exactly where it should be and that by correcting that for myself, I can then have the fortitude to drive that in my followers, seems like an easy choice. So, goodbye chico-sticks and random cookies that I am eating just 'cause I have never had a cookie from that place before…

> Here is where I run into an annoying self-realization (and realize that this book in particular has been a journaling exercise).

With all that said, there are aspects where it is more about intent than a specific action. I had a follower who was going for her master's degree, which I both have never done nor do I have interest in. So it is not necessary that I "do that thing" to keep her on track. Instead, "Do what you agree to do, keep your commitments, follow through" is what I am driving.

I often hear people make fun of the person who is still living in mom's basement but call themselves "master", and I understand that. OK, I have been that guy. The concept, though, is valid—how can you call yourself a Leader when you have yet to lead yourself?

And finally, there is the opposite spectrum, where I am unclear how a follower can really trust a Leader who does not have a strong relationship with the creed of "lead by example". But I'll leave that to the followers to explore when they answer this question.

[Later note: I am officially breaking the rules of the book in what you are reading right now, as it was written after the thirty-minute period. A few days after this, I told dawn that starting Sunday she is stepping on the scale and I wanted to see the number be less than it was the week before until it gets to a more healthy number. I said that when the scale is set up, before you put it away, I am stepping on there as well because I need to reduce my weight as well.]

How do you view a "Do as I say, not as I do" style of leadership?

dawn:

Some people may be a little confused with the reality of a power exchange relationship, in that they think Leaders just get to do what they want and followers have to ... well, follow. But over time they will learn that some things work better than others to create that Leader/follower dynamic.

For me, Dan rarely gives me orders to do something that he's not willing or able to do himself. For example, if he wanted me to meditate every day, he would meditate every day. If he wanted me to be polite on social media and not snarky, that's the way he would be on social media. He sets the example he wants me to follow.

Does that apply to everything? If he wants me to do the dishes, would he make sure he was able to do the dishes? With Dan, he takes a bit of pride in knowing how to do things for himself, so he knows how to do the dishes. But in our relationship it's one of my duties because it creates the feeling of following, not because he doesn't know how.

I know this of Dan, so I don't feel like I'm being taken advantage of like what happened in my vanilla relationship many years ago. Sometimes we have different skill-sets, and that can be why I do things vs. him doing things or vice versa. But Dan doesn't "not" do things because he's lazy, or because he's taking advantage of my following.

If I was in a relationship that was a "Do as I say, not as I do" style ... I know me. I'd become very resentful. If I was required to be polite even when I didn't want to be, but he was able to be rude and abrasive with people ... nope. That means he doesn't have the strength to be my Leader. It means he's projecting what he wants, but not willing to do the work himself. I don't see that as a strong leader. I'm a strong follower. I need a strong leader or I won't be able to submit or follow.

> But if he's not willing to lead by example, I'm going to constantly question why I should be doing it.

If he's giving me orders to do things but not doing them himself ... as in meditating each day ... I see it as not really important to him. If it's not important enough for him to do it, why should I? I mean, really ... why should I? Let's say he wants me to exercise daily, but he's not willing to lead by example, I'm going to constantly question why I should be doing it. In a fantasy world, that's not the way it happens … he speaks a demand and I follow. But, in reality, why should I? I'm not a child that is in a relationship that I can't walk away from. Will I try to follow his demand regardless? For me, dawn, right here right now, yes, I'll try at least at first, because that's the relationship I want. He says. I do. But it will be a struggle for me.

Do I want to be in a relationship where I follow regardless of what I'm told? Absolutely. Do I want to be in a relationship where I don't question him? Absolutely. But that comes with trust, and trust comes with experience. It comes from knowing he's willing to put as much work into the relationship, and me, and our power exchange as I am. It comes from knowing I follow because I trust him and his judgment. "Do as I say, not as I do" is not going to get me to that spot in our relationship where I can automatically follow like I/we want. I will do my best. It will be a struggle. And one day, it might not be enough.

Chapter 28: Challenges From Others

How do you handle it when someone questions or challenges your dynamic?
Kevin:

It really depends (and just how many of these questions am I going to start with that phrase, I wonder...) on what part of my dynamic they are questioning and their purpose for doing so.

If they are questioning out of curiosity or confusion, then I'm usually happy to help them understand. Katie and I are presenters for a reason! We are glad to help folks understand what we do and why we do it. We don't just hang out exclusively with other 20-year couples and have our elite relationship conversations (whatever those are)— we hang out with folks who are just starting an Authority Transfer relationship, or are even just considering one. We enjoy answering those basic questions about how and why we make our relationship sing. Part of that is our shared orientation toward helping and service, and part of that is that keeping the foundation elements fresh in our minds means that we are less likely to become complacent or neglectful of them.

When someone "questions" our dynamic in a more insulting, aggressive, or judgmental way the response is initially similar, I suppose. We are inclined to assume the best about people and so we try to imagine that the person simply lacks the skill to ask appropriately, or to express their issue in a productive way. We are usually willing to hear out their attempt, and then we try to explore whether they are fearful for Katie, or believe we are sinners against something holy to them, or that our presence in the universe undermines all the progress in liberating women from the tyranny of male oppression. Or some other thing. Those are all legitimate concerns to discuss in thoughtful ways, with no anger or menace or defensiveness necessary. No need to treat us like pariahs, or aberrations.

The end result of exploration of their intent and meaning is sometimes a shared understanding that all is not as it seemed. I'm not an abusive asshole and I treasure Katie beyond measure ... so our dynamic is not about oppressing her simply because she carries around the vagina I own. Heh. Sometimes the end result is that Katie and I listen to their concern, attempt to explain or reassure, and then attempt to disengage when we realize that their "questions" are not about seeking understanding, but are more about having a tool to judge us, or impose their viewpoint on us.

> Sometimes the end result is that Katie and I listen to their concern, attempt to explain or reassure, and then attempt to disengage when we realize that their "questions" are not about seeking understanding, but are more about having a tool to judge us, or impose their viewpoint on us.

We stand fairly stable in our dynamic after 20 years. We believe it is healthier than most egalitarian relationships of which we are aware (with very few exceptions). We believe it is enhancing our growth, health, and well-being. We believe it is an expression of trust, responsibility and love in a world currently pretty lacking in all three. That said, we are usually open to an honest exploration of some part of what we do. For instance, we have very few "rituals" as we understand them in the Authority Transfer/Kink/BDSM subculture. Why is that? Would we be happier or more successful or have new awareness or be improved in any way by adding rituals to our toolbag? Maybe so! If someone asked us "Why don't you make use of rituals when they are so gosh darn wonderful?" we would honestly take the time to both explain our current position, but also take time to self-reflect and evaluate whether that would be additive to our experience.

(A funny aside—a few times someone has questioned our dynamic in a class full of people while we were presenting. On those rare occasions there has been a gasp of horror from the rest of the audience, since they can tell the person just doesn't get it at all. A room full of people there to try to understand our dynamic find it pretty shocking to have someone take a shot at our dynamic. One of the best: "Which one of you is actually in charge?")

Katie has an absolutely brilliant statement that totally captures everything I just said, but in a single sentence, which I've been tempted to steal for this writing. If she doesn't use the hell out of it in hers, then I'll get permission to break the rules and come back after our writing time is done to share that in a few sentences.

[She did use it! So no need for me to steal her brilliance … at least not this blatantly.]

In sum—we handle questioning gently and respectfully, then walk away comfortable in our unique and authentic expression of our relationship.

How do you handle it when someone questions or challenges your dynamic?
Katie:

This has happened to us—at munches, at dungeons, at events, while we are teaching classes. As International Power Exchange title holders—*dun* dun dun—being questioned and challenged was part of the process. It was expected.

Now, after all these years, I am ready and calm when the challenge or criticism arises. Truly it is a gentle wave on my shore rather than a rip-tide that has me tumbling and searching for footing.

When I was fresh to the role, I admit it was difficult. I was finding my place, we were figuring out what the relationship was going to be, Kevin was finding his style of Leadership.

I truly believe I am much the same follower as I was back then as regards interactions and responses. But I had no touchstone or example to use as the evidence that I was doing it "right." So when folks would call me bratty—which I am not—or tell Kevin he needed to get ahold of his girl, or say "You're not much of a submissive, are you?" I would question myself more than I already was. Those early years are full of discovery, introspection and yes, unsurety if you have any humbleness at all.

Kevin and I interacted in a joyful, playful and loving manner—we do not alter that from home to social situations. We are who we are. This was very contrary to many of the public appearances of Masters and slaves at BDSM gatherings where there are often high protocols or posturing for the sake of other people or formal occasions. We just continued to be authentic to ourselves.

Back in the early years our reaction was often to be quiet and take the shot. Our reaction today is to still be very calm but answer concisely to any challenges.

The following statement has been said to us many times, once as we were teaching a full class at an event. "Which one of you are in charge?"

A typical answer from Kevin would be, "She serves me exceptionally well." From me, "I am not submissive in personality, but I absolutely have given Kevin authority over me."

We will try to figure out if they are ignorant (uninformed) or ignorant (a rude twat). Uninformed we have all day for. Ignorant, we need a quick response so that anyone who has heard the shot can hear the reply for them to process and take away from the situation.

Folks have MANY times told Kevin he needs to get me in line.

> We will try to figure out if they are ignorant (uninformed) or ignorant (a rude twat). Uninformed we have all day for.

This is almost always because I am quick with my humor and very energetic. They will say, "Why do you let her get away with that?" He will answer, "Are you kidding? I designed her that way. That's not a bug, it's a feature!" I love this response. It is joyful and funny without being defensive and confrontational. It also makes me feel like a treasure when someone is being rude and ugly.

We've been to a munch where someone smacked the back of his hand into the palm of the other (try it so you get the message) every time I was witty or made a quick reply to someone. He did this gesture staring Kevin in the face each time. Does this make us go home and have a big discussion and change who we are and how I serve him? No, that guy's a fool who probably has never had a follower for more than a year.

People are rude. People are uninformed and have only been exposed to the fantasy version of this relationship style. People are struggling with their own insecurities and sometimes their need to stand on top of others to appear higher in the community.

None of that has a negative effect on who Kevin and I are. In fact, it often highlights to us that we have something to treasure. Part of treasuring it is to be secure enough in ourselves to not let others' opinion shake us. At the same time, we strive to be humble enough to hear feedback when we are with other introspective, long-term couples.

How do you handle it when someone questions or challenges your dynamic?
Dan:

People have questioned our power exchange dynamic (is it valid, is it abuse in another form) over the past twenty years, but it is far more rare than you might imagine. That is, that we know about. When people question it indirectly—meaning not to us, but about us—then I simply ignore it. Or if they question it without actually caring, just judging it in the form of a question when they have no interest in what I actually answer, I just move on. (Actually, I have a specific phrase that I use, a fairly polite phrase that translates in my head to "I hear you, you're wrong, and I'm not engaging because fuck off.")

When people question our dynamic directly—be it anything from "That seems unhealthy," or "I could never let someone," or "I see what you are showing me but I don't believe you," and they do it in a way that invites conversation, I have a conversation. I have no need or desire to prove anything—or, said another way, I have no attachment to someone believing we are a happy, healthy, full-time total exchange of power. I know we are. I have two decades of proof that it works. This allows me to easily engage in conversation if a conversation is warranted. Ask me how this can possibly be healthy, or challenge that dawn is a doormat, and I'm happy to chat about that and show you my reality. As long as it is a conversation with mutual back-and-forth listening. When they stop listening because they have already judged our relationship "wrong", then see "fairly polite phrase" from above.

> I have no attachment to someone believing we are a happy, healthy, full-time total exchange of power.

I will point out that we are not public about our dynamic in some venues—my workplace has no clue that with a word dawn is sucking my cock, or, more commonly, making me a peanut butter sandwich. Our family—older children with families of their own—do know but prefer to not talk about it, and we avoid "sir" and overt symbols around them. And we simply do not have "vanilla" friends. That is not good or bad, but why invest in hanging out with people where we have to hide who we are?

It really is as simple as that. I love talking about power exchange. So when you want to talk about it, great, let's talk. When you stop listening, I'll switch topics to sports ball or candy bars we can only find in Canada.

How do you handle it when someone questions or challenges your dynamic?
dawn:

Not only have I had people question our dynamic, but question my submission enough to hold an intervention, or show up at my house to make sure I'm OK. One of these people was actually in the kink community and another one was not, but now is.

Even though this relationship dynamic is seen as part of the kink community, it's not understood by a lot of people in it, let alone non-hierarchical people that only hear about relationships needing to be 50/50 or egalitarian or they aren't healthy.

I've had more than one person tell me that they didn't think our relationship was really a power exchange relationship because they had never seen me punished, or because they've seen me running around with a clipboard, in charge of whatever was going on. That just tells me they don't "see" the nuances of our relationship. After this many years, we aren't high protocol anymore. Though it was during the years of high protocol when the interventions took place.

I've even had people think that I was the one in charge of the relationship at the beginning. That tells me they really weren't paying attention. The example I'm thinking of is when I had walked into a meeting space before Dan, reserved two chairs for us, and then told him where they were when he walked into the room. No one knew us yet and they assumed I was in charge. What they hadn't seen was that Dan had told me outside to find us two seats and let him know where they were. That way he could go around introducing us, knowing we had a place to sit when things got started.

These moments have happened over the years. But in reality, are they important? If someone questions our dynamic, is it really any of their business?

Dan and I have created a designer relationship that works for us. We didn't know it at the time, but we are … a term a friend of ours uses … relationship hackers. We knew that the so called "egalitarian" relationships we had been in before didn't work for us and we had no interest in trying something like that again. After reading some "erotica" … OK, porn … I had become intrigued and turned on by the dynamics that were presented in what I was drawn to. I wanted to try it. Dan wanted to try it. We gave it a go, with some stumbling involved as we created a fantasy relationship that had to fit into our reality.

During our second year of our contract when the theme was High Protocol, and the kink community member came to our house on a pretense of borrowing one of our old computers, just to check up on me and make sure I wasn't being abused … it was my first experience with realizing that even the kink community didn't understand what we were creating. I'm not angry at her. She cared about me and needed to check in. She took me outside and asked me if I was OK. I literally laughed, probably shouldn't have, and told her that I was absolutely fine and living the life of my dreams.

> We've designed and continue to design what is right for us. It doesn't need to be right for anyone else.

A couple years later, another intervention happened with a woman not in the kink community who didn't understand our dynamic or submission. That was a 3-hour conversation of me trying to explain what I get out of our power dynamic. Finally, I blurted out that as a feminist I was allowed to do what I wanted that brought me happiness and following a Leader that I trusted was exactly what I wanted and brought me happiness. She sat back, agreed, said if I had stated that at the beginning it would have saved us three hours, and now has had a couple of hierarchical relationships herself, from both sides of the slash.

And what about the person that said he didn't believe we were in a power exchange dynamic because he had never seen me punished? Well, Dan and I do have a punishment dynamic, but it's my goal to never have anyone see me punished. I can probably name on one hand the number of times I've been "punished" in our 20 years. Corrected, yes. Disciplined, occasionally. Punishment is for serious infractions that shows an issue with our dynamic, and therefore isn't needed as much.

And honestly, like I said before, our dynamic and the way we do it and whether someone thinks it's the "right" way or not, really isn't anyone's business … until we decided to run for title, that is. In the Leather world, there are title runs where people put themselves in front of judges on purpose. Ten years into our relationship and this is what we decided to do. We ran for the Master/slave title. We put ourselves and our relationship in front of seven people from the Leather/kink/fetish community. We answered questions. We had our dynamic picked apart. All so that we could win a title and backpatch for our vests.

It was not so that our relationship would be deemed worthy by anyone else. We didn't really care about that part. We are confident enough in what we've created for ourselves. But in the Leather world, a lot of emphasis is placed on titles, and that way we'd be able to cross some bridges into the Leather world and be able to teach more classes on hierarchical relationship structures.

We won our regional title, we did not win International. No big deal. We used those experiences to reflect on the relationship we have designed and to modify it. Relationship hackers. We've designed and continue to design what is right for us. It doesn't need to be right for anyone else.

Section 6: Bonus Questions

As part of launching this book, we ran a very successful crowdfunding campaign. One of the reward levels allowed the supporter to pose a question to the authors for inclusion in the book. The folks who chose that reward sent us a handful of questions and Kevin worked with them to choose the one that best fit the tone of the book without significant overlap with other chapters. The other authors remained blind to the questions entirely. After a month, the two questions were randomized and each was written in the spirit of the rest of the book—no prep, no discussion.

We appreciate the extra financial boost of their contributions, but perhaps even more so we appreciate the two excellent questions we had the privilege to answer and include in the book!

This is a heartfelt "Thank you" from all four authors to Mitch Moore for his question (#29) and to Emma & Eris for their question (#30).

29) What are the skills and tools that an AT relationship provides to help each other work through bad habits, sensitivities and past baggage and improve future choices and behaviors?
30) What is the most challenging irreversible decision you've made as the Leader or followed as the Follower in your authority transfer relationship?

Chapter 29: Defusing the Past

What are the skills and tools that an AT relationship provides to help each other work through bad habits, sensitivities, and past baggage, and improve future choices and behaviors?
Kevin:

We have discussed in various ways some of the tools of AT relationships throughout the book, I think. However, this question focuses our attention on challenges and baggage we bring from the past, and ways to intervene such that they can be corrected or healed and not infect the future success and happiness in the relationship. That might be a different set of tools!

> We become more adept at seeing ourselves—but we also become better people through having ongoing support in knowing, from an outsider's viewpoint, what we are like.

The first tool that comes to mind is my early directive to Katie that I was the source of the only valid information about whether she is doing OK. She might have historical voices playing in her head like a record player that say that she needs to do X, or she is not good enough at Y, or that she has some failing or another. That voice, that message from her past, no longer had the right to influence her beliefs about herself. I was the only valid source of information about those topics. She might have (actually HAS had) people judge her for being witty and zany—frankly telling me that I should get a rein on her. Or implying that her humor and wit was inappropriate. My order to her is that those opinions of other people do not matter. I am the source of judgment about whether her behavior is appropriate. Related to the question, this means that I can listen to her and hear the messages she takes to heart, whether from past interactions or current, and I can use my love and admiration for her as the filter for those messages. I can use my authority as her Leader to take the power out of those and render them impotent.

We also attend not just to communication, but to meta-communication. When it appears that she is reacting to a situation not based on the reality of the current experience, but instead through a filter or learning from the past, I can stop our interaction and process the communication as it is occurring. Asking questions is a valuable tool for exploring that experience. Her oath of transparency means that she is obligated to stop and try to do the mental work to figure out why she is reacting in a particular way that seems out-of-place compared to the situation. Why is she suddenly frustrated? Rather than continue an interaction with her frustrated, I can pause the interaction and explore that frustration. She does the hard work of seeking inside herself and then trusting me enough to share what she finds. Perhaps that interaction reminded her of an old boss who was very critical. Perhaps she was feeling the same sense of frustration at not being valued she felt when interacting with family. Those things can be brought into the light and dissolved. I can use my authority as Leader to help her release those historical voices and interact with the present in a more mindful and current way.

One of the powers of our relationship is that we are loving, respectful mirrors for one another. We admire and adore our partner. That means that when a thing is not going correctly for them, we have a desire to intervene—to help them find their way through. We have a desire to help them be their best. Being a mirror means that I can say to Katie, "Hey, you seem frustrated," and the trust and love (and obligations of AT) require her to pause and explore that. She does not resort to denial or defensiveness. She accepts that if I see her as being frustrated, then that is a valid perception she must take seriously and try to understand. She believes in the purity of my motive in being a mirror for her—that I am honestly and accurately telling her things about herself that she might have trouble seeing or being aware of otherwise. The power and benefit of having an accurate and respectful mirror in your life cannot be overstated. It is super rare to have that right to be that mirror for someone. It is also super rare to have a person willing and able to be that mirror for your benefit. Seeing oneself lovingly reflected allows each of us to hone our behaviors. We become more adept at seeing ourselves, but we also become better people through having ongoing support in knowing, from an outsider's viewpoint, what we are like.

Katie and I have the trust and the sense of responsibility to honestly debrief through all the events we experience. We try to take our various experiences and process them and distill from them the lessons we feel are valuable. Having the ability to discuss our experiences together and process them for the wisdom each of us can glean lets us release those things that might hold onto us or drag us down. We can become unattached to the event or the experience and instead move forward with the lesson and the wisdom it provided. Each of us can own, or take responsibility for, the ways that we behave and the things that we bring to our shared experience. Whether our actions are beneficial or bone-headed, we can discuss and process them, and own the responsibility for what we have brought. That allows us to have appreciation and admiration for each other, but also allows us to have forgiveness and grace. We can dance our way through our shared lives—doing amazing things, or fumbling and floundering, and know that each of us will support the other, take responsibility for our parts, and treasure our partner for being at our side.

What are the skills and tools that an AT relationship provides to help each other work through bad habits, sensitivities, and past baggage, and improve future choices and behaviors?
Katie:

A big question with many parts. I am going to break it down to help think things through, and italicize the skills and tools.

Bad Habits: I had this bad habit of only relying on myself. Exclusively measuring what was possible in my daily life based on my time and ability. Fiercely pursuing independence at a very high level—like to the point of buying cars for my past husband, but putting them in my name "just in case." Managing the accounts and making sure that my income was enough if I finally had the courage to show him the door.

This relationship style with Kevin quickly began to address that level of independence by highlighting time and again that we were a team. As I came to *recognize his skills and experience in life* that were in addition to mine. A silly example is the first time our washing machine broke down. Old katie said, "I hope we have enough in the bank to pay the repairman," because that's what taking care of things on my own would look like. Kevin said, "This is easy, I will repair it for just a few dollars," and did. I was astonished. I had never had a clever handy person as a partner.

This is a habit that still has little crumbs laying around in my life. I have to *stop and think,* "He loves to help and contribute. It's not all up to me."

Sensitivities: Ack! I am sensitive about my scars and the damage done to my body by a childhood accident. I never felt sexy. I have never felt like I move with grace or appeal. I have brought a difficult issue into our relationship—one that Kevin addresses with incredible *kindness and encouragement.* As my Leader, he recognizes that I need to be more secure in how I look and my appeal, but he also has the tricky responsibility to not push me so far out of my comfort zone that I am robotically obeying and surviving.

Past baggage: Huh ... don't sensitivities and bad habits usually come from past baggage? Baggage. Baggage as in burdens and things that I am packing around from the past? I grew up in a household where modesty was my mother's main goal. This was attained in the children by never complimenting or praising anything we did. Criticism was worth sharing. Affection, appreciation and words of encouragement did not exist. I had very low self-esteem no matter how much I accomplished, and this continued into adulthood. Successful business, beautiful healthy children, a clean and organized house— none of it had personal worth attached.

This relationship style has me in a wonderful place as regards the above baggage. Kevin is my Leader. He is the one I turn to in order to know if I am enough. If I am low and doubting, *my trust in his feedback and praise gives me courage.* Kevin will say things such as, "I said you did great. That is your truth. Those other words inside your head are not accurate." This power in the wrong hands would equal gaslighting and abuse. This power and authority I give over to him equals me being stronger, sexier and with far better self-esteem. (I will break the fourth wall here and say, "Dear reader— choose wisely.")

Future choices and behaviors: It just keeps getting better. Yes, there are still low spots for me. Sometimes I sink into a place of being extremely dissatisfied with myself and disinclined towards energy and joy. Rarely, but it is not gone. We are both aware. We know it is temporary and Kevin's firm and loving leadership helps the journey back up again. I choose to *believe him.* I choose to trust him. Like the CEO that has led a company to incredible success, but every once in a while the company stumbles a little and needs additional effort to reset and thrive. This relationship style has given me the framework to be healthier, to heal from past misuse, to *trust deeply,* to *set aside independence* and learn how to be a valued member of a powerhouse team.

> This power and authority I give over to him equals me being stronger, sexier, and with far better self-esteem.

What are the skills and tools that an AT relationship provides to help each other work through bad habits, sensitivities, and past baggage, and improve future choices and behaviors?

Dan:

One common theme in all of my relationships is growth. We might start with a mix of past baggage, old wounds, and unskillful behavior … but the expectation is that these are temporary states that we, as a team, will move beyond.

This question could perhaps be reframed to ask "How do you do that?", and of course it varies for each situation. But one tool that comes to mind that is essential is courage. I didn't hear much about this in my formative years, but the courage to grow is huge. We sit in our misery and complain about how much it sucks … but sometimes the fact it is familiar feels like a better choice than the "doing" to get somewhere else.

This is a gift of power exchange—I could "loan" dawn courage by making her do things. Better stated, we knew she had a desire to change. So when I commanded her to go seek a counselor or journal about a fear or reveal a fantasy, she wasn't doing anything she didn't already want to do—she just wanted that extra nudge. She could then hang onto "Well, I don't think I need to, but if you want me to, *sir,*" and then go do the thing she knew was the right thing to do.

> We might start with a mix of past baggage, old wounds, and unskillful behavior … but the expectation is that these are temporary states that we, as a team, will move beyond.

A tool we have created lately is one called "grains of rice", and this is a powerful one for addressing sensitivities. The idea of it is that sometimes, small things—those that we dismiss as unimportant, as not worthy of conversation, or something I should be able to just let go of—can become something more if you ignore them. Or, like a grain of rice in a bowl … one is easy to ignore. But a second and a third and at some point you have a problem.

The way it works is we simply have a designated time and ask each other if we have any grains of rice. We share these tiny things—at least, they feel tiny—and give them voice. It is not an issue to be fixed nor a problem to be solved. But it is acknowledging that you didn't say thank you when I brought you a coffee or your comment about my hat was kinda rude sounding. No big deal—but on the other hand, it is the practice of another tool for these situations, *speak the unspeakable*.

This tool—speak the unspeakable—is simply the acknowledgement that nothing should have to be hidden from each other. That no issue or thought or idea or annoyance needs to be locked away. Having this agreement with each other—and reminding ourselves that we do have it—is a great practice to avoid mistrust or miscommunication or the dreaded "I didn't know how to tell you."

What are the skills and tools that an AT relationship provides to help each other work through bad habits, sensitivities, and past baggage, and improve future choices and behaviors?

dawn:

I came into this relationship with a lot of baggage. Not only past baggage, but bad habits, anxiety, lack of trust in people and lots of anger because of that past baggage. When I stumbled across D/s relationships and saw the trust that was involved and the transparency that was needed and how the Leader could be the type of person that put his own ego aside and put the relationship first, and that I could be cherished, I knew that was the style of relationship that I desired.

I needed that in my life. I didn't want to be the person I had become. I needed to be able to trust someone on such a deep level so that I could find my true self.

When Dan and I started looking into this separately, the first thing that happened was I shared all my baggage with him. This wasn't on purpose and it wasn't a test and it wasn't with the idea of an AT relationship in mind. It just happened as the result of a workshop we were attending together on something totally unrelated. But it happened at the same time I had found kink and power exchange and had decided that my vanilla relationship wasn't working. Later, I truly felt the Universe was pushing me in a certain direction.

Dan listened to me and trust started developing between us. He saw that I could be vulnerable with him and I saw that he could be trusted. He shared that he needed to be responsible for someone and I shared that I didn't think I could grow as a person unless I had someone I could trust enough to submit to.

So we decided to give this a try. We found that the vulnerability, transparency, honesty, trust, accountability, fearless communication and dedication involved in this style of relationship were powerful tools in our growth as people and as a couple. We are highly growth oriented and use the dynamics of our hierarchical relationship to push our growth.

> We found that the vulnerability, transparency, honesty, trust, accountability, fearless communication, and dedication involved in this style of relationship were powerful tools in our growth as people and as a couple.

When I knew I needed help on my healing path, Dan pushed me to make that call to a professional. When I wanted to become a Clergy, Dan pushed me into taking that step. Dan has pushed me many times over the years. He pushes because he knows what I want and need and he has the ability to do so.

Because we work on being trustworthy, I know that I can trust however he pushes me. He has our and my best interest at heart, which works well with the fact that I have our best interest at heart.

I guess we could be in any sort of relationship and it would be built on growth, but something about being in a power exchange relationship gives it some extra oomph. Not only am I in a relationship that holds me accountable for my actions, my actions are a reflection of my Leader. There is no reason to play games like there was in my vanilla relationships.

If he sees me with a bad habit, he'll point it out. If he sees something that would help us grow, he points it out. Well, we both point it out, as we are a team. A team with a clear leader.

Surrendering to his leadership has provided the space and opportunity for me to become the person I always wanted to be.

Chapter 30: Irreversible Decisions

What is the most challenging irreversible decision you've made as the Leader or followed as the Follower in your authority transfer relationship?
Kevin:

This is interesting to me because many of the decisions I make are the result of a long series of discussions with Katie. She is sometimes (often?) the genesis of the ideas we pursue because I am more content to simply do as we are successfully doing, and she is inclined to look for new and expansive opportunities. All that goes to say that my final decision is often the final "stamp of approval" on an extended process of exploration and negotiation. I was trying to think of an irreversible decision where I acted 100% autonomously without any input from Katie and it was truly just me acting in an irreversible way and imposing that decision on our relationship. I can't think of any.

An irreversible decision that comes to mind is the purchase of a 1940 house for renovations. We bought it thinking it would be a relatively gentle rehab, as it was a really cute little bungalow. The more we did the more we either wanted or needed to do. And it truly was irreversible. Almost always, once you own a home you really need to either stay in it a significant period of time or make some serious upgrades or you absolutely lose a fortune. So we owned the home and started figuring out the wide spectrum of things that really needed improvement to make a reasonable price improvement on the sale.

> ...It is possible to never repeat that same bad decision again ... so that's the best I could do: take care of Future-Katie.

That house was so hard on us. We were doing the majority of the renovations ourselves. We spent two years of hard labor there—much of it without air conditioning in the sweltering heat of Kentucky summer. The whole spectrum of skills and labor: demolition, plumbing, laying floor tile, new fixtures in one bathroom, new shower surround, turning a closet into a second bathroom, new kitchen, refinish the hardwood floors ... on and on. We were exhausted. And some projects were harder than we originally expected. Some were outside of our current skillset.

Katie cried sometimes. I had to lead us through a decision that had us trapped and suffering for two years. There was no way to simply walk away, without it being a total disaster for our finances. We could not hire out the labor if we wanted to break even (or better) on the sale. I (we)had to continue to do the labor required for the renovations, but I also had to be supportive and understanding of the misery of my sweet girl.

It was an awful time. I knew that I had not protected us. I knew that I had endorsed and approved a decision that was dominating all our attention and energy. I knew that I had set us on a path that was physically risky—both in terms of risk of injury (from tools and ladders, etc.) but also risky in terms of heavy wear and tear on our bodies. We shoveled tons of gravel. We spent hours on hands and knees doing tile work. I spent hours crawling around the ceiling joists in an attic. Katie spent countless hours with a paintbrush or roller in her hands. We were sore and tired. I had led us into a seemingly endless task ... and it sucked.

And every time we took a rest day, we simply extended how long we were trapped in that hell. Every time we took a weekend off or took time to let our wrists recover from some job ... we were extending the time until it was finally over.

Incredibly, we sold the home four months before the renovations were complete. We were then on a ticking timeline. We had a contracted date by which the house must be completed in order to make the sale. We had buyers looking over our shoulder and wanting updates. We had to bring the buyers into some of the decision-making process rather than just letting me (or us) make the choices we might normally make. This added a pressure and a complication that I did not anticipate. I thought it would be a relief to have the home pre-sold ... and it was just an intensification of the hell we found ourselves in. No rest. No days off. Just pushing through and having the buyers watching every choice we made. Needing to justify to them when we stopped work early, despite it being our project.

So, I compounded my original bad decision by adding a sprint to the end of it. I took some of the power out of my hands and put that power into the hands of people that did not feel an obligation to protect my Follower.

As we neared the end of that project, I told Katie that it was our last renovation (for money) ever. She needed to hear from me that limit was in place. She needed to know that when we finished that house, we were actually done for all time. I decided that we needed to find other side-hustles to make some money and not take on projects that add stress and risked our bodies.

That decision was painful and irreversible. But it did come to an end, and it is possible to never repeat that same bad decision again ... so that's the best I could do: take care of Future-Katie.

What is the most challenging irreversible decision you've made as the Leader or followed as the Follower in your authority transfer relationship?
Katie:

*[**Note during editing**: Due to an error in transcribing the question I mistakenly answered "What is the most challenging irreversible decision I made as a follower?" My apologies. I believe my answer still has wisdom and value. Our journal-blast method of writing has this in place now as canon. - katie]*

I am going to use the word irreversible like a piece of clothing. Some clothes are reversible, some are not—but sure you can wear them backwards. It's just not going to go well, feel right, and folks will look at you like "Hey, what??"

My decision to not lead when my personality is very much one to be independent, rely on my own organizational skill and methods has been a decision with pervasive effect. Almost everything in my life runs differently because of it. My relationship with Kevin has been built on that foundation. How we pursue goals and achievements in life has been affected by it.

Even now—21 years later—I daily have to use personal discipline to "rein in" my inclination to charge forth and do as I think best.

I know I am not always right. I know my ways and inclinations are not necessarily the best. I also know that Kevin and I have vastly different methods and approaches to almost everything. If we were individually accounting our budget for the month and doing math, our spreadsheets would look totally different with the same bottom line. If we were individually tasked to organize shutting down a business, selling a house, moving across the country, our list of sequences, priorities and methods would not match. But either of us could accomplish it with success.

And that's the distilled wisdom to this decision I have made. I will not lead, though I have the skills, intelligence and experience to do so. I will support, make suggestions, and follow. I have chosen a leader who is different from me, but not less.

It is a challenging decision because it has never stopped. Each day I renew that decision. Ongoingly, I support and step into my role. My way has not become more like his and vice versa has not happened either. We continue to be different dominant personalities with strong leadership tendencies.

> My ego is bullshit and I need to bring a wheelbarrow and shovel into each day.

He might say, "No, we are not going to sell off our stuff in storage in Kentucky and move only our treasures to Arizona. We are loading a moving truck with all the things and sorting it in Arizona instead." I might say, "I think we should rent a place in Kentucky, sort through every box, go to some flea markets and only move the best of things with us. Job complete."

Who is right? Who cares? Both ways work.

One of us has agreed to decision making, responsibility, managing the accomplishment of goals and priorities. The other has agreed to be amazing in supporting and working alongside to success.

A main part of the peace and unity we have experienced at a tremendous level is both of us staying aware of this issue. This struggle in my head. This management of tasks. And none of that struggle is because he is less capable. I chose to follow because he is amazing. My ego is bullshit and I need to bring a wheelbarrow and shovel into each day.

I have chosen wisely. I must behave with integrity, not getting tied up in the details. What matters is the results, the relationship and my Leader feeling empowered and adored.

What is the most challenging irreversible decision you've made as the Leader or followed as the Follower in your authority transfer relationship?

Dan:

For me, one of the hallmarks of being a good leader is that you make decisions. That is likely a no-brainer but, let's be honest, sometimes making a decision is not what I want to do. When I've been working all day, trying to keep up with projects and deadlines, and finally after a long day, I get to leave it behind. Only to have my follower ask "What do you want for dinner? Do you want to go out tonight? Should we watch the last episode of Lost?" And those are supposedly easy decisions, we are not getting into the power exchange tricky ones yet.

Yet, in our house, they are all a sort of power exchange decision. I am Leading, and each time I am not leading … then I am not Leading. You might start with an "I dunno" or "I don't care" or "Whatever" and then one day you've lost the momentum and the trust of your Follower. And although you might think I am exaggerating to make a point, in truth, slipping into a vanilla life can start that small.

Then we get to the Big Decisions. We can't afford the mortgage, so sell the house. Or let's go on an adventure and live in an RV full time. One day I announced I am becoming a Buddhist monk. No, I'm not. Yes, I am. Or … the dog is in pain, we are putting her down. I make major decisions in our house with some regularity. Many of them are financially impacting—this year, I've got us going to two different events and talking about a third that are overall going to cost us thousands of dollars. But others affect our lives in other ways. Like I am looking for a different job. Or we are going to leave where we are and drive East with no clear plan. These are all decisions I made that although my Follower gets input, I pull the trigger on.

> But the reality is these decisions are not hard or challenging when I am in my seat of power.

The key to making these decisions is that I own the responsibility of making them. And if they are bad decisions—we hate RV living, we can't actually afford the event, the new job is unstable—I own the responsibility of fixing that as well. To argue with my previous paragraph, this is the real hallmark of a good—hells, great—Leader. You made decisions, and you own the result when it doesn't go the way you thought it would. And you recover.

But this question is about those "one and done" types of decisions. Not just challenging, but irreversible as well. Certainly making the decision to put the dog down qualifies as both. But that isn't really the answer to this question. Yes, it was challenging and clearly irreversible, but it was also Right. I knew it was the right decision, and that we needed to do it, and it was not easy for dawn or I, but it was what should be done.

Staying on the theme of dogs, our next pupper, some 10 years later, we decided to rehome. This was way tougher. On one hand, the dog had serious anxiety issues around travel and as we are moving (RV living) every few weeks was very stressful for her. This you might suggest is not irreversible—we could ask for the dog back. But … it isn't a decision you flip around on. You see, the only reason I would reverse that decision would be for my own selfish desire to have my puppy with me. Regardless of the impact it has on her, I love my dog and enjoy how excited she gets when I come in the door (in all fairness, she gets just as excited when a stranger comes to the door, but it felt special just the same).

Life is a decision. I started and ended relationships, changed jobs, went through seven different places to live in the same city. And they are all irreversible. See, time does that. You might break up with someone and change your mind and get back with them … but it isn't the same. You might order your Follower to make you coffee, then decide you only want cold coffee, then no coffee, then back to cold coffee. And you think "This is the same cold coffee," but it has a different story to it now, and is not the same experience for everyone.

Most challenging, irreversible decision? Getting married, kicking out a kid, faking my way into a job I am not qualified for? Collaring dawn? Collaring someone that ended up being someone not suited to me? Advising the daughter of my collared slave that her mom was gone, and it was time to pull the plug?

Maybe if I wrote this chapter yesterday, or tomorrow, it would be easy to answer (like "should have decided to have bought bitcoin when it was still just something geeks knew about"). But the reality is these decisions are not hard or challenging when I am in my seat of power. This will be the third indicator of a great Leader. You know. You know buying a new, bigger RV is the decision. And that staying with the job for 20 years was right ... but it isn't anymore. Or that dawn is ready to go to New Orleans on her own. And tonight, I'll have chicken with mild salsa, we will watch the movie Get Out, and then leave me alone while I kill zombies with Kevin.

What is the most challenging irreversible decision you've made as the Leader or followed as the Follower in your authority transfer relationship?

dawn:

OK. I'm drawing a blank. Someone in the other room *[Kevin note: we have always sat around the same table while writing but could not for these last two]* started typing right away. I still have nothing. Do I sit here with my head in my hands like Dan is doing? Or just start typing?

Typing it is. Though, I don't know what to write. I'm having a problem with the word "irreversible". I don't feel like anything is "irreversible". Well, unless someone passes or something is destroyed.

> But I got rid of the stuff because he said so, and I trusted it would turn out OK.

We've moved many times. We've started businesses together. We've ended businesses together. We've become full-time RVers. But none of these feel "irreversible" to me. And those that are, I don't remember being a challenge.

When Dan decided that we weren't going to produce our weekend events, PXS (Power Exchange Summit) and BTL (Beyond the Love) anymore ... that was a challenge, for sure. I enjoyed creating and producing those events. And I totally resisted when he had brought it up the year before, but the following year he made the decision and put his foot down. But I don't see it as "irreversible". We could start them up again at any time, if he wanted to.

When we closed The Space, that was a challenge, but not something I did as a Follower. I helped make that decision as a co-director and it was the right one to make because of Covid.

Probably the closest thing I can think of that was a challenge and irreversible was downsizing when we became full-time RVers. That has been my biggest struggle. So many things I sold and gave away—fetish clothes I had started collecting after the weight loss, furniture I had spent so much time on finding the right pieces to feel at-home with, office items, craft items, books ... the list goes on. Dan is a minimalist and I am not. I really, really did not want to get rid of everything: the podcast studio, the cars, the motorcycle. Holy cow, getting rid of the motorcycle was hard. But I got rid of the stuff because he said so and I trusted that it would turn out OK. Luckily, I found good homes for the stuff, which made it a bit easier. And it's only "irreversible" because I can not get that particular stuff back. I can replace most of it if I wanted to.

But it was absolutely a struggle. I didn't want to have to replace things if the RVing didn't work out. I wanted a safety net of having my things. What if the RVing didn't work out and we bought a house and had nothing to put in it? What about the money involved in replacing everything? I had a poor childhood. You don't get rid of things that can be used later or you might not have the money to replace. Dan had a different experience and different ideas.

And ... what if living in a 30-ft. box on wheels didn't work out with us as a couple? I personally would have nothing to my name.

I had to overcome this personal fear and anxiety, and take it on trust and faith that this would work out. Either his decision to RV was going to work out, or if it didn't, he'd still take care of the situation.

It was the right choice on his part. Since then, we've been to many, many, places, met a lot of people and had a lot of fun. I don't miss the stuff, except the motorcycle, and now have a hard time even wanting stuff because it would have to fit in a 30-ft. tiny home on wheels.

Conclusion

With many of these writings we found that we had more we wished we had time to say. Writings end. Chapters end. Sections end. And finally the book must come to a close. When all our time is gone and we only have one hour left for two final writings, what are the things we want to share? Below, find our concluding thoughts:

31) What advice do you have for folks wanting to start an AT relationship?
32) What was your experience like doing this project?

Chapter 31: Getting Started

What advice do you have for folks wanting to start an AT relationship?
Kevin:

The list is so long!

Know yourself, and your needs.

Be able to clearly communicate your own wants and needs, and listen attentively to those of your partner.

OK, those foundation bits out of the way, I believe the single most important piece of advice is to expect your relationship to evolve, and that you should work to help it evolve to be pragmatic and joyful. I think that people try to desperately cling to their fantasy instead of finding ways to make their relationship realistic and sustainable, while still maintaining the hot and sexy elements that probably caused them to explore the relationship style in the first place. If you latch onto unrealistic expectations, you will jeopardize the opportunity to build a relationship that is truly extraordinary.

Another bit of advice—realize that the odds are not great and that you must search for your AT partner in a very specific way. In a "normal" dating process you need only to determine if you are attracted to someone, then decide if you think you want to hang out with them a lot and share bank accounts. For Authority Transfer you not only have to agree that each of you will occupy a particular role, but you also have to be certain that the style of relationship and the roles that form it are what you desire.

We know lots of folks who say "I am a Master" and find someone who says "Great! I want a Master because I am a slave." Yeah, maybe. But what do you mean by those things? As a Master, do you want to be in a position to micro-manage every aspect of the Follower's life, or do you want to delegate and barely have to think about that decision again? Do you want to be a harsh disciplinarian requiring strict compliance and rigorous attention to ritual, or do you want to be a warm and sensuous Leader that gently guides their Follower? As a Follower, do you want to be nurtured, appreciated, and have a shared priority of personal growth, or do you want to be used, ignored, treated as property, and ordered to wear obvious and blatant nipple jewelry to your place of employment? None of those choices or options are wrong or bad. But it is really unfortunate and causes a lot of heartache to have a gruff and demanding Leader who, through failure to discuss thoroughly, ends up treating some soft-hearted Follower like a recruit at boot camp. Neither one is really satisfied. Just finding someone who does the complementary role to your own does not mean you will be happy.

> Remember that AT relationships are custom-made, unique, and carefully designed to be an outgrowth and melding of the authentic people who form it.

Remember that AT relationships are custom-made, unique, and carefully designed to be an outgrowth and melding of the authentic people who form it. You simply cannot live the AT relationship designed by some other couple. At best, you might find some other couple who live a life and have a relationship you admire, on whom you can model your unique relationship. Katie and I deeply admire Dan and dawn. We wouldn't last a year together if we had to use their AT guidelines for our relationship. Even though we are closely aligned, and what they do resonates very closely to us, it is unique to them and trying to live in their relationship would be foolish.

Other advice? Go to classes on Authority Transfer—and use that to prime the pump for your own exploration and discussion, not to tell you how it should be done. Do journaling and share it with each other to explore topics and come to understand each other (like your priorities, etc.).

Recognize you will fuck up, and that's probably OK. You cannot be the perfect Follower or the Omnipotent Leader. Find ways to discuss mistakes, admit to yourself and your partner you shit the bed, and move forward with humility and resolve to learn from it and do better.

Realize that BDSM is probably a pretty terrible foundation for a long-term relationship. If all you have in common is the desire to play hard and fuck hard, you'll have a great couple of years, but reality hits you hard, bro. BDSM is (usually) best when held as an exciting supplement to a great relationship, not as a foundation for the relationship.

Frick. Out of time! So many tips left to share!!

What advice do you have for folks wanting to start an AT relationship?
Katie:

My advice to folks starting their journey into a non-egalitarian style of relationship? Don't do what we did at the start. Kevin and I jumped in the deep end with no experience, very little knowledge and no connections to anyone who was giving it a go.

My advice is to start with introspection and self-awareness. This relationship is intentional and deliberate in its best form.

Journaling alongside your partner on aspects of the relationship style and then sharing what you wrote. Conversations that are structured this way allow a person to say what they are thinking to completion. And encourages the listener to hear without getting wrapped up in replies.

Journaling prompts such as: What is appealing about being a Leader or follower? What aspects do you find intimidating? How do you picture daily life, sex, conflict resolution with this dynamic?

Seek out classes, events, other couples who have this type of relationship that seem aligned with where you would like to journey. Look for good books. Dodge the fantasy movies and books—they are great fap material, but reality requires more. As a couple, consume this kind of information and then discuss the parts that are appealing, hot, undesirable, scary.

As you actually start to enact in this manner with each other, do not become too attached to making everything work. Don't be rigid as you discover and explore.

> Make sure that who you are taking advice from are people you respect—couples who have evidence of success.

I remember a couple that thought it was very hot for the follower to sleep at the foot of the bed on her own mattress on the floor. It charged up the dynamic for both of them. This rule lasted until she got sick and the leader realized that having her sleep on the floor fevered and shivering was just wrong. As a firm protocol it made no sense. This was an interaction that belonged in certain circumstances but not always.

Time and again people create protocols and orders that they think will be hot and keep each one mindful of their role. Then they slowly get lazy because it doesn't appeal as much as they thought, or it gets annoying and a burden. This is likely to happen. Take the time to consciously "retire" protocols and orders that just aren't working. It's not a failure. It's discovering who you are.

You might stumble on an action, a statement, an order that is unexpectedly profound. Recognize when this happens. This is authentically you. Share that with your partner. Talk about if you can fold that into your interactions.

When Kevin addresses me in a certain way, I have a response he expects from me. When I am having a tough day, we have found a way for me to share that information with him. We have many key phrases that communicate quickly with each other. Most of them highlighting our roles and respecting the dynamic.

I encourage people to try a day of full authority transfer. Have your follower ask for everything. A glass of water. To leave the room. To go pee. To eat a meal. Take that authority to the bedroom and play and fuck. Take it out into public and find fun ways to be subtle and still in your roles. After the day is through, journal about it. Write about the best parts. Write about the parts that were icky or felt like they didn't fit. Then share those journals with each other and explore what the next day will look like.

Some folks write contracts with each other. That is an awesome way to have a commitment to roles and responsibilities. I always encourage folks to not have them be of too long duration. Signing aboard for a year of something you have never experienced before is going to go sideways and set you both up for failure. Try a month with review and rewrite if necessary. Then three months with a repeat.

We have friends who use the business model of CEO, COO like Kevin and I. They actually have weekly "business" meetings each Sunday morning at a restaurant with brunch. They discuss the week past and the week ahead. It's an opportunity for recognition of service, for decisions to be made. It also is a really effective way to prevent complacency and sliding into old habits.

I believe every Authority Transfer couple would have different advice on getting started. Their guidance is coming from their inclinations and style. Interview as many as you have available. Figure out which pieces sound right for you. Make sure that who you are taking advice from are people you respect—couples who have evidence of success.

Don't choose a fitness coach that is hacking up a nicotine lung and hugging a box of donuts.

What advice do you have for folks wanting to start an AT relationship?
Dan:

I've been to many Leather events and seen all kinds of people in authority transfer relationships. Master/slave is common in Leather, but so is Daddy/boi, Owner/property, Handler/pet, Dom/sub, and lots more. I felt like most of them just kind of showed up that way, knew their role, and fit right in. That of course is far from the truth—because that view missed the transformative journey that got them to that point.

So before I offered advice, I'd ask, "Why?" What makes this feel like you; what do you think you'll get out of it; are you taking this journey alone or with a partner? Whose idea was it? There are no wrong answers to any of that, but those answers would likely lead to what advice I'd give them.

It would start with writing it down. What is a Leader to you? What is a follower to you? And no quoting from a book or an internet forum post—what is it to you? Because our language of kink and power exchange and authority transfer all share some common words that have different meanings (when you say you are a sub, do you mean a bottom in the bedroom or a service-oriented person?). So, I advise you to write it down to be clear for yourself.

Next I would ask more about the story of how they got to wanting to try it. Someone read a book and thought it was hot? Or you went to a kink event and noticed some people in collars and deferring to someone? Contrary to what some people I know would suggest, being inspired by fictional writings to try it for real isn't bad. And the door for a lot of us. My story with dawn started in porn—but a style of porn where the images conveyed surrender and control beyond just physical bodies.

> Find some peers you can bounce things off of. Being able to talk about stuff you are experiencing is a great benefit.

Following that, I would advise them to take it easy. Slow down. Much like new relationship energy, some will find that this homecoming - this idea of AT relationships - fills the bit of empty they always felt but never knew what belonged there. So before you divorce your spouse and quit your job so you can move closer to the mecca of power exchange, treat what you found as a fine bottle of wine. In other words, rushing it will likely cause it to be less pleasant, and may even lead to disaster. So don't worry about a title or how you are going to identify on an internet forum. Keep it simple and lean into Dom and sub, since those are very flexible terms but give you a general role.

Now, time to start hanging around. And get involved. This is best accomplished in real time with local groups. In Columbus, OH, which you may not think of as a center for kink or power exchange, we had two yearly power exchange weekend events, multiple power exchange discussion groups, as well as formal dinners and other AT friendly happenings. See what is in your local city and area. If you are not near any real time events, then get involved virtually. I say this as "better than nothing" advice, because the low energy and effort some virtual offers require means the people running it may not be people you want to model yourself after. I don't want to get bogged down by my issues with online forums so I'll leave it as a reminder that what people say they do and who they actually are may not align.

Next up, get more involved. Not just attending stuff, but being part of the community. That can mean anything from picking up chairs after a meeting to offering some other skill set to help things progress. And if there is nothing in your area? Start a group. Yep, you don't need to be a great people leader, just say "On Tuesday we are going to meet at the Common Grind Coffee Shop and talk power exchange—anyone else want to attend?" Now, this is more complex than I am suggesting as issues of ego and scheduling and such are part of it, but someone has to step up, why not you?

I am a big fan of peer mentoring (which I am nearly sure dawn is going to mention—and if neither of us do, I'll have to sneak back into this document after everyone else is asleep) but I'll still say, find some peers that you can bounce things off of. Being able to talk about stuff you are experiencing is a great benefit.

Finally, remember what this is like. You are coming to a new world, unsure of what to expect, without any preconceived notions about how things should be. This is called beginners eyes. Keep that in the years that follow. Remember the joy you felt when you stumbled upon us and thought "I belong".

What advice do you have for folks wanting to start an AT relationship?

dawn:

- ❖ Be consistent
- ❖ Find a role model
- ❖ Read
- ❖ Figure out your "why"
- ❖ Figure out what your expectations are
- ❖ Discover your needs, wants and desires
- ❖ Find a peer mentor
- ❖ Meet real people, not just online

❖ Join a MAsT group or something like it
❖ Join a support group if there is one in your area
❖ Surround yourself with like-minded people

I've started this half hour's writing with a list and I'm not sure if that is what I'm going to stick with just yet, let's see. If nothing else, it will help me organize my thoughts, since I have so much advice on the tip of my tongue.

The first big piece of advice I would give is to figure out your "why". Why do you want to be in an AT relationship? Is it authentic or are you trying to fix something? Do you have any experience or did you read *50 Shades of Gray* and it gave you a tingle? It's possible. I know people that have started their AT relationship specifically for this reason. Some are still together, some not. And honestly, that's how Dan and I found our interest in power exchange and kink. There were books at the time like *The Story of O, The Claiming of Sleeping Beauty*, the *Marketplace* series ... and also stories on Literotica. I think that site is still around. Regardless, figure out your "why". That will be super important on the tough days when you wonder if you should throw in the towel.

Once you figure out the why, start designing the relationship. I personally highly recommend a contract. If nothing else, it will help you create a pretty solid foundation that you can look back on later. Figure out your needs, wants, desires and expectations. Put it in writing and take a look at it.

Another big piece of advice I can think of, is to surround yourself with like-minded people. You can join kink social media or AT social media or whatever, but it's not going to be the same as being around people that LIVE this lifestyle. Many people have ideas. Many people have theories or thoughts on how it SHOULD be. But when you live this life, you'll find out that theories aren't a lot of help. Armchair dominants sitting on the other side of a screen aren't much help. You'll need to be talking to people that are really living this life and you'll not know that until you meet in person and see how they live. If possible, find people that you can hang out with outside of events. For a lot of us, they use events as a place to really fall into their roles and it's more like a scene rather than how they really live. Make sure they aren't just projecting how they want to be, online or at an event. We've run across people like that before. What they were showing of themselves when people were watching was much different than their actual home life, and yet they were giving advice to other people when their own relationship was a hot mess.

You'll want to find people that are new like you so that you'll have peers going through the same sort of experiences, and you'll want to find people a few years ahead of you so that you can see what there is to look forward to. This way when you are going through struggles you'll see that others have survived.

Why is this my biggest piece of advice? As you may have read elsewhere, Dan and I didn't have role models. At the very, very beginning, it was just us and our fantasies. We had no one to discuss this with except a couple members of NLA (National Leather Association) that had tried power exchange before. Actually, one of those people gave us some great ideas for our contract, based on what she hadn't done in her relationship that hadn't survived.

Being the only ones we knew that were trying this relationship style was lonely and confusing. Then, we found two other couples that were giving this a try. I'm not even sure how we found them, probably through the new kink group that was forming in the area. The six of us got together and created a D/s support group. Even though we were all different, it was nice to be able to talk about things honestly and get some head nods. With the group, more people joined. Many at the same level as us and some even newer. Then, we met someone new to the area that had been in this dynamic for more than five years! What a relief! I could ask the other submissive all kinds of questions, and even though her answer was mainly some form of "What does your Master say to that?" that was usually exactly what I needed to hear.

So, find people. Find support. Surround yourself with like-minded people. Maybe attend an event or two. Join something like a MAsT (Masters And slaves Together) group for support. Find a mentor. I'd stay away from someone you only know online. And I highly suggest a peer mentor. Dominants for Dominants, and submissives for submissives. Dominants "training" submissives just to get sex is a thing to watch out for.

Once you've got the foundation built and you're rolling, remember to be consistent. There is a saying: "Meditate when it's easy, meditate when it's hard." Well, the same works in a power exchange relationship. "Stay in your roles when it's easy, stay in your roles when it's hard." If you are building your communication methods around your power exchange dynamic, dropping your power exchange to try and fix something can actually damage the relationship itself. I've so much more to say about that and hopefully, I'll have time to come back to it. [But time ran out. We do talk about this in our classes though.]

> The first big piece of advice I would give is to figure out your "why".

But I also want to mention, don't let others judge you. A power exchange relationship has the potential to be just as healthy as a vanilla relationship. And as such, just as unhealthy as one. It's a valid relationship style that you don't need to defend to anyone. If you are both happy and growing and it's consensual, it's no one else's business. You'll find people not only in the vanilla world that don't agree with a hierarchical relationship, but you'll also find them in the kink world. Again, another reason to surround yourself with like-minded people.

Chapter 32: This Project

What was your experience like doing this project?
Kevin:

This whole dealio was awesome!

We decided it might be fun to do this thing during one of our many "sitting around chitterchats" (thanks for the new word, Dan). Then in a typical Katie way, she started exploring and planning for how that might unfold and offered a framework for managing which questions get into the book. Sure, if we decided to do the book, that might be a good way to manage it. Then we did a test writing together and had a great time doing it. Suddenly we were headed to a writing retreat with a spreadsheet full of questions. The funny part? Last night, with all the topics complete, we finally started to think about the business end of this.

This process has been an extension of the ways we usually hang out with Dan and dawn. Deep topics often get pulled apart when we are together, but usually in a more interactive way. In this case, each "speaker" prepared their opinions in advance and got to share them uninterrupted. A very cool variation on a theme.

The more this project moved forward, the more convinced I was that it was not only a great way to inspire my own personal growth and introspection, and a great way to hear from respected peers about their relationship choices, but also of value to other people. Hopefully people that like long sentences, in my case.

The rules we set out as guidelines for this project turned out to be invaluable. The "random topic with zero warning" means we didn't do any pre-writing and our thoughts were fresh and real. The "no talking" means we didn't have the intent or slant of the writing influenced by how others heard the question. The "30-minute time limit" meant we had to crush out the words, firehose style, without much time to consider typical essay structure or even clarity. This forced it to be much more like a journal entry. Each of our choices turned out to be so valuable to us. I think that it enhanced the content, but it also enhanced the experience of doing the project.

Was it fun? That might be the wrong word? I looked forward to doing each writing. One of the times we did two-in-a-row, instead of spreading them out, I was totally knackered. I was not looking forward to the next writing, until I woke up the next morning and found myself excited to go!

It was valuable though. I learned a lot from this process. I discovered things about my own beliefs because I was forced to put my thoughts into words. I was forced to pay attention to some places where I questioned my abilities, or recognized room for improvement. I learned some things from Katie—even though we are aligned and communicate frequently. This project showed me even more places where her perspective on our world is very different from mine. And obviously I learned some things about Dan and dawn, and also from Dan and dawn. I know them better, but I also was able to use their words as a way to gain a new viewpoint outside my own.

The fun came as the chapters took shape. Imagining someone, you, reading these words and feeling like they were valuable. Imagining someone reading a chapter and feeling relief that they are not the only one who feels like humor and silliness is OK in a Leader, or that monkeys are terrible creatures.

There is some hesitation though, if I'm being honest. This is some pretty raw and vulnerable stuff—where I show my flaws or express a doubt about my leadership. There are a lot of bluntly stated opinions here. While it is intended to be about me and mine, it can be taken as harsh, or judgmental, or whatever. Even if folks aren't offended, they absolutely do have a closer look at who I am, my fears, my failings, my lusts. My life is pretty bare in these words, revealed for every person to see, and that brings pause. Somebody better find these words helpful, 'cause running around nude just to be pelted with rocks is not my kink.

This feels kind of like a relationship bootcamp. We met around the writing table at 7a.m. every morning. We met again after dinner almost every night. And we hammered out the words. This was a strange kind of work. Grueling yet invigorating.

Five minutes left of this—probably final—writing for this book. What is important to say?

I hope that this has given you as much value as it has given me. I hope that it makes you question the choices you make as a Leader or Follower and shakes you out of complacence. I hope that my stories of my path have helped you find new treasure or at the very least reassure you that your path is right for you. My biggest wish is that the love Katie and I feel and are able to express because of the tools and techniques of Authority Transfer, matches the love you are able to create in your life.

What was your experience like doing this project?
Katie:

Ever write a conclusion to a book with a 30-minute time limit and no time to fine-craft it? Well, we decided to keep the flavor of the book in our closing statements. Not complaining, I like things fast and rough. Last verse same as the first.

It has been less than three weeks of writing and answering one or two questions a day. Waking up at 6am on our "vacation" week with Dan and dawn so we were coffees in hand, sitting at our computers ready to create by 7. As dawn sat down sleepily this morning for our final session, she said, "I'm going to answer the question, What does the inside of your eyelids look like?" And she reclined her chair and began to Rip Van Winkle on us.

We have written in the RV together, at picnic tables, around the campfire. We did one session at a coffee shop, which we thought would be a change of scenery, and it was. It also was the main route for constant transport trucks. The noise was deafening. We would like you to attach whatever chapter you believe to be our weakest to that situation.

For me this has been a recording and an expansion of the way we often visit with Dan and dawn. Each of us shining in our own personalities and styles. The love and acceptance of each other. The deep, personal—and before now private—conversations we have together. There has been much laughter. Loud, brain chemical improving laughter. There have been tears, sometimes because it was so poignant and loving, sometimes because it hurt.

In past visits, by the time we get together for a weekend or a week visit we have texted back and forth a list of topics we want to discuss. Political topics, personal struggles, health and wellness, life changes. Real topics.

The list is always in funny code so only the person adding a topic knows what the hell it is. A list could look like:

- ❖ Frog freezing
- ❖ Don't touch that next time
- ❖ Cheese in my belly
- ❖ Repeat like burps
- ❖ Clear the table and reset

Then, while we visit, we work our way down the list lounging about in random locations. So this writing was an extension of those interactions. An expansion.

For me it has been a joy. Especially because the style of the book allowed me to write as I think. To zip out my responses and reactions just the way I would talk about it. I didn't have to craft it for a class and rewrite it so many times my soul got shaved out of each sentence. My writings are congruent to who I am and what my journey has been like with Kevin.

I know this book isn't going to be some financial windfall. That wasn't the purpose. Like a busker on the street, we do what we have some level of skill and knowledge of, and hope to find enough in the hat to continue.

The purpose is that we share so you can discuss with your partner. Have introspection into yourself. Perhaps even find peace in our struggles and perseverance. Read our words of when we fucked up, how much it hurt, how we found our way back to healing. And in those words find hope or tools that will aid you in tough spots.

Laugh. Fucking laugh out loud! Shoot chicken noodle soup out your nose, spew root beer on your book. Then take pictures of the mess and link us on social media. Laugh at our silliness, our fuckups, our tilted view of situations, at the joy we have in our relationships. Then seek out and stir joy into your relationship.

Do not survive. Thrive! And if we have helped you do that in some small way, all is worth it. And remember:

- ❖ If your shoes are on fire, get a flounder and cook it.
- ❖ Find your own "For Fuck's Sake katie!" and use it as a term of adoration. I suggest, "What the twatting twiddle, (*insert name here*)!"
- ❖ Never call your leader a Plodding Possum.
- ❖ Don't ride in cowboy position, tuck your feet under you and spring off the cock like it's a pogo stick.
- ❖ Don't fuck up your strawberry.

What was your experience like doing this project?
Dan:

This was, I think, my idea. I had just finished reading the book *The Dude and the Zen Master* by Bernie Glassman and Jeff Bridges. Basically the premise of the book is they sit around and talk about Zen concepts over a weekend retreat and capture the results. Although we did not emulate that per se, it brought to mind the general concept of "take an authority transfer question and discuss" (or in the case of this book, personally reflect). So two years prior to me sitting here now, we sat in other chairs around a table and did a test run of "pick a question, you get 30 minutes, lets see what happens." We were all pleased with the results.

Fast forward to three weeks ago and we started this writing retreat and my initial feeling about it was ... dread. You see, dawn and I had just finished another book and I felt pretty spent. I was actually wondering if I had anything else to say on authority transfer, power exchange, or relationships in general. With that as background, let's talk about how it went.

Write, share, write, share. After day two I suggested that this was too personal to share. Not in a bad way, but in a way that it felt very vulnerable and special and something we should cling onto and hold tight to our bosom. After day three, I reversed course and said we need to get this out and into other people's hands because I genuinely felt we had somehow created something that could be of great value to people. I've repeated that more than once throughout the process.

The other aspect which was really special to me is that unlike our other books, I don't care as much about how you will digest what I have to say. What I mean is, this is for me a number of journal entries on my experience or perception. So instead of saying "In my opinion, it could be wise if you want to grow as a Leader to consider...", I instead said "If this ain't happening, then there is a way to go to be a good Leader." The first version is valuable because you want to engage and inspire your reader. The second version—what you find everywhere in this book—Is just me talking about me and you can dig it or not. Maybe instead Kevin's voice makes more sense. I guess what I'm saying is, two things can be true—one, I really believe this is going to be a great resource for our community. And two, when I was behind the keyboard, I was writing for myself.

The good news is we have already started on and made great headway on the icky stuff! Who is handling this, if the book makes money how do we handle it, by basically saying "Hey, Katie, you are good at that, go do it?" and such. I make spreadsheets, so I did that.

Finally, what if for whatever reason this book never makes it out there? In that scenario, I have absolutely no regrets how I spent this weekend with my heart pals Kevin and Katie. Every morning we not only wrote and shared vulnerable aspects of ourselves, but we also shared our thoughts about what each other wrote. Our own friendship has deepened not only by our time together but by working on a project we are all passionate about - and dealing with the bumps that came up. I'm not actually sure at the moment what those bumps were, but we must have had some, right? We've been very easy on each other. During our time together, we've had two different tragedy level events hit the national news and one chapter got pushed back a week. Things like that have just helped us come to trust each other on a deeper level.

Finally, I've run out of time to talk about the time we have not been writing. Great food, walking our dogs, trying different board games and outdoor games (I am better at bocce ball than disc golf - wait, dawn was on my team and she is good at bocce ball - but I digress). Yoga, sitting by the fire, talking about health and challenges and orgasms. All without that messy business of sexual foursomes.

What was your experience like doing this project?
dawn:

As I sit here yawning, I realize this is probably the last morning of us sitting here writing together. Everyone else has been bright eyed and bushy tailed during the last three weeks as we meet at Kevin and katie's RV at 7a.m. to tackle the first question of the day. I've yawned my way through the morning ones and have had an easier time with the evening ones.

We've actually discussed doing a book together for over a year at this point and couldn't figure out how to do it. It's hard enough to do two voices when Dan and I write together, but we figured out our flow. So, with Kevin and katie we figured out something that seems to work for us ... journal style.

But what to write about? Especially since Dan and I have already written a couple of books?

Kevin and katie have a long list of questions from their years of facilitating roundtables, so a spreadsheet of questions that we all vote on is born. If there are enough questions that three or four of us voted on, those get used. Put the numbers on a slip of paper and put in a little bowl. Each time we meet, one of us draws a number. We set two timers, one for 25 minutes as a 5 minute warning and another for 30 minutes. When the one for 30 dings, hands up, typing done.

Others in the group enjoy that randomness. I never really got used to it. I don't like being put on the spot without knowing what I'm writing about. Even now, I want to go back and change everything I've written here to make it more concise and well ... pretty.

Instead, because there is only a half hour and no time to go back and rearrange and make things smoother, I tapped into the real guts of the question. I treated it like a journal entry and some days what came out was the painful stuff with no time to soften it. I was able to tap into the emotions instead of feeling like I was writing a class to share a learning moment. Sometimes memories came up that I'd forgotten about.

Some mornings, I sat here for the first few minutes of the timed writing and just closed my eyes, hoping for something to speak to me. Other times I couldn't type fast enough. A few times I even asked myself if I should share something, doesn't matter, no time to think.

Five-minute timer would ding. Shit! Do I have any more to write? Do I have time to read over what I've got to make sure it conveys what I wanted and isn't just a mash of words? Do I have the time I need to just get this last little bit out? I didn't always.

Timer goes off. We all sit back with a sigh, sometimes of frustration as there was more we wanted to type, or with a sense of completion ... of "that's some good shit right there."

Then it was time to share. So not only did we answer the question in our writing, we then read out loud to the others. Whomever drew the number for that writing round would start the reading.

Some of these pieces were deep and we'd listen and support the one reading as they shared. Giving a moment at the end of the reading for the reader to process what they had spoken. Then, give feedback. This feedback could be as simple as, "Wow, great stuff," with a fist bump, to "Did you know you used the wrong word there, you probably meant this one instead?"

At first, we were just sharing with each other what we had written for the book, but after a few of these readings, I realized we were really getting to know each other at a deeper level. Hell, even Dan and I were learning a bit more about each other based on how we remembered and wrote about different memories and situations.

Sometimes, we'd share and part directly after the writing as there were chores to do and Dan needed to log into his day job. Sometimes the discussions would go on into the evening as we pulled it apart after the writing and sharing was over.

I sit here this morning, listening to everyone else clicking away, knowing I haven't conveyed how much of a growth opportunity ... yep there is the 5-minute bell ... that this has been for me. I'm assuming it has been for everyone else as well. But it's been huge for me. I'm just hoping I've shared things that will be beneficial for others as well.

You get to see how two authority transfer couples have made it two decades differently, and how we overcame so many hurdles as couples and individuals in and with our relationship dynamics.

Appendix 1: Book Titles We Considered

1. 20 years, 2 couples, 30 minutes, 30 questions
2. 20 years, 30 minutes, 30 questions
3. 80 years in 30 minutes
4. 80 years of Authority Transfer Relationships
5. An Authority Transfer Choose Your Own Adventure!
6. An Intimate Reflection
7. Ask Us The Hard Shit
8. Authority Transfer Reflections
9. Authority Transfer Relationships
10. Cowboys, Tentacles, Oatmeal Smoothies and Other Stories on Authority Transfer Relationships
11. Four Love Letters to Authority Transfer Relationships
12. Insight - We put that shit on everything.
13. Intimate Reflections
14. Leading and Following
15. Leading and Following in Love
16. Love Letters to Authority Transfer Relationships
17. Navigating a Negotiated Relationship
18. Negotiated Hierarchical Relationships
19. Negotiated Inegalitarian Relationships
20. Our honest reflections
21. Skip the Flowers, Here are the Roots
22. Straight from the Heart
23. The Scholars and the Fool
24. The Experts and the Fool
25. Three Experts and a Fool
26. Three Scholars and a Fool
27. Twenty Years, Four People, Two Relationships
28. Uncensored Answers to the Toughest Questions
29. Uncensored Authority Transfer Journals
30. Uncensored Authority Transfer Relationships
31. Uncensored Journals
32. Uncensored Journals on Authority Transfer Relationships
33. Uncensored Writings

Appendix 2: Make the Grade

Pick your favorite author for each chapter then add it all up and see who wins the game! You can tell them how great they are when you meet them next. But who gets the vote? The person most similar to you? The one who made you think the hardest? The one that makes you want hot sex? The one that makes you florp soda out your nose? THERE CAN BE ONLY ONE!

	Dan	dawn	Kevin	Katie
Foundations				
1: What makes Authority Transfer relationships worth the effort?				
2: What were the biggest hazards in the first couple of years of your relationship?				
3: How important is sex, eroticism and intimacy in your relationship?				
4: These roles are not a social norm. How do you have peace with them?				
Interactions				
5: What actions/tools do you use to maintain the dynamic on a daily basis?				
6: Is your relationship goal and growth driven? How do you attend to that?				
7: Can and do you inspire your partner into their role?				
8: How do you give feedback to your partner?				
9: How do you encourage and support open communication?				
10: What is your experience with leading as the Follower, and following as the Leader?				

	Dan	dawn	Kevin	Katie
11: How do you attend to "reaction" and "resistance" in your relationship?				
12: How do you interact in public? Talk about the subtleties of your role.				
13: How important is BDSM play and scenes in your dynamic?				
Mental and Emotional Gymnastics				
14: Transparency, vulnerability and openness - what do these mean in your relationship?				
15: How do you manage the sacrifices necessary to make this relationship work?				
16: Are manipulation, coercion, or underlying motives part of your interactions sometimes? Why?				
17: How do you reconcile empowerment and independence with transferring authority?				
18: Is anything off-limits in your relationship?				
Struggles and Challenges				
19: Share a time you fucked up and how it was resolved.				
20: How do you deal with being disappointed or causing disappointment?				
21: You want to fuck but they don't - what do you do? Now reverse it.				
22: What does a shitty day look like in your relationship?				
23: Tell us about a significant disagreement and how it was resolved.				

	Dan	dawn	Kevin	Katie
24: Describe a time your partner was compromised in their ability to fulfill their role. How do you manage when it happens?				
25: Have you ever been in a slump with your partner? How did you resolve it?				
Myths and Reality				
26: Does it matter who's stronger, smarter, makes more money or any of the other regular power issues?				
27: How do you view a "Do as I say, not as I do" style of leadership?				
28: How do you handle it when someone questions or challenges your dynamic?				
Bonus Questions				
29: What are the skills and tools that an AT relationship provides to help each other work through bad habits, sensitivities and past baggage and improve future choices and behaviors?				
30: What is the most challenging irreversible decision you've made as the Leader or followed as the Follower in your authority transfer relationship?				
Conclusion				
31: What advice do you have for folks wanting to start an AT relationship?				
32: What was your experience like doing this project?				
Grand Total				

www.ingramcontent.com/pod-product-compliance
Lightning Source LLC
Chambersburg PA
CBHW020825270326
41928CB00006B/447